101 Trends

Every Investor

Should Know About the

GLOBAL ECONOMY

Joseph P. Quinlan
Kathryn L. Stevens

CB

CONTEMPORARY BOOKS

Library of Congress Cataloging-in-Publication Data

Quinlan, Joseph P.
    101 trends every investor should know about the global economy /
Joseph P. Quinlan and Kathryn L. Stevens.
      p.   cm.
    ISBN 0-8092-2976-5
    1. Investments, Foreign.   2. Competition, International.
3. Economic history—1945–   I. Stevens, Kathryn L.   II. Title.
HG4538.Q56   1998
332.67'3—dc21   97-46461
                                               CIP

The graph on page 165 includes technical details of country selection, weighting
and index construction, which are available from the following sources:

Rosensweig, Jeffrey A. "A New Dollar Index: Capturing a More Global
Perspective," Federal Reserve Bank of Atlanta, *Economic Review*, June/July 1986,
71:6, pp. 12–22.

Rosensweig, Jeffrey A. "Constructing and Using Exchange Rate Indexes," Federal
Reserve Bank of Atlanta, *Economic Review*, Summer 1987, 72:3/4, pp. 4–16.

Hunter, Karen R. "Inflation and the Dollar Index," Federal Reserve Bank of Atlanta,
Economic Review, September/October 1990, 75:5, pp. 32–43.

Cover design by Scott Rattray
Cover image copyright © 1996 William Whitehurst/The Stock Market
Interior design and illustrations by Amy Ng

Published by Contemporary Books
A division of NTC/Contemporary Publishing Group, Inc.
4255 West Touhy Avenue, Lincolnwood (Chicago), Illinois 60646-1975 U.S.A.
Printed in the United States of America
International Standard Book Number: 0-8092-2976-5
98   99   00   01   02   03   BA   10   9   8   7   6   5   4   3   2   1

This book was written in loving memory of Carolyn A. Quinlan and is dedicated to Chris, William, and John McCormack.

Contents

CHAPTER 3   INVESTMENT

CHAPTER 4   TRENDS IN GLOBAL COMPETITIVENESS

CHAPTER 5   SIZING UP SOME GLOBAL INDUSTRIES

CHAPTER 6	GLOBAL ODDS AND ENDS

Acknowledgments

We are especially indebted to Richard Hagle, formerly of NTC/Contemporary Publishing Group, who had the vision and persistence to get this project launched. Tim Lee of Morgan Stanley Dean Witter provided valuable support in the early phases as well. In bringing this book to completion, we would like to acknowledge the contributions of Susan Moore-Kruse, project editor, and her team at NTC/Contemporary. A special thanks also to Matthew Carnicelli of NTC/Contemporary Publishing Group.

In the course of researching and preparing this book, we have become obliged to a number of institutions, both private and public. We drew from sources all over the world and extend our thanks to those that gave us permission to cite their figures. In particular, we would like to thank Raymond Mataloni of the Bureau of Economic Analysis, U.S. Department of Commerce, for his invaluable assistance in gathering information on U.S. foreign direct investment flows.

William T. Stevens provided encouragement and wisdom over the course of this project, which we would like to highlight.

Finally, writing a book is a difficult endeavor not only for the authors but also their families. So for their unwavering support and good humor throughout the project, we are particularly indebted to Karen, P.J., Brian, and Sarah Quinlan, as well as Chris McCormack.

Introduction

It's the economy, stupid.

—James Carville, Democratic campaign adviser

Mr. Carville was only half-right. It's really about the world economy, a point brutally driven home in 1997 when a currency crisis in far-off Thailand ultimately sparked a global sell-off in the world financial markets and precipitated a slowdown in world growth. Very few countries have been spared Asia's pain, including the United States.

That a currency debacle halfway around the world could reverberate back to the United States underscores the realities of our time: owing to the accelerating rate of global economic and financial integration, no country is an island, not even the world's largest, the United States. Virtually every investor, institutional or retail, and nearly every business, large or small, are influenced by trends in the world economy. The food we eat, the cars we drive, the money we borrow, the clothes we wear, even the air we breath—all of these are increasingly shaped and driven by external forces. We live in a global village, although few realize it.

This book attempts to define the global village and the world economy we live and work in. It has been written for a global audience, although we admit writing with a bias toward the American reader. Why? Because at a time when the United States is being heralded as the economic champion of the world, it is even more critical for Americans to recognize the predominant trends of the global economy and realize that their future is tied and linked to events beyond America's borders. America's integration with the world economy has never been greater, and with luck, it will only become stronger in the future.

The Organization of This Book

This book serves as a general introduction to the global economy. The format is designed to give you a quick, easy, and succinct picture of the prevailing key trends. More for the novice than the expert, this book, in our opinion, is just a starting point toward a greater understanding of the world in general. Given the subject matter, many of the graphs and tables presented to illustrate the text contain figures that are dated. We apologize for this shortcoming, and as heavy data users ourselves, realize the perils of old data. However, the tables and graphs serve as a framework in understanding the dynamics of the global economy, so we urge readers to focus in on and understand the trends that are set forth. We also suggest that you take particular notice of the data sources, as well as the key terms and organizations in the Appendix. The terms are important to recognize and understand; the organizations are the sources of statistics and additional information.

The book is divided into six chapters. The first chapter centers on global output and discusses salient trends in world production and growth. Entries include the role and position of the United States in the world economy, global growth leaders and laggards, the rising importance of the developing nations, and statistics on the world's richest and poorest nations. Global population trends are also covered.

Chapter 2 focuses on the dynamic forces of global trade. Leading world exporters and importers are discussed, as is the interplay of trade and the U.S. economy. Global investment flows are the focus of Chapter 3. The first half of the chapter highlights foreign direct investment inflows, while the latter portion reviews the more volatile and liquid form of capital flows—portfolio investment.

Chapter 4 tackles a more contentious and subjective matter—global competitiveness. With the input of various surveys, wage comparisons, and productivity studies, we present the strengths and weaknesses of the United States relative to its chief competitors among both the developed and developing nations. Chapter 5 hones in on a dozen industries, and the relevant companies, that are of global significance. Chapter 6 is entitled "Global Odds and Ends" and serves to cover many loose ends not found in the other chapters. We think the reader will find the entries, ranging from the overseas Chinese of Asia to influential religions, provocative as well as interesting.

As a special footnote, one trend that looms large over the world economy, but not included in this book, centers on the looming millennium problem for computers. Because computers will not be able to distinguish between the year 2000 and the year 1900, many experts fear massive computer malfunctions as the new century dawns. Quantifying this trend is difficult given the wide-ranging impact of computers in the world economy. Suffice it to say the Year 2000 problem is significant and should be watched carefully by investors.

CHAPTER 1

Output

Overview

Although a singular concept, the global economy is made up of many different parts. These parts are discussed in this chapter. Of particular importance is the fact that the United States, while still the largest economy in the world, no longer dominates or sits astride the globe. The rebuilding of Europe and the industrial rise of Japan over the Cold War era diminished the economic weight of the United States. The industrialized nations still account for the majority of global output, yet investors should recognize the incessant rise of the developing nations.

Led by Asia, the developing nations have been growing two to three times faster than the industrialized nations over the past decade. China, Malaysia, Thailand, Poland, Chile, Indonesia, the Czech Republic, and Turkey have been at the forefront of growth within the developing countries. Though it is not widely known, the developing nations already account (based on purchasing power parity rates) for more than 45% of world gross domestic product and will most likely account for more than half of world output in the not-so-distant future. Economic size, for now, remains in favor of the industrialized nations, but for how long is uncertain, given faster growth rates among the developing nations. More on that in the pages ahead.

Also ahead are entries on the world's richest and poorest nations. Global wealth is still concentrated in the industrialized nations, and the countries of Africa remain the poorest of the poor. Another entry underscores the economic power of the transnationals versus the nation-state; in an era of rapid globalization, strategic alliances, and technological change, some companies now generate more in sales each year than the total output of many countries. This chapter likewise includes a special look at China's economy.

The final entries hone in on global population and demographic trends. One constant of the global economy is the inexorable rise in world population. Sometime in late 1998 or early 1999 the global population is expected to exceed 6 billion people. The good news is that the rate of population growth is slowing in virtually all regions of the world. One entry centers on global urbanization while two others focus on important global demographic trends. One of these is the rise of Asia's "MTV Generation," a cohort of new consumers that will make their influence felt in the world economy. The second lies with "global graying," or the aging of the world's population, which carries all types of implications for investors.

☐1☐ Global Growth–the Long View

There have been five distinct phases of global growth and development in the twentieth century. The first phase encompasses the years 1900–13, although this period of buoyant world trade, robust capital flows, and large international migration began in the mid-nineteenth century. This was a period of accelerating global interdependence, with the share of exports in world output rising to 11.9% in 1913, a level not reached again until 1970.

World GDP (gross domestic product) growth expanded by an annual average rate of 2.8% during 1900–13, with the United States one of the most dynamic emerging markets of the time and among the fastest growing economies of the world. Global growth, however, slowed in the second distinct period of this century. This phase, 1913–50, was marred by two world wars, a world depression, and a general collapse of the world trading system.

The outbreak of World War I and its aftermath destroyed the productive capacity of Europe, led to an estimated 25 million deaths in Europe, and triggered a series of quantitative restrictions on trade and capital. Inflation was rampant. A gold exchange standard was reinstated in 1925, although the attempt to restore financial stability failed. In mid-1930, the United States passed the Smoot-Hawley tariff, which raised duties on imports by 23%. Not surprisingly, other nations retaliated with their own tariffs and quantitative controls, causing global trade and growth to plummet. The world depression resulted in an 18% decline in aggregate output of the industrialized nations, with America taking an even bigger hit—U.S. output declined 28% during the 1929–32 depression.

If the second phase was the darkest of the century, then the third phase, or the so-called Golden Age of 1950–73, was the high-water mark of the twentieth century. Robust growth was bolstered by strong multilateral institutions, steady flows of capital to the developing nations, the rebuilding of Europe and Asia following the devastation of war, rising government spending, and robust capital investment.

The good times ended in the early seventies. The fourth phase, 1973–88, saw a marked deceleration in growth and a sharp acceleration in inflation in the industrialized nations, triggered by the sudden and dramatic rise in world oil prices in 1973. The Bretton Woods system, which had provided a stable, international fixed exchange-rate system over most of the Golden Era, collapsed in August 1971. Currency volatility subsequently increased. Rising oil prices led to higher levels of external debt for oil importers. Balance-of-payment difficulties surfaced in various parts of the world. The 1980s turned out to be the "Lost Decade" for Latin America.

The fifth phase of global development commenced in the late 1980s and continues today. In many respects, the current period of global growth resembles the first—global economic interdependence has accelerated sharply over the past decade, and the level of trade to world GDP continues to climb, rising to more than 21% in 1996. The accompanying graph charts the annual rise in GDP in the twentieth century for the OECD (Organization for Economic Cooperation and Development) countries and developing nations. With the collapse of communism, more countries with more people are participating in the global economy. Trade and investment liberalization have become the global norm. Capital flows to the emerging markets have soared. New technological advances have facilitated greater trade and investment flows among nations, just as railroads and steamships helped promote global integration and interdependence more than a century ago.

The world economy, therefore, has come full circle as the new millennium approaches, with many of the salient features of today resembling those in the first decade of this century.

World Real GDP Growth, 1900–97
(% Annual Average Growth)

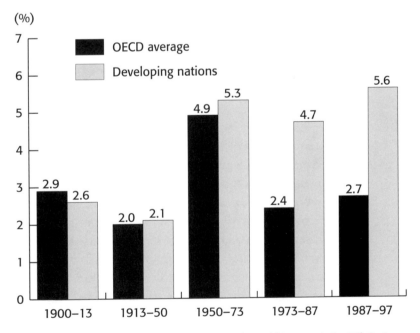

Source: © OECD, 1989, Development Centre Studies, The World Economy in the 20th Century. Reproduced by permission of the OECD; International Monetary Fund

2 │ The Shape of the World Economic Pie

America's global economic supremacy was unchallenged following the end of the Second World War. With the industrial base of Europe and Japan devastated by war, America was home to the largest economy in the world, accounting for roughly half of total world output. The United States still maintains the top ranking today, although the nation's share of world economic output, 20.4% in 1997, is much smaller now than a half century ago.

Global economic power is more diffused today, as the pie graph shows. Following decades of rapid growth and the development of world-class industries, Japan has emerged as the second largest economy in the world, making up nearly 8% of world output. Germany ranks third, but the nation's economic power is embellished by the fact that Germany lies at the core of the European Union. The aggregate output of the 15-member economic group is roughly equal to that of the United States. Combined, and based on purchasing power parity (PPP) estimates, the United States, the European Union, and Japan account for almost 50% of world output.

Among the developing regions of the world, developing Asia is the undisputed giant, accounting for 23.1% of total world output. In dollar terms (see the accompanying table), China is the largest economy in Asia after Japan and ranks number seven in the world. South Korea is the third largest economy in the Pacific Rim, followed by Australia, India, and Taiwan. It is particularly noteworthy that in the aftermath of World War II, Japan and virtually all of Asia lay in ruins. From the ashes of war, however, Asia has risen dramatically over the past 50 years and now accounts for over 30% of total world output, well ahead of the United States and Europe.

Rounding out the rest of the world pie, Latin America makes up nearly 9% of global output. The largest economy in the region by a wide margin is Brazil, ranked number eight in the world, ahead of such nations as Canada and Spain. Mexico is the second largest economy in Latin America, followed by Argentina. On a global basis, Mexico and Argentina ranked numbers 16 and 18, respectively, in 1997. The Middle East, home to one of the most important strategic commodities of the world, oil, makes up less than 5% of total world output. Similarly, the combined output of Central Europe and Russia equates to less than 5% of the world aggregate. Russia, though, the largest economy in the region, is the 15th largest economy in the world.

Of the world's 20 largest economies, 8 are from the developing world.

The Global Economy: World GDP Shares*, 1997

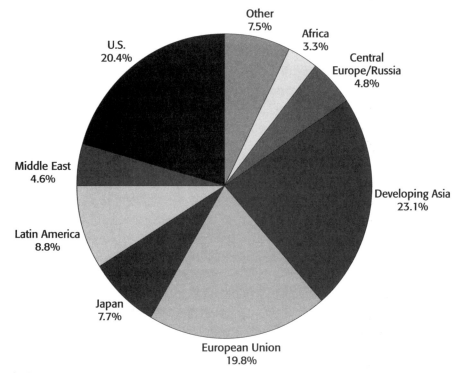

*PPP basis

Source: International Monetary Fund, World Economic Outlook, May 1998

The World's Largest Economies, 1997
(GDP at Market Exchange Rates)

Rank	Country	US$ Billions	Rank	Country	US$ Billions
1	United States	7,341.9	11	South Korea	483.1
2	Japan	5,149.2	12	Netherlands	402.6
3	Germany	2,364.6	13	Australia	367.8
4	France	1,533.6	14	India	357.8
5	United Kingdom	1,152.1	15	Russia	356.0
6	Italy	1,140.5	16	Mexico	341.7
7	China	906.1	17	Switzerland	313.7
8	Brazil	710.0	18	Argentina	295.1
9	Canada	570.0	19	Taiwan	274.0
10	Spain	563.2	20	Belgium	265.0

Source: National sources; World Bank

3 | The Size and Cycles of the World Economy

Whether measured at market exchange rates or at purchasing power parity rates, global output has steadily expanded over the past decades. As presented in the first graph, world output totaled $3.1 trillion in 1969 (at market exchange rates) but rose roughly fourfold to $12 trillion in 1980. By the end of the 1980s, world output had expanded to $20 trillion, a 69% increase from the beginning of the decade. Output reached nearly $30 trillion in 1997, marking a tenfold increase from the level of 1969.

While world output has advanced fairly consistently over the past decades, the annual rate of growth has varied. Real (i.e., adjusted for inflation) world GDP increased by nearly 6.9% in 1973, the last year of the so-called Golden Era of growth. The twelvefold rise in oil prices in 1973 contributed to the difficult years of 1974 and 1975. Since then, the world economy has experienced three distinct economic expansions or cycles—1976–82, 1983–91, and 1992 to the present. The second graph illustrates world GDP growth over 1970–97. The weakest year occurred in 1982, when high interest rates in the United States and Europe led to global growth of 1.2%. Since 1970, world GDP has expanded by an annual average rate of 3.7%.

The current global expansion is hardly a record setter. This relatively subpar cyclical performance reflects many variables, including lingering and structural economic difficulties in Japan, very weak levels of growth and high unemployment in Europe over most of the decade, and the underperformance of the U.S. economy compared with other expansions. The decade started with Canada, the United Kingdom, and the United States slipping into recession. As these nations began to recover, a number of other key countries—France, Germany, Italy, and Japan—stumbled, depriving the world economy of momentum. In the industrialized nations, government policies emphasizing price stability over growth have also contributed to this period of weak activity.

For most of this decade, robust growth in the developing nations has offset the weak performance of the industrialized nations, preventing a sharp deceleration in global growth. On average, the developing nations have grown two to three times faster than the industrialized nations in the 1990s. Even though Asia stumbled in 1997, the developing nations still grew by an estimated 5.8% in 1997, versus growth of 3% in the industrialized nations.

World Output

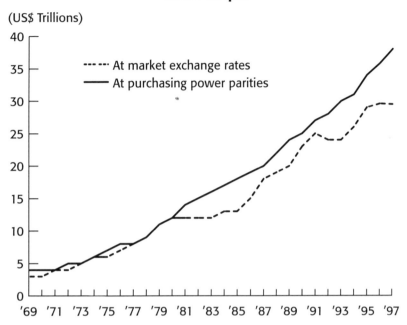

Source: International Monetary Fund, World Economic Outlook, May 1998

World GDP Growth

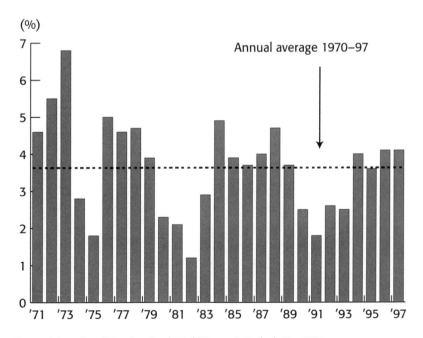

Source: International Monetary Fund, World Economic Outlook, May 1998

4 The Developing Nations as a New Engine of Global Growth

Prior to the 1990s, economic growth in the developing nations was closely aligned or in sync with that of the industrialized nations, with business cycles in the latter typically leading those in the developing nations. Domestic demand in the industrial nations helped promote export growth in less developed regions of the world, which in turn stoked the economic engines of such nations as South Korea, Singapore, Taiwan, and Chile. The United States, because of its size and demand for imports, was so important to the economies of the developing nations that it was often said that when America sneezed, the rest of the world caught a cold.

Today, America, along with Europe and Japan, remain key markets to the developing nations, as well as critical sources of external finance and technology. Yet, the developing nations have increasingly struck out on their own this decade, becoming, to a degree, "decoupled" from industrialized nations. The developed nations expanded by an annual average rate of 2.3% over the 1990–97 period. The developing nations, however, grew by 5.9% over the same period, staking a claim as a legitimate new engine of the world economy during the nineties.

The relative strength of the developing nations has been underpinned by a number of factors, including rising per-capita incomes and the steady rise and formation of a middle class in many countries. Free-market reforms that have promoted better macroeconomic management and more realistic trade and investment policies have fueled growth as well. Also contributing have been soaring private-capital inflows to the developing nations and higher levels of intraregional trade in Asia, Latin America, Africa, and Central Europe, a trend that has helped to not only promote export growth in general, but also reduce the developing nations' trade dependence on the richer nations.

The importance of the developing nations to the world economy has grown over this decade and will assume even greater significance in the years ahead. Near-term prospects, of course, have been diminished by Asia's economic problems. Still, the developing nations' share of world GDP could surpass that produced by the industrialized nations by the early part of the next decade. Currently, the developing nations' share of world output is roughly 45–47%, much higher than most investors realize.

Real GDP Growth: Developing Versus Industrialized Nations

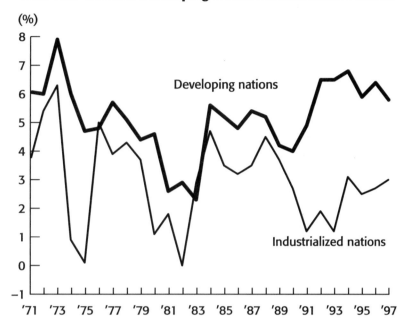

Source: International Monetary Fund, World Economic Outlook, May 1998

Developing Nations: Share of World Output
(GDP at Purchasing Power Parity)

(%)

F = Forecast

Source: International Monetary Fund, World Economic Outlook Database, May 1998

5   Shadow Economies, Corrupt Countries

Measuring the total output of a nation is an imperfect science, even in countries where government statistics are considered credible. Unreported economic activity (alas, the underground economy or black market) is a characteristic of most countries and is usually an outcome of rising tax and social security burdens as well as excessive government regulations. These factors can ultimately drive business "underground" and drive taxpayers to hide their income. What emerges is a "shadow" economy, which can take on significant magnitudes.

Italy's shadow economy, for instance, is estimated to be equivalent to nearly 26% of total gross domestic product (see the bar graph). Right behind Italy is Belgium, whose shadow economy is estimated to be greater than 21%; Sweden (18.3%) and Norway (17.9%) follow. The shadow economy of the United States is estimated to be roughly 9.4% of total output. Among the developing nations, unreported economic activity is even more widespread and common. In Russia, the shadow economy is estimated to be as large as the official one.

In many developing nations, the size of a shadow economy can depend on the level of corruption within a given country. Corruption is a difficult variable to measure, although Transparency International and Gottingen University release an annual ranking of the world's most corrupt and least corrupt nations (see the accompanying table). The index is not a direct measurement of the level of corruption, but rather an assessment of the level based on the input and perceptions of people working for institutions and businesses in the country. *Corruption* is defined as the misuse of public power for private benefits.

Against these standards, Nigeria was perceived to be the most corrupt nation in the world in the last survey. Bolivia and Colombia followed. Four of the largest emerging markets in the world—Mexico, Russia, India, and Indonesia—were also on the top 10 list.

What conditions or factors promote corruption? According to the International Monetary Fund (IMF), variables that may contribute to corruption include trade restrictions, price controls, government subsidies, multiple exchange rates, and low wages to civil servants. The consequences of corruption range from slower economic growth to the misallocation of resources.

Corruption also leads to lower levels of investment and reduced effectiveness of aid flows through the diversion of funds. Prior to being run out of power, Zairian leader Mobutu Sese Seko reportedly robbed the nation of billions in foreign-aid dollars. Inadequate public revenues, adverse budgetary constraints, and a poorer quality of infrastructure are also symptoms of corruption.

Size of the Shadow Economy as a Percentage of GDP, 1994

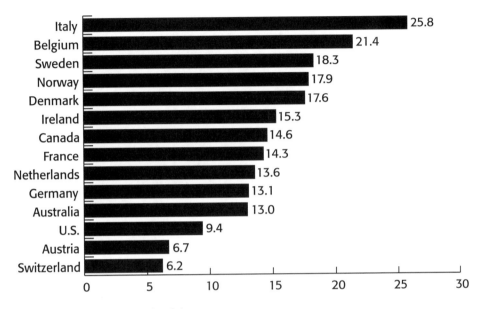

Source: Friedrich Schneider, University of Linz

The Corruption Perception Index
(Based on a Scale of 0 to 10, with 10 Being the Least Corrupt)

Rank	Most Corrupt	1997 Score	Rank	Least Corrupt	1997 Score
1	Nigeria	1.76	1	Denmark	9.94
2	Bolivia	2.05	2	Finland	9.48
3	Colombia	2.23	3	Sweden	9.35
4	Russia	2.27	4	New Zealand	9.23
5	Pakistan	2.53	5	Canada	9.10
6	Mexico	2.66	6	Netherlands	9.03
7	Indonesia	2.72	7	Norway	8.92
8	India	2.75	8	Australia	8.86
9	Venezuela	2.77	9	Singapore	8.66
10	Vietnam	2.79	10	Luxembourg	8.61

Source: Transparency International

6 | World Growth Leaders

For the balance of the past three decades, the developing nations of Asia have led the world in terms of growth. Yet the world's fastest growing economy over the 1965–96 period was neither China nor Singapore, which are among Asia's most dynamic performers. Ironically, the growth champion is out of Africa. Botswana, according to figures from the World Bank, claimed the top honor by growing at a 13% average annual pace over 1965–96 (see the graph). Landlocked, with a population of 1.4 million people, Botswana is blessed with one particular commodity—diamonds. The country is one of the world's largest suppliers of gem-quality diamonds, which accounts for up to 80% of their export revenue.

Regional honors go to Asia, which, out of the world's top 10 fastest growing economies over 1965–96, placed seven nations in the elite ranking. Behind Asia's rise are a number of critical variables including outward-looking trade policies, high rates of savings and investment, and a strong emphasis on education in many nations. All three attributes will assist the region as it struggles to rebound following the financial crisis of 1997.

Over the 1965–96 period, South Korea (ranked third) edged out China, although over the nineties the biggest story has been the emergence of the mainland as one of the most dynamic economies in not only Asia, but also the world. Since 1979, following China's turn toward the West, the country has seen its economy rise by nearly 9% per year. Per-capita incomes, while still low, have nearly quadrupled in the last 15 years. By some estimates, China is on course to emerge as the largest economy in the world by the early part of the next century.

Reflecting decades of solid growth and rising per-capita incomes, Singapore is now considered a developed nation by the IMF (International Monetary Fund). So too is South Korea. Not listed is Taiwan, which is excluded from the World Bank figures. Yet, as many familiar with Asia know, Taiwan has long been one of the region's most dynamic economic performers.

Of the 25 countries listed (excluding the United States, which is shown for comparative purposes), notice the subpar ranking of India relative to its dynamic Asian neighbors. Brazil has been among the fastest growing economies of Latin America over the past three decades, although the country's average annual rate of growth (4.6%) is well below its competitors in Asia.

Among the developed nations, Japan achieved the strongest level of growth during 1965–96, with annual growth averaging 4.5%. However, the nineties have been particularly harsh to Japan, and the country has fallen near the bottom of the growth league among the industrialized nations.

The World's Fastest Growing Economies
(% Average Annual Growth of GNP, 1965–96)

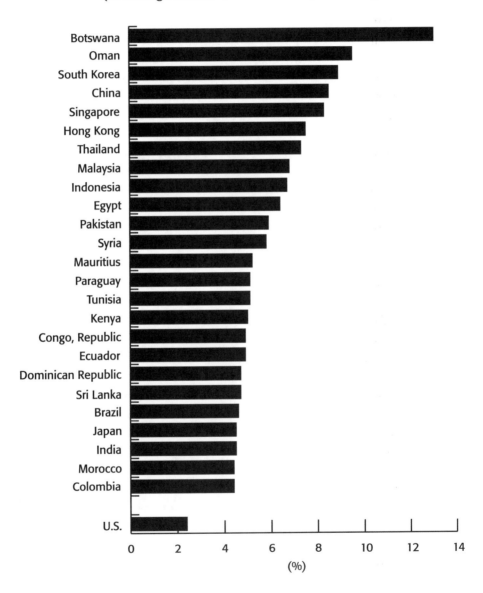

Source: World Bank, World Development Indicators, 1998

7 The World's Growth Laggards

The second half of the twentieth century has been a period of sustained economic prosperity for the world at large, notwithstanding various "shocks" that have slowed the pace of global growth at times. The rebuilding of Europe, Japan's remarkable industrial emergence, U.S. economic leadership, an open trading environment—all of these variables and more underpinned an average annual rate of global growth of over 3% during the 1965–96 period.

Not surprisingly, though, not all countries have kept pace. Many have floundered over the past few decades while others have flourished. The former group, the world's laggards, are highlighted in the accompanying chart.

What is surprising, as well as disheartening, is that against a backdrop of sustained global growth, some nations (Nicaragua, Congo, Iraq, and Bulgaria) actually went into reverse (growth contracted on an average annual basis) over 1965–96 while the rest of the world went forward. A handful of countries did not even muster 1% average annual growth over the 1965–96 period. The upshot? Minimal or no growth is a recipe for poverty and a steady decline in the standard of living, a tragic fate of millions of people around the world.

Various factors account for the dismal performance of the laggards. Yet there is one common denominator to this group: a great deal of their economic misfortune was homegrown or of their own doing. Civil war, external conflicts, widespread official corruption, misguided economic policies, the misallocation of resources, political instability, and bureaucratic ineptness—all or some of these variables have contributed to the fortunes or misfortunes of the world's weakest economies at some point in the past three decades. To be sure, external shocks or events, like the dramatic spike in oil prices followed by the collapse in commodity prices, have made the road to growth difficult for many. Note that many of the laggards have yet to truly develop manufacturing capabilities and remain to this day overly dependent on one or two primary commodities. For Bulgaria, Poland, Hungary, and Romania, economic development was long stifled by the Cold War and the iron embrace of the former Soviet Union.

On a more positive note, some of the laggards have turned the corner and have achieved growth rates far in excess of their historic averages over the past few years. Poland, for instance, one of the first nations in Eastern Europe to grasp the mantle of reform, is now one of the most dynamic nations in greater Europe. Hungary has exhibited strong growth rates as well over the past few years and is one of the most popular locations for multinationals. Argentina, like Poland in Eastern Europe, has been at the vanguard of economic reform in Latin America in the 1990s, behind only Chile in pursuing a massive restructuring of the economy.

While confronted with many challenges, these countries have broken free from the cycle of slow or no growth over the 1990s. The same cannot be said for many nations in Africa, Central America, and the Middle East.

The World's Laggards
(% Average Annual Growth of GNP, 1965–96)

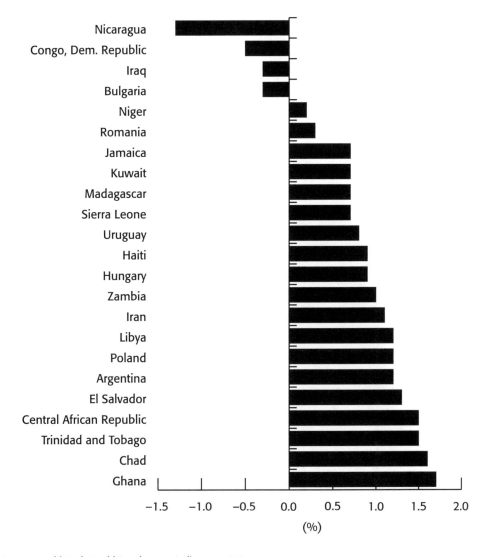

Source: World Bank, World Development Indicators, 1998

8 The Wealth of Nations

Being the largest nation in the world does not necessarily translate into being the richest. Many marketers fantasize over the large, untapped markets of India, Brazil, and China, while not realizing that these countries are well endowed with people but with very little purchasing power. To the contrary, some of the world's wealthiest nations are small, industrialized nations with relatively small populations. It is nations such as Singapore, Switzerland, Hong Kong, Belgium, and Austria, as the accompanying table reveals, that have some of the highest output-per-capita incomes in the world, a good benchmark determining a nation's standard of living.

One exception is the United States. Among the large industrialized nations, the United States was ranked number one in 1996, with a GNP-per-capita income of $28,020. Over the 1991–96 period, America's per-capita income grew by 2% on an average annual basis, versus 1.8% in Japan. The per-capita income of the latter was $23,420 in 1996.

The GNP-per-capita income of the European Union was $18,609 in 1996, although this figure masks wide regional disparities. At the top of the scale are the small, wealthy industrialized nations already mentioned. In the middle of the pack are Europe's larger economies such as France ($21,510), Germany ($21,110), the United Kingdom ($19,960), and Italy ($19,890). Oil-rich and thinly populated Norway had a per-capita income of $23,220 in 1996, the highest among the Scandinavian countries.

Below the European Union average in 1996 were Spain, Portugal, and Greece, the region's southern countries that, while rapidly industrializing, still maintain large farm and agricultural sectors. The per-capita income of Greece, $12,730, was the lowest in Europe, just below Portugal. Ireland's per-capita income was also below the European Union average.

Compared with its neighbors in the North American Free Trade Agreement, Mexico's per-capita income is roughly one-fourth that of the United States and one-third of Canada's. Ranked 37th, Mexico is not included in the table. Chile is ranked 28th and has the highest per-capita income in Latin America ($11,700). Brazil ranked 46th in 1996 ($6,340), while Argentina ranked 32nd ($9,530).

Among the developing nations of Asia, the wealthiest nations are the small city-states of Singapore ($26,910) and Hong Kong ($24,260). Surprisingly, Israel is one of the wealthiest countries in the Middle East, ranked 19th in 1996, ahead of the oil-rich United Arab Emirates. Slovenia and the Czech Republic are among the wealthiest in Eastern Europe.

GNP per Capita, 1996
(Purchasing Power Parity Basis)

Rank	Country	US$
1	United States	28,020
2	Singapore	26,910
3	Switzerland	26,340
4	Hong Kong	24,260
5	Japan	23,420
6	Norway	23,220
7	Belgium	22,390
8	Denmark	22,120
9	Austria	21,650
10	France	21,510
11	Canada	21,280
12	Germany	21,110
13	Netherlands	20,850
14	United Kingdom	19,960
15	Italy	19,890
16	Australia	19,870
17	Sweden	18,770
18	Finland	18,260
19	Israel	18,100
20	United Arab Emirates	17,000
21	Ireland	16,750
22	New Zealand	16,500
23	Spain	15,290
24	Portugal	13,450
25	Korea	13,080
26	Greece	12,730
27	Slovenia	12,110
28	Chile	11,700
29	Czech Republic	10,870
30	Malaysia	10,390

Source: World Bank, World Development Indicators, 1998

9 | The World's Poorest Nations

The poorest of the poor reside in Africa, a cruel irony, given the region's abundance of natural resources. That Africa lags the rest of the world in terms of development is well known. But less recognized is the fact that the per-capita income levels of some African states in the 1950s were on par with South Korea and many countries in Asia. However, the latter have largely thrived, notwithstanding Asia's dearth of natural resources, while resource-rich Africa has floundered.

The disparity in development is due to a number of reasons, ranging from rapid population growth in Africa to higher education and literacy rates in Asia. While Asia has been adept at promoting domestic savings, attracting foreign investment, and encouraging external trade, most of Africa has not, and has paid a severe penalty as a consequence.

The region attracts very little in the way of foreign capital and has yet to truly appear on the radar screen of multinationals and portfolio investors. Terms of trade in African countries, long-time exporters of primary commodities, have declined sharply over the past decades. The result has been chronic trade deficits in many countries and the ongoing need to either borrow money from abroad or seek financial assistance from the industrialized nations.

Misguided government policies and poor economic management have greatly exacerbated the problems of many countries. Government policies that favor the state over the private sector, large monopolies over private companies, and imports over exports have combined to leave many African states as the world's poorest nations. Compounding matters, official aid has been squandered or pilfered in the past.

Asia, for its part, is not without problems. The proportion of those living in poverty continues to decline, though the sheer number of people living on less than a dollar a day—the common international poverty line—is staggering. In South Asia alone, nearly 515 million people lived on less than a dollar a day in 1993, according to the World Bank. Another 445 million were considered impoverished in East Asia. Interestingly, using the common international poverty line, some 60% of the world's poor reside in just two nations—India and China. A dozen countries, each with more than 10 million people living in poverty, account for 80% of the world's poor. The group, in addition to India and China, includes Brazil, Nigeria, Indonesia, the Philippines, Ethiopia, Pakistan, Mexico, Kenya, Peru, and Nepal.

Health problems have greatly contributed to the woes of the world's poorest nations. Malnutrition, notably among women and children, is all too common in many parts of Africa. In many African nations, there remains a lack of doctors, drinking water, medicines, medical instruments, and electricity. The AIDS epidemic remains a huge impediment to development.

Looking forward, there are grounds for cautious optimism regarding Africa's future. Trade and investment ties with other regions of the world are being strengthened. Political stability is becoming the norm in many key states, notably South Africa. And multinationals, albeit slowly, are beginning to view the region more favorably as market-based reforms become more popular.

GNP per Capita, 1996
(Purchasing Power Parity Basis)

Rank	Country	US$
132	Mozambique	500
131	Ethiopia	500
130	Sierra Leone	510
129	Burundi	590
128	Rwanda	630
127	Malawi	690
126	Mali	710
125	Yemen, Republic	790
124	Congo, Dem. Republic	790
123	Zambia	860
122	Nigeria	870
121	Chad	880
120	Tajikistan	900
119	Madagascar	900
118	Niger	920
117	Burkina Faso	950
116	Bangladesh	1,010
115	Uganda	1,030
114	Guinea-Bissau	1,030
113	Angola	1,030
112	Nepal	1,090
111	Kenya	1,130
110	Haiti	1,130

Source: World Bank, World Development Indicators, 1998

10 The Rise of Global Transnationals

One of the most significant trends of the world economy centers on the rise of what the United Nations calls *transnationals*, or global firms that are spread throughout the world and that operate complex and intricate production chains. Transnationals are powerful agents of global change and are most often associated with the rise of globalization. Through expanding levels of cross-border trade and investment flows, companies such as Ford Motor, Volkswagen, and Honda increasingly influence the trade, employment, and ultimately, income levels of nations.

The global reach and impact of transnationals is outlined in the accompanying table. As of 1996, some 44,000 transnationals, with almost 280,000 foreign affiliates, were in operation. Note from the table that the sales of affiliates were greater than world exports of goods and services. According to World Bank estimates, the share in world output of transnational affiliates rose from 4.5% in 1970 to 7.5% in 1995. These global behemoths now generate more in sales than the total output of some nations, a trend depicted in the accompanying graph.

Which party—countries or companies—wields ultimate power has become a contentious issue during the 1990s. Some people argue that the balance of power lies with transnationals, who are free to roam the globe for the best deal, in the best location. Others counter by arguing that the states, which set the rules of the game and control access to local markets, drive and dictate the actions and policies of the transnationals. The debate continues, and will no doubt continue into the twenty-first century.

What is less uncertain is the change in government attitude toward transnationals over the past decade. There was a time (in the late 1960s and early 1970s) when transnationals were scorned and loathed. Today, most nations are out courting and cajoling these global giants—shifting the balance of power, according to many, in favor of transnationals. Where some governments nationalized or directly assumed control of foreign companies in the 1960s and 1970s, the buzzword of the 1990s has been privatization, whereby state-enterprises are being sold off to private investors. In all but a few nations in the world, foreign direct investment incentives have been enhanced to attract the attention and capital of transnationals.

For transnationals and governments alike, the fate of both parties has become intertwined and linked, with cooperation rather than conflict in the interest of all parties and investors.

The Rising Might of Transnationals
(US$ Billions)

	1995	1996
FDI inward stock	2,866	3,233
FDI outward stock	2,811	3,178
Sales of foreign affiliates	5,933*	6,412†
Gross product of foreign affiliates	1,363*	1,557†
Total assets of foreign affiliates	7,091*	8,343†
Exports of goods and services	5,848	6,111

*1993
†1994

Source: UNCTAD

Nation-States Versus Transnationals
(Company Net Sales Versus Country Nominal GDP)

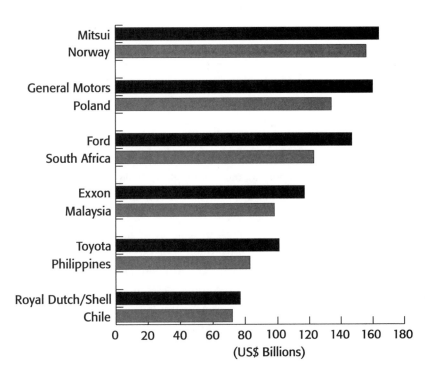

(US$ Billions)

Source: IMF; company data

11 The Many Markets of China

All too often, China is viewed as one massive market, with over 1.2 billion people eager to indulge in Western goods. This vision, however, has led many companies astray, since China is not one market, but rather a collection of markets, as the accompanying table highlights.

Business activity in China revolves around the provinces and a few select coastal cities. The policies and directives of the central government are important, but the success of many foreign companies lies more with understanding the local power structure and market conditions.

The average annual per-capita income of China was $622 in 1995. This figure, though, masks broad disparities in market size and, more important, wealth among the provinces. In general, the coastal provinces and cities have been more outward-looking and outward-oriented and have therefore enjoyed faster rates of growth and income relative to the provinces in the interior.

Guangdong province has emerged as one of the most dynamic economies of China over the past 15 years by leveraging its proximity to Hong Kong, a critical source of capital and manufacturing know-how. Both the aggregate output ($64.7 billion in 1995) and population (69 million people) of Guangdong are greater than those of many developing nations, which is why the southern Chinese province is an Asian "economic tiger" in its own right. Jiangsu and Shandong are two other provinces with a market economy, population base, and per-capita income greater than those of many countries.

Shanghai is the most economically vibrant city in China. The gross domestic product of the city is roughly equal to the total output of Vietnam. Shanghai's population of 14.2 million people is double Hong Kong's. Per-capita income was roughly $2,085 in 1995, more than three times the national average and well ahead of such nations as the Philippines and Indonesia.

China's poorest provinces are in the interior, where trade and investment contacts with the rest of the world have been at a minimum. Interior provinces such as Gansu and Tibet have also lagged behind the rest of the nation on account of poor infrastructure, low education levels, and a dearth of development funds from the central government. Because such a wide gap exists in income and wealth between the exterior and interior, the mainland's markets remain relatively fragmented and differentiated along provincial lines. This is the first trend investors should recognize regarding China.

China: GDP, Population, and Income by Province

Province	GDP (US$ Billions)	Population (Millions of People)	Per-Capita GDP (US$)
Guangdong	64.7	68.7	941.9
Jiangsu	62.0	70.7	876.6
Shandong	60.1	87.1	690.5
Sichuan	42.5	113.3	375.0
Zhejiang	42.4	43.2	981.0
Henan	36.1	91.0	396.8
Hebi	34.3	64.4	532.1
Liaoning	33.6	40.9	821.0
Shanghai	29.6	14.2	2,085.4
Hubei	28.7	57.7	498.2
Hunan	26.4	63.9	413.2
Fujian	26.0	32.4	801.9
Heilongjiang	24.2	37.0	654.8
Anhui	24.1	60.1	400.9
Guangxi	19.3	45.4	425.3
Beijing	16.8	12.5	1,341.8
Yunnan	14.5	39.9	363.7
Jiangxi	14.5	40.6	356.8
Jilin	13.6	25.9	524.1
Shanxi	13.1	30.8	426.3
Shaanxi	12.0	35.1	342.5
Tianjin	11.1	9.4	1,176.7
Xinjiang	10.0	16.6	604.8
Inner Mongolia	10.0	22.8	439.3
Guizhou	7.6	35.1	215.8
Gansu	6.6	24.4	272.5
Hainan	4.4	7.2	607.8
Ningxia	2.0	5.1	400.8
Qinghai	2.0	4.8	413.3
Tibet	0.7	2.4	280.5
National Total	**693.0**	**1,203.0**	**622.0***

*Average

Source: China Statistical Yearbook, 1995

12 Global Prices—from Inflation to Deflation?

Inflation has been relatively tame for most of this decade. No, the scourge of rising prices has not been permanently put to rest. However, as the accompanying graph underscores, many countries around the world have been successful in reducing inflation in the 1990s, bringing the average rate of global inflation down to 7.4% in 1996 and to roughly 5.6% in 1997. In the industrialized nations, average inflation slowed to just over 2% in 1997, down from 2.5% in 1996. The deceleration in prices over the past few years has been so pronounced that fears of deflation—a sustained fall in the overall price level—emerged in late 1997.

Global inflation rose sharply following the first oil price hike in the early 1970s and the second hike late in the decade. The first oil shock occurred just as many economies were near the peak of their expansions, with capacity constraints exerting upward pressure on wages and prices. As a result, the global rate of inflation soared from 9.8% in 1973 to 16.3% in 1974.

Inflation moderated over the second half of the 1970s, although the second oil price hike of 1978–79 carried a heavy inflationary impact again. The global rate of inflation rose from 11.1% in 1978 to 17.7% in 1980. Thereafter, commodity prices declined in real terms over the 1980s, although the combination of rising wages in the developed nations and soaring levels of inflation in some emerging economies, such as Mexico, Brazil, and Argentina, sustained a double-digit level of global inflation over the 1980s. Another episode of sharply rising global inflation occurred in 1990, brought on by the global synchronized economic expansion of the late 1980s and the temporary increase in world oil prices following the Iraqi invasion of Kuwait in 1990. Hyperinflation in some emerging markets only added fuel to the fire, and global prices rose to nearly 35% in 1990, the peak of the past quarter century.

Since 1994, the rate of global inflation has slowed significantly. Indeed, as measured by the IMF, it averaged just 4.8% in December 1997 and 5.1% in February 1998, one of the lowest annual rates since the 1960s. What accounts for the stellar inflation performance of the 1990s?

A number of factors have converged over the past decade to compress inflation around the world. In the developed nations, falling worker wages, productivity improvements, and intense global competition brought on by trade and investment liberalization have contributed to lower prices. Weak world commodity prices have been a factor as well. In the United States, fierce import competition, the renewed strength of the U.S. dollar, productivity enhancements, and moderate wage gains have combined to keep a lid on prices.

Inflation in many developing nations remains above the global average, although the decline in prices in many emerging markets, including the one-time hyperinflation victims of Brazil and Argentina, has been impressive. Fiscal consolidation, financial market vigilance, exchange-rate adjustments, a greater openness to trade and foreign investment—all of these variables have converged to impose more price stability on many developing nations.

Recently, Asia's economic crisis of 1997–98 has been a key driving force behind the deceleration in global prices. Slower growth in Asia helped trigger a sharp drop in world prices for primary commodities in late 1997 and early 1998. In addition, the region's competitive devaluations have produced a reduction in U.S. dollar prices of goods manufactured and exported from the region. In fact, some worry that Asia's economic problems and attendant need to export products could trigger a bout of global deflation. The last episode of global deflation occurred in association with the Great Depression of 1929–33.

The discernible drop in global inflation over the 1990s has been one of the most important and impressive features of the world economy. But has the deceleration in prices gone too far? As history has proven, falling price levels, or deflation, can be just as disruptive and punitive as rising prices.

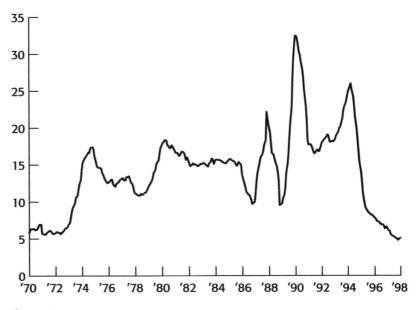

Monthly World Inflation
(Consumer Prices, % Change Year to Year)

Source: IMF

13 | This Crowded Earth

One constant of the global economy is the inexorable rise in world population. Mother Earth was home to roughly 1 billion people in 1800; according to Census Bureau projections, the world's population will total 7.6 billion by the year 2020.

The population of the globe is currently expanding by roughly 80 to 85 million people every year. At this annual increment, the world's population will top 6 billion people by the year 2000 and 7 billion around 2011. The 5 billion mark was surpassed in 1987.

The dozen years spanning 1987 through 1998 represent one of the shortest time spans in history needed to add another billion people to the earth. It took more than a century, from 1800 to 1925, for the world's population to increase from 1 billion to 2 billion. But as the first graph illustrates, succeeding increments of 1 billion took 35 years, 14 years, and 13 years.

While the absolute number of people in the world continues to rise, the rate of population growth is forecast to slow across all regions at the turn of the century. Global population growth peaked at 2.2% per annum from 1962 to 1964 and has since slowed, helped by rising education levels among women and improved living standards around the world. The rate of world population growth fell to 1.8% in 1975, 1.6% in 1990, and 1.4% in 1996. The annual rate of growth is expected to drop below 1% per annum during the first quarter of the next century.

World population growth is now concentrated almost entirely in the developing nations, a trend that will steadily raise the share of humankind residing in the poorer nations in the future. In 1950 nearly two-thirds of the world population lived in the developing nations; today 80% live there.

The U.S. Census Bureau estimates that the world's population grew by an average annual rate of 1.4% over the 1990s. Yet, the rate of annual growth was 1.7% in the developing nations, versus 0.4% in the developed nations. In the latter group, the most significant trend lies with fertility rates that have fallen below replacement levels. In other words, in many countries birth rates are now lower than the average of 2.1 children per woman needed to keep a population merely stable over time.

As the second graph depicts, Italy now has one of the lowest birth rates in the world, with a projected fertility rate of 1.2 children per woman over the 1995–2000 period. Germany, Spain, and Greece have marginally higher rates, 1.3, while the average rate of births per woman in Europe is 1.5. Japan has a similar rate. The United States has one of the highest fertility rates among the developed nations.

Total World Population

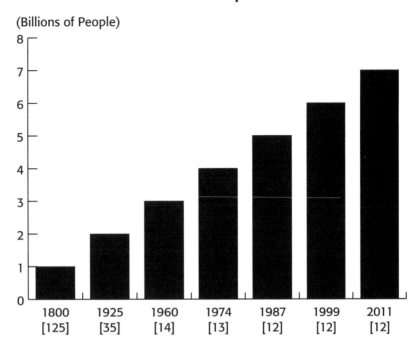

(Billions of People)

| 1800 | 1925 | 1960 | 1974 | 1987 | 1999 | 2011 |
| [125] | [35] | [14] | [13] | [12] | [12] | [12] |

[ ] = Number of years required to add 1 billion people

Source: World Bank; Census Bureau

Average Births per Woman

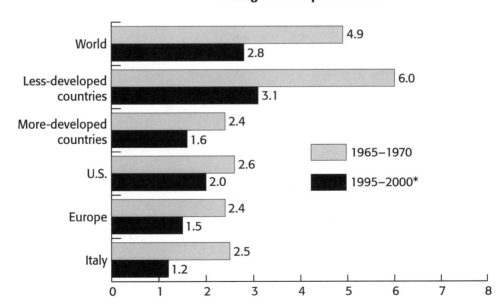

1965–1970
1995–2000*

*Projected

Source: United Nations 1996 World Population Prospects

14 Where Do All the People Live?

Most of the world population lives in the developing countries of Africa, Asia, and Latin America. In fact, 8 out of every 10 people currently live in these regions, and because birth rates in the developing nations are well above those in the more advanced nations, 95 out of every 100 persons added to the world population live in the developing nations. If present trends continue, the developing nations will comprise 84% of the total world population in less than 25 years.

As the table shows, China accounted for approximately 21.3% of the world's population in 1996, more than the combined share of the developed nations (20.3%). China's population of 1.2 billion in 1996, combined with India's 952 million people, easily makes Asia the most populous region of the world. More than half of the world's population (51%) reside in just six countries—China, India, the United States, Indonesia, Brazil, and Russia. Given that India's population is expected to increase by 337 million people over the next 25 years, versus an increase of 207 million in China, India's population will approach China's by 2020 and is projected to surpass China's by 2040.

By region, Asia is home to 3.3 billion people, or 57% of the world's population. Africa, home to 13% of the world population, ranks second. Roughly 8.5% of the world's population is in Latin America and the Caribbean. Western Europe accounts for 7% of the total, while the United States, with a population of just over 266 million people, accounts for approximately 5%.

Asia has the most people in the world, although sub-Saharan Africa and the Near East and North Africa have emerged as the regions with the highest projected population growth rates during the next quarter century. Growth rates in sub-Saharan Africa are expected to remain above 2% through 2020, helping to boost the region's population of 600 million people today to nearly 1 billion by 2020.

Besides ongoing changes in fertility and mortality rates—or the so-called natural increase in population—trends in migration also are instrumental in determining a nation's population. In general, population growth is largely determined by natural increase in the developing nations, while international migration plays a key role in boosting growth in the developed nations.

The United States remains the destination of choice, with roughly 6 million more people entering than leaving the country since 1990. This represents the largest number of net immigrants for any country in the world. After America, Germany and Russia are the major migrant destinations.

Share of World Population
(%)

Region	1970	1996	2020
Less-developed countries	72.9	79.7	83.6
More-developed countries	27.1	20.3	16.4
Sub-Saharan Africa	7.8	10.3	13.5
Near East and North Africa	3.9	5.1	6.4
China (Mainland and Taiwan)	22.5	21.3	18.9
Other Asia	29.7	33.2	35.0
Latin America and the Caribbean	7.7	8.5	8.5
Eastern Europe and the New Independent States	9.5	7.2	5.8
Rest of the world	18.9	14.4	11.9

Source: U.S. Bureau of the Census, International Database

The World's Most Populous Countries

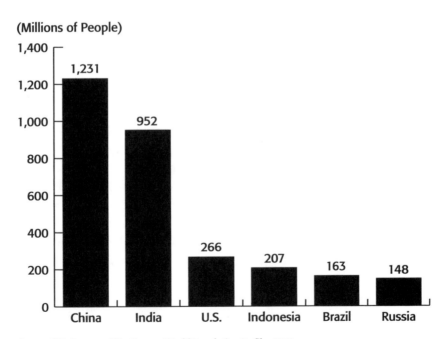

(Millions of People)

Source: U.S. Bureau of the Census, World Population Profile, 1996

15 The Coming Boom of Global Cities

The twentieth century has witnessed an unprecedented rise in the proportion of people living in urban areas. At the start of the century, only 13% of the total world population lived in the cities or in areas classified as urban. By the turn of the century, however, 48% of the world population, or nearly 3 billion people, will reside in the cities. According to official figures, by 2020 60% of humankind will live in urban areas.

As you can see by the first table, New York was the largest city in the world in 1950, with a population of 12.3 million people. At the time, no other city had a population greater than 10 million. By 2000, however, the United Nations (U.N.) expects 20 cities to have a population in excess of 10 million. The bulk of these megacities are in Asia.

Currently, city dwellers are the most common in the developed nations, where three-quarters of the population live in urban areas. Yet, nearly all the future urban population increase will be in the developing nations. With people lured by the prospects of a better job and modern amenities, the level of urbanization in the developing world is projected to rise 1.5% annually over the 1995–2015 period, above the world average rate (1%). A key exception is Latin America and the Caribbean, where 74% of the population are already domiciled in the cities, making the region the most urbanized of the developing world.

Over the next two decades, the fastest rate of urban growth will occur in Asia and Africa, whose current levels of urbanization, 34.6% and 34.4%, respectively, are below the world average (45.2%)

Asia, in particular, is about to go urban in a big way. Based on projections from the United Nations, Asia's urban population is expected to increase by a staggering 1 billion people over the next 20 years. Between 1995 and the year 2000, the U.N. projects that Asia's urban population will increase by 210 million people. Thereafter, it expects the region's urban population to expand by 231 million people between the years 2000 and 2005, by another 252 million (roughly the population of the entire United States) between 2005 and 2010, and by 268 million between 2010 and 2015.

People, notably youths, are leaving the farms for the cities in Asia for the same reasons people migrated to the urban areas in the United States more than a hundred years ago. The lure of the city lies mainly in the potential of higher wages, job opportunities, and access to material goods not yet available in rural areas.

The World's Largest Cities, 1950 and 2000
(By Population Size, in Millions of People)

Rank	City	Country	1950	City	Country	2000
1	New York	United States	12.3	Tokyo	Japan	28.0
2	London	United Kingdom	8.7	Mexico City	Mexico	18.1
3	Tokyo	Japan	6.9	Bombay	India	18.0
4	Paris	France	5.4	São Paulo	Brazil	17.7
5	Moscow	Russia Federation	5.4	New York	United States	16.6
6	Shanghai	China	5.3	Shanghai	China	14.2
7	Essen	Germany	5.3	Lagos	Nigeria	13.5
8	Buenos Aires	Argentina	5.0	Los Angeles	United States	13.1
9	Chicago	United States	4.9	Calcutta	India	12.9
10	Calcutta	India	4.4	Buenos Aires	Argentina	12.4
11	Osaka	Japan	4.1	Seoul	Republic of Korea	12.2
12	Los Angeles	United States	4.0	Beijing	China	12.0
13	Beijing	China	3.9	Karachi	Pakistan	11.8
14	Milan	Italy	3.6	Delhi	India	11.7
15	Berlin	Germany	3.3	Dhaka	Bangladesh	11.0
16	Philadelphia	United States	2.9	Metro Manila	Philippines	10.8
17	Saint Petersburg	Russia Federation	2.9	Cairo	Egypt	10.8
18	Bombay	India	2.9	Osaka	Japan	10.6
19	Mexico City	Mexico	2.9	Rio de Janeiro	Brazil	10.6
20	Rio de Janeiro	Brazil	2.9	Tianjin	China	10.2

Source: Population Division of the Department of Economic and Social Affairs, United Nations Secretariat, "World Urbanization Prospects: The 1996 Revision."

Asia's Urban Population
(As a % of Total Population)

Country	1960	1994	2000
China	19	29	35
Hong Kong	85	95	96
India	18	27	29
Indonesia	15	34	40
Malaysia	27	53	58
Philippines	30	53	59
South Korea	28	80	86
Thailand	13	20	22

Source: U.N. Human Development Report, 1997

16 | The Rise of Asia's "MTV Generation"

One of the most dynamic global demographic trends of today concerns the world's youths, notably young people in the developing nations. Half the population in the developing nations are under the age of 23, versus the median age of 36 in the developed countries. This helps explain the strategic thrust of many multinationals, which view the developing nations as the last commercial frontier. By the year 2000, according to the World Bank, the global "MTV Generation" (those between the ages of 10 and 24) will number over 1.6 billion.

The largest concentration of youths is in Asia, where the World Bank estimates that the number of people between the ages of 10 and 24 years old will top 1 billion by the year 2000 (see the accompanying graph). Given the sheer size of this massive emerging market, and the fact that many consumer-related industries in the United States and Europe are either oversupplied or stagnant and mature, the future of many multinationals lies with Asia's youths. Their desires, tastes, and spending habits are crucial to the long-term prospects of McDonald's, Procter & Gamble, General Electric, and many other consumer-related product companies.

Asia's youths, or emerging MTV Generation, differ substantially from their parents and grandparents. The latter were tasked with rebuilding war-torn nations following the destruction of World War II. This required long hours at work, individual sacrifice, high savings, and a mindset that favored production over consumption.

In contrast, members of Asia's MTV Generation are growing up in an era of relative prosperity, not poverty, not withstanding Asia's current economic slowdown. Think of the parents and older generations as the "builders" of Asia; the children as the "buyers." This group is more attuned to Western goods and norms and has developed a taste for Coke and Chicken McNuggets. Eating out is less of a novelty and more of a mainstream event. Computers and wireless phones are becoming standard hardware.

As a by-product of Asia's success, this generation is better educated and more willing and able to travel abroad. Traditional norms remain important, though leisure time, convenience, individualism, indulgence, spending, and other Western habits permeate this group. Brands are very important, giving a competitive edge to companies with widespread global brand awareness. These same trends are becoming more pronounced in Latin America.

Asia's army of youths is roughly 4 times greater than Africa's, almost 7 times larger than the number of youths in both Latin America and Europe, and 16 times larger than the number in North America. In some nations such as China, Indonesia, Vietnam, the Philippines, and Malaysia, the MTV Generation makes up 30% or more of the population. In both China and India, the number of people aged 10 to 24 is 300 million or higher, a figure greater than the total population of the United States. In the United States, the so-called MTV Generation makes up 20.1% of the population. The number is 17% in Japan and 16.7% in Germany.

Against this backdrop, the rise of Asia's MTV Generation represents one of the most important demographic trends in the world, and it will undoubtably play a featured role in the future profitability of many multinationals.

The Global MTV Generation*
(Population Ages 10 to 24 Years)

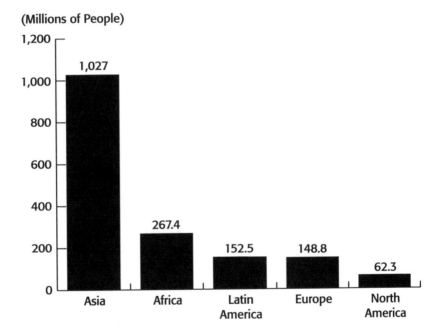

(Millions of People)

*By the year 2000

Source: World Bank

17 Global Graying

The fastest growing segment of the world's population is elderly people, a trend that will become more pronounced over the next few decades in both the developed and developing nations. Indeed, the number of persons aged 65 and over will increase at a rate more than twice as fast as total population between 1996 and 2020.

The median age—the midpoint that separates the younger half from the older half—of the world population was 26 in 1996 but will rise to 31 by 2020. Currently, half the population in the developed nations is under the age of 36, versus under age 23 in the developing nations. By the year 2020, the median age in the former will be 42 and will be age 29 in the latter.

While global graying is a sign of economic progress and medical triumph, it also represents one of the most important challenges for societies around the world. The aging of the world's population is already straining the national budgets of many countries and will force major reform in public pension and retirement sytems not only in the United States, Japan, and Europe but also in key emerging nations such as China, Mexico, and Brazil. Pay-as-you-go retirement systems—or systems funded by taxes on current workers rather than from the earnings of investment pools—threaten to be undermined by such factors as longer life spans, early retirements, and slower labor-force growth. Accordingly, the "support ratio" of workers to retirees continues to fall in many nations, including the United States, where the ratio has declined from 16 workers in the 1950s to little more than 3 workers today.

Japan has one of the fastest growing elderly populations among the industrialized nations and will go from being one of the youngest of the main industrialized nations to one of the oldest over the next decades, causing the country's elderly dependency ratio to soar and to top its counterparts.

A serious challenge for Japan and virtually every other country in the world is to adjust policies to accommodate their respective aging populations. The traditional way of looking after the aging segment—social security or state pensions—is becoming too expensive. Under the pay-as-you-go system, countries are running out of people to pay the contributions. Accordingly, support is building to privatize pension systems. Compulsory contributions into personal pension accounts are becoming the norm around the world. Moves to increase the number of funded systems, rather than pay-as-you-go systems, are also afoot. In short, preparing for older populations is one of the most pressing issues before the world economy.

Percentage of Population Aged 65 and Older

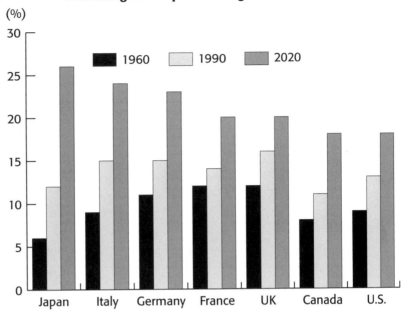

Source: © *OECD, 1996,* Social Policy Studies, Ageing in OECD Countries, A Critical Policy Challenge No. 20, October 1996. *Reproduced by permission of the OECD.*

Elderly Dependency Ratios
(Population Aged 65 and Older as a %
of Working-Age Population)

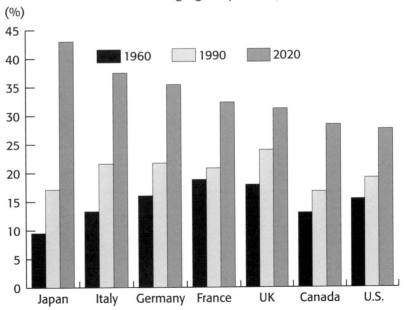

Source: © *OECD, 1996,* Social Policy Studies, Ageing in OECD Countries, A Critical Policy Challenge No. 20, October 1996. *Reproduced by permission of the OECD.*

CHAPTER 2

Trade

Overview

Global trade is one of the most important variables of the world economy. Trade, in addition to investment, is the conduit by which countries, companies, and individuals interact on a global basis. In general, trade benefits consumers by giving people a greater choice of competitively priced goods to choose from. Growth in global trade has been a key factor behind the rising standard of living for millions of people over the past 50 years. As a benchmark, total world merchandise trade amounted to $58 billion in 1950. In 1997 world merchandise exports and services totaled $5.3 trillion and $1.2 trillion respectively.

This chapter discusses a number of relevant trends ranging from the role of trade in the world economy to specific commodity export patterns. We have identified the world's leading exporting and importing nations, global service leaders, the top suppliers to the developing nations, and countries waiting in line to join the World Trade Organization (WTO), the multilateral institution that governs the global trading system.

We have devoted a few pages to the role of trade in the U.S. economy, a sensitive, yet not well understood, issue in America. Suffice here to say that trade is an increasingly important component of the U.S. economy and is, in general, beneficial to American workers. Although it may sound counterintuitive given America's large trade deficit, the United States is among the most competitive exporters in the world. In addition, America's breadth of exports is unparalleled, while its trade deficit is not as formidable viewed from the perspective we present. The United States, thus, has everything to gain from a free and thriving global trading system, and conversely, much to lose from a weak and fragile trading environment.

The role of U.S. foreign affiliates is critical to the global success of American multinationals, a little known fact highlighted in trend 32 and 34.

Given the benefits derived from trade, it is important for investors to recognize what countries are integrated into the world trading system and what countries are not. Pay particular attention, therefore, to entry 25, which summarizes the "globalization" of countries, notably those among the developing nations.

The import demand of the developing nations, the structural shift in Japan's trade, and the rise of regional trading blocs are also highlighted in the following pages. So too is the role of intrafirm trade, which is probably one of the most important, yet least recognized, global trading trends of today.

18 | World Trade and the Global Economy

Trade plays a pivotal role in the world economy. Indeed, world trade has consistently expanded at a faster pace than world output for more than a decade. World output rose by an annual average rate of 3.4% between 1979 and 1988 and by roughly 3.1% between 1990 and 1997. Growth in world trade volume was stronger—4.3% on average over the 1979–88 time frame and an estimated 6% over 1990–97. In some years, notably 1994 and 1995, the rate of growth of world trade has been almost three times faster than world output (see the first graph). In continuation of historical trends, merchandise exports grew at a much faster pace than world output in 1997, rising 9.5% versus 4.1% output growth.

As a result, the share of world trade to world output has climbed significantly since the mid-1980s, which is illustrated in the second graph. The ratio stood at 16.7% in 1986 but has since climbed to 18.6% in 1990 and a record 21.6% in 1996. This represents one of the fastest increases in trade as a percentage of output since the early 1970s, when the spike in world oil prices led to an equally sharp hike in dollar-denominated global trade. Then, an exogenous shock led to a higher percentage of trade in world output. Over the 1990s, however, trade has assumed a more prominent role in the world economy owing not to a singular event, but rather to long-term, secular forces.

Numerous variables have converged over the past decade to boost trade, including greater trade liberalization in the developing nations and lower transportation and telecommunications costs. In addition, the proliferation of intraregional trade agreements as well as the successful conclusion of the Uruguay Round of global trade talks have been a catalyst for global trade. So too has the demise of communism, which opened new markets in Russia, Poland, Hungary, and other places around the world. The collapse of the Berlin Wall alone added millions of new consumers to the world economy and complemented the opening of China in the late 1970s. Economic reform measures in India and across Latin America have brought to the fore even more consumers and traders.

In general, the 1990s has seen the blossoming of trade in the developing nations. But trends in the developed nations have been just as important in promoting world trade growth. They include the following: the extended economic expansion of the United States, the world's largest consumer of imports by a wide margin; robust levels of foreign direct investment among the developed nations; surging trade in high-tech products; and the turn toward a stronger U.S. dollar in mid-1995 that helped revive export growth in Japan and Germany.

Growth in the Volume of World Merchandise Exports and GDP
(% Annual Change)

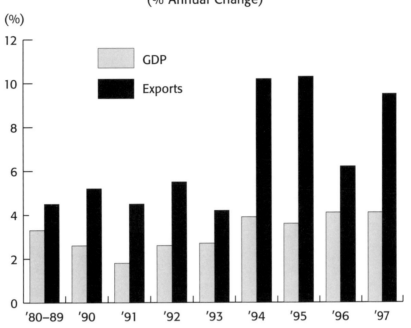

Source: IMF *World Economic Outlook, May 1998*

World Trade as a Percentage of World Output
(At Constant Prices)

(%)

Source: *International Monetary Fund*

19 The Strongest Traders of the 1990s

The value of world trade decelerated in 1996 and 1997 on account of the strength of the U.S. dollar, which resulted in a sharp decline in dollar export and import prices. Measured by volume, however, world trade remained robust in 1997, Asia's financial crisis notwithstanding. Indeed, the volume of world merchandise exports grew by 9.5% in 1997, the second highest rate recorded in more than two decades.

One key trend in world trade lies with Latin America, which has experienced somewhat of a trade renaissance in the 1990s. Stronger levels of real growth, rising foreign direct investment flows, and trade liberalization efforts are just some of the variables that have contributed to the region's much improved trade performance of this decade. As shown in the first table, export volumes grew by 8% on an annual average basis during 1990–95, and by 11% and 12.5% in 1996 and 1997 respectively. Import growth was even stronger, notably in 1997, when import volumes surged by 21.5%, the strongest in the world. Despite this strong trade performance, a key question to emerge is whether or not the robust levels of exports and imports can be sustained given the region's current account deficits and the appreciation of the real effective exchange rates in many key Latin American countries, such as Brazil. Both variables could hamper Latin America's trade performance in the years ahead.

Other key trends shown in the first table include the following: Like Latin America, import volumes in North America outpaced export volumes in 1997. Europe's main exporters enjoyed an 8% rise in export volumes in 1997, one of the strongest annual growth rates for the region this decade. Export volumes in Asia also accelerated in 1997, with Japan experiencing a sharp turnaround in export volumes, thanks to the weaker yen. Exports rose 9.5% versus a 0.5% decline the year before. On the downside, import volume growth in Japan and Asia slowed significantly in 1997 and 1996 relative to the first half of this decade. Import volume growth in 1997 was roughly half (5.5%) the rate of average growth over the 1990–95 period (10.5%). Finally, note the revitalization of trade among the transition economies (Cental Europe and Russia) in 1996 and 1997.

By value, and on a country basis, China experienced the strongest level of growth in exports in 1997, with exports rising by over 20% to $182.7 billion (see the second table). Mexico, Brazil, and the United States followed, with all three achieving double-digit export growth in 1997. Ireland and the United Kingdom were the top exporters in Europe.

In terms of imports, some of the world's best markets for foreign goods in 1997 were in such key emerging markets as Mexico, Brazil, Poland, Taiwan, Russia, Turkey, and India. Among the industrialized nations, Canada, Ireland, and the United States ranked as the strongest importers. The United States ranked last among the top 10, although note that U.S. imports in 1997 (nearly $900 billion) were greater than the combined imports of the nine other countries listed. Such is the importance of America to the world trading system.

World Merchandise Trade by Region
(Volume, % Annual Change)

	Exports			Imports		
Region	1990–95	1996	1997	1990–95	1996	1997
North America*	7.0	6.0	10.5	7.5	6.0	12.5
Latin America	8.0	11.0	12.5	11.5	11.5	21.5
European Union	5.5	4.0	8.0	4.5	2.5	6.5
Transition Economies	4.5	7.5	11.0	1.5	14.5	16.0
Asia	7.5	3.5	11.5	10.5	5.0	5.5
Japan	1.5	–0.5	9.5	6.5	2.0	2.5
Asia†	11.0	6.5	10.0	12.0	4.5	5.5

*Canada and the United States
†Taiwan, Hong Kong, Korea, Malaysia, Singapore, and Thailand

Source: World Trade Organization

The Fastest Growing Exporters and Importers, 1997
(US$ Billions, Annual % Change)

Exporters	$ Billions	%	Importers	$ Billions	%
China	182.7	21	Mexico	112.5	23
Mexico	110.4	15	Brazil	65.7	15
Brazil	53.0	11	Canada	201.0	15
United States	689.0	10	Poland	42.0	13
Ireland	52.4	8	Taiwan	113.2	12
United Kingdom	280.1	7	Russia	48.0	11
Indonesia	53.4	7	Turkey	46.8	10
Canada	214.4	6	India	40.6	9
Taiwan	123.0	5	Ireland	39.1	9
South Korea	136.6	5	United States	899.2	9

Source: World Trade Organization

20 | The World's Export Champions

Competing for global customers is a difficult and herculean task, and no one does it better than the United States. The accompanying table shows current leaders in the trade. America exported $689 billion in goods in 1997, which is more than what many countries produce in a year. America accounted for 12.6% of total world exports for the year, the number-one ranking.

A number of variables account for the top ranking of the United States, with one factor being the steady depreciation of the dollar over the second half of the 1980s and the first half of the 1990s. Yet, a cheaper currency, which enhances the price competitiveness of tradable goods, is not the only reason behind America's export success of the nineties. Breadth of exports, with the export mix of the United States ranging from apples to auto parts to aircraft, is another component. So too is America's commanding technological lead in such products as computer software, medical equipment, and other advanced technology goods. Global demand, notably in the developing nations, continues to rise for such products, boosting the overseas sales of U.S. goods. All of these variables have sustained relatively strong export growth since the U.S. dollar began to appreciate significantly beginning in mid-1995.

Germany is number two in global exports, exporting $512 billion worth of goods in 1997. German exports center on chemicals, capital machinery, textiles, and automobiles. Exports from Japan, totaling $421 billion in 1997, are composed primarily of automobiles, automobile parts, consumer electronics, and other related products. Combined, the United States, Germany, and Japan accounted for roughly 30% of total world exports in 1997.

It is interesting that out of all the nations of the world, only 16 countries have the wherewithal to export more than $100 billion worth of goods in a given year. The United States was the first country to export $100 billion or more of goods, in 1975. Other industrialized nations (Germany, Japan, France, the United Kingdom) followed over the second half of the 1970s and the balance of the 1980s. Not until Hong Kong breached the $100 billion mark in 1987 did a developing nation belong to the exclusive trading club.

The 1990s, at least up until 1997, has seen the entry of just six new members to the $100 billion club, with four of the six, to no surprise, from the trade-oriented Pacific Rim region. China, whose exports totaled just $9.5 billion in 1978, the year before the mainland "opened" to the world, exported more than $100 billion in goods in 1994 and now ranks, including Hong Kong's trade, as one of the world's largest exporters.

The development strategies of South Korea, Taiwan, and Singapore have long emphasized an outward orientation toward exports. To a large degree, the strategy has paid off handsomely, given that all three nations, whose combined exports totaled just $3 billion in 1965, exported more than $100 billion each in 1995. The newest members of the $100 billion export club include Spain and Mexico. Spain's entry into the European Union and expanding trade links with South America helped boost exports from $24.3 billion in 1985 to more than $100 billion in 1996. Owing to strong demand in the United States and the weak peso, Mexico's exports topped $100 billion for the first time in 1997.

Future candidates for the club include Sweden, whose exports reached $82.4 billion in 1997, and Malaysia, whose exports reached $78.7 billion in the same year.

The $100 Billion Export Club, 1997

Country	$ Billions	% Share of World Merchandise Exports
United States (1975)	688.9	12.6
Germany (1976)	511.7	9.4
Japan (1979)	421.1	7.7
France (1979)	287.8	5.3
United Kingdom (1980)	280.1	5.1
Italy (1987)	238.9	4.4
Canada (1988)	214.4	3.9
Netherlands (1988)	193.5	3.5
Hong Kong (1987)	188.1	3.4
China (1994)	182.7	3.3
Belgium-Luxembourg (1987)	167.6	3.1
South Korea (1995)	136.6	2.5
Singapore (1995)	125.0	2.2
Taiwan (1995)	121.9	2.1
Mexico (1997)	110.4	2.0
Spain (1996)	104.3	1.9

( ) = First year that exports exceeded $100 billion

Source: World Trade Organization

21 The United States as the World's Leading Importer

Just as the United States is the world's leading exporter, so it is also the world's top importing nation, and by a significant margin. Where the United States, Germany, and, to a lesser degree, Japan vie somewhat closely for the honor of being the world's export champion, it is no contest among the top three when it comes to imports—the United States consumed nearly $900 billion in imports in 1997, or 16.1% of the world total. That is not only greater than Germany and Japan combined but also a figure that exceeds the total imports of the 15-member European Union (excluding European Union intratrade).

After the United States, Germany and Japan are the next largest import markets. As shown in the table, Germany's share of world imports was 7.9% in 1997; Japan's was 6.0%. The bulk of Germany's imports come from Europe, while an increasing percentage of Japan's imports come from Asia. Combined, the United States, Germany, and Japan accounted for 30% of world imports in 1997. The industrialized nations, in total, account for nearly two-thirds of world imports.

The aggregate imports of Hong Kong and China totaled $350 billion in 1996, making China one of the largest import markets in the world. As a footnote, however, the actual dollar amount remains uncertain, given the double-counting that occurs when determining the imports and exports between Hong Kong and China.

Asia's newly industrialized nations are major world importers as well. Note that the aggregate imports of Taiwan, South Korea, and Singapore, with a combined gross domestic product of $850 billion, were greater ($390 billion) than Japan's ($338 billion) in 1997, whose economy is roughly six times larger ($5.1 trillion). Not surprisingly, then, weak import demand in Asia's newly industrialized nations, as well as Japan, carries global ramifications.

By a wide margin, Mexico is the largest importer in Latin America. The country's imports totaled $112.5 billion in 1997, well above Brazil's imports ($65.7 billion), whose economy is more than twice the size of Mexico's.

What nations are the most dependent on the U.S. market? Mexico and Canada stand out, with both nations' exports to the United States accounting for more than 80% of their total. Close investment and manufacturing ties among the NAFTA (North American Free Trade Agreement) partners is a significant factor behind the export dependence of Mexico and Canada on the United States.

The nations of Central America and the Caribbean are also overwhelmingly dependent on the United States for exports. More than 75% of Haiti's exports were shipped to America in 1997, while Honduras sent more than 70% of exports to the United States in the same year. Among the larger nations of the world, roughly 28% of Japan's exports were consumed by the United States in 1997. Germany is far less dependent, with the United States accounting for less than 10% of Germany's total.

The World's Top Importers, 1997

Rank	Country	Value (US$ Billions)	% Share of World Imports
1	United States	899.2	16.1
2	Germany	441.5	7.9
3	Japan	338.4	6.0
4	United Kingdom	307.4	5.5
5	France	266.8	4.8
6	Hong Kong	208.7	3.7
7	Italy	208.6	3.7
8	Canada	201.0	3.6
9	Netherlands	177.1	3.2
10	Belgium-Luxembourg	155.5	2.8
11	South Korea	144.6	2.6
12	China	142.4	2.5
13	Singapore	132.4	2.4
14	Spain	122.7	2.2
15	Taiwan	113.2	2.0
16	Mexico	112.5	2.0
17	Malaysia	78.6	1.4
18	Switzerland	75.8	1.4
19	Australia	65.8	1.2
20	Brazil	65.7	1.2

Source: World Trade Organization

22 Top Global Exports—Computers and Chips Move to the Forefront

World merchandise trade is dominated by manufactured goods, whose share of world exports jumped from 54% in 1980 to 73.3% in 1996, as the accompanying table conveys. Manufactured exports encompass many products, including iron and steel, chemicals, and semimanufactured items. The share of these goods in global exports continues to decline or stagnate, save chemicals, whose share of world exports has increased modestly over this decade, from 8.7% in 1990 to 9.3% in 1996.

The robust growth of manufactured exports over the past 15 years has come from rising exports of machinery and transport equipment. This group's share of total world exports stood at 25.8% in 1980 but climbed to 35.8% in 1990 and nearly 39% in 1996.

Machinery and transport equipment exports are broken down into three segments by the World Trade Organization. One is "other machinery," whose share of world exports fell slightly between 1990 (17.6%) and 1996 (17.4%). A second category is automotive products, whose share of world exports also fell between 1990 and 1996, a trend that reflects greater in-country assembly and manufacturing among the world's largest automobile companies.

The third and most explosive category is office machinery and telecommunications equipment, which includes such high-tech goods as computers, semiconductors, printed circuit boards, telecommunications equipment, and other related goods. Think of these products as information-age exports. They played a rather insignificant role in world exports in 1980, yet office machinery and telecommunications equipment exports are now valued at more than $625 billion a year and account for more than 12% of total world exports, up from 8.8% in 1990 and just 4.2% in 1980. Over the 1990–96 period, world exports of office machines and telecommunications equipment grew by 13% on an annual average basis, following 18% annual average growth over 1985–90.

The torrid pace of growth was due to a number of factors, including strong capital investment, particularly in the United States, but also around the world as more and more companies strive to boost productivity via machines. Falling prices, strong computer demand from households, and the ongoing convergence of computer, communications, and consumer electronics technologies have also contributed to robust trade levels.

The outlook, meanwhile, remains rosy, given the prevailing trends just mentioned. In addition, countries all over the world are upgrading their telecommunication infrastructures, while the global demand for computers remains very strong. Adding more fuel to the growth of high-tech exports is the International Technology Agreement, which was hammered out in 1996–97 under the aegis of the World Trade Organization. The high-tech trade deal, signed by countries representing more than 90% of trade in information technology, will lower tariffs on a range of high-tech products in four stages and play a key role in sustaining the prominence of high-tech exports in world trade. Indeed, the World Trade Organization estimates that trade in office machinery and telecom equipment will rise to $1 trillion annually by the year 2000. The WTO agreement to liberalize international trade in basic telecommunications services should also prove to be a boom to world trade in telecom equipment.

The advent of the information age and the attendant robust expansion in high-tech exports have been critical to the growth of manufactured exports and world trade in general. Note from the table that exports of office and telecommunications equipment is now one of the largest segments of global trade, surpassing exports in agricultural products, mining, autos, and fuels.

World Merchandise Exports by Product
(% Share of Total Exports)

	1980	1990	1996
Agricultural products	14.7	12.2	11.5
Food	11.0	9.3	9.0
Raw materials	3.7	2.9	2.5
Mining products	27.7	14.3	11.2
Fuels	23.0	10.6	8.1
Manufactured goods	53.9	70.6	73.3
Chemicals	7.0	8.7	9.3
Machinery and transport equipment	25.8	35.8	38.8
Office/telecom equipment	4.2	8.8	12.2
Automotive	6.4	9.4	9.2
Textiles	2.7	3.1	2.9

Source: World Trade Organization

23 Leading Global Exporters by Commodity

The accompanying table lists the world's leading exporters by commodity and reveals, to a large degree, the competitive strengths of each country. One of the most notable features is that of the five major commodities listed, the United States is the only nation to rank in all five categories, testimony to America's export breadth and global competitiveness.

By a wide margin, the United States is the globe's top farmer, accounting for more than 13% of total world food exports in 1996. That is down, however, from the level of 1980, reflecting in part the growing agricultural efficiencies of Argentina, Poland, Brazil, and other large developing nations. Note that of the world's top five food exporters, all are from the industrialized nations. They accounted for roughly 40% of total world farm exports in 1996.

The world's top chemical exporters again are all from the advanced nations as well. Germany ranked number one in 1996, with a world share of 14.2%, down from 17.1% in 1990. America's global export share was double that of Japan's. Collectively, the top five chemical exporters accounted for nearly half of total world exports.

The United States was the leading exporter of machinery and transportation equipment in 1980, dropped to third place in 1990, but regained its top rank in 1996. The cheap dollar earlier in this decade, coupled with U.S. restructuring efforts to boost productivity, led the comeback.

The top exporters of office machinery and telecom equipment differ slightly from those of other commodities. The United States and Japan top the list. But two of the top five—Singapore and Taiwan—are developing nations. Taiwan's strength, among other variables, lies with its educated workforce and small, nimble technology companies.

However, it must be noted that much of what Singapore exports is to a large degree manufactured and exported by American or Japanese multinationals operating in Singapore. The presence of the United Kingdom in the top rankings reflects the country's competitive wages and corresponding ability to attract foreign investment from the world's leading high-tech companies.

As for the world's top exporters of automobiles, the race is being won by Germany, ranked number one with a share of 18.5%, followed by Japan. The share of the United States has remained relatively stable over the past 15 years, despite wide swings in the exchange rate. The majority of Canada's automobile exports are autos produced by the U.S. "Big Three" in Canada and then shipped to the United States and other markets. The top five exporters accounted for over 60% of total world auto exports in 1996.

Leading Exporters by Commodity
(% Share in World Trade)

Rank	Exporter	1980	1990	1996
	Foods			
1	United States	17.8	13.5	13.8
2	France	8.0	10.5	8.7
3	Netherlands	6.6	8.3	7.3
4	Germany	4.5	6.1	5.6
5	United Kingdom	3.5	4.1	4.0
	Chemicals			
1	Germany	17.2	17.9	14.2
2	United States	14.9	13.3	13.3
3	France	9.4	9.6	8.6
4	United Kingdom	8.7	8.0	7.4
5	Japan	4.7	5.3	6.1
	Machinery & Transport Equipment			
1	United States	17.0	15.1	15.4
2	Japan	14.5	16.7	14.4
3	Germany	16.3	17.3	12.8
4	United Kingdom	7.6	6.2	5.8
5	France	7.0	6.5	5.8
	Office Machinery and Telecom Equipment			
1	United States	20.2	17.3	16.7
2	Japan	21.1	22.4	15.0
3	Singapore	3.2	6.4	10.3
4	United Kingdom	6.4	6.5	6.2
5	Taiwan	3.2	4.7	5.7
	Automobile Products			
1	Germany	21.1	21.9	18.5
2	Japan	19.8	20.8	15.9
3	United States	12.7	10.2	11.7
4	Canada	6.9	8.9	9.5
5	France	9.9	8.2	7.3

Source: World Trade Organization

24 The Rise of Global Services and Global Service Leaders

International commerce is dominated by trade in goods, with world trade in merchandise goods topping $5 billion for the first time in 1995. In 1997, world merchandise exports rose to $5.3 billion, up 3% from the prior year. Trade in commercial services, while not as large as merchandise trade, is just as dynamic. As the bar graph shows, world service exports have increased steadily over the past decade, topping $1 trillion for the first time in 1994. World service exports rose to $1.3 trillion in 1997, accounting for roughly 20% of total world exports.

Services are poised to gain a larger share of world trade in the future. Government deregulation of various service sectors, the globalization of production, rising service-based activities, and, in particular, the rapid diffusion of information technology—all of these variables are expanding the boundaries of tradable services and promoting cross-border trade in software programming, manufacturing design, education, health care, entertainment, insurance, and financial services.

This trend bodes well for the world's top service exporter—the United States. Services figure prominently in the U.S. trade picture, with service exports the second largest category of U.S. exports (capital goods exports are number one). According to figures from the U.S. Commerce Department, U.S. service exports totaled more than $250 billion in 1997, which is more than the total exports of most nations. More important perhaps, while America runs a chronic trade deficit in goods, it consistently generates a service trade surplus. From a modest level of just $100 million in 1985, the U.S. trade surplus in services rose to $30.7 billion in 1990 and hit a record $85.2 billion in 1997.

Travel, passenger fares, and freight and port services have traditionally made up the bulk of U.S. service exports. However, the "other private services" category, a collection of activities including information services, education, computer and data processing, financial services, and medical care, has emerged as one of the fastest growing components of U.S. service exports. Exports of "other private services" hit $83 billion in 1997, up from $40.6 billion in 1990 and $20 billion in 1986. As these services become more internationally "tradable," U.S. companies are primed to reap the rewards.

As the world's largest service exporter, America accounted for 17.8% of world commercial exports in 1997, with the United Kingdom a distant second (see the accompanying table). (Note that the U.S. government valued U.S. service exports in 1997 at $253 billion versus the $231 billion tally of the wto.) Relative to Japan and Germany, U.S. service exports in 1997 were more than triple the level of Japan ($68.4 billion) and Germany's ($72.3 billion). Japan, a country strong in selling manufactured goods overseas, is weak in service exports.

World Exports of Commercial Services

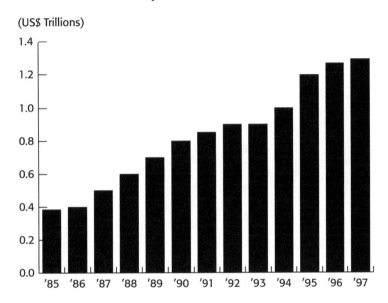

Source: World Trade Organization

Leading Exporters and Importers of Commercial Services, 1997

Rank	Exporters	US$ Billions	% Share	Rank	Importers	US$ Billions	% Share
1	United States	230.7	17.8	1	United States	151.4	12.0
2	United Kingdom	84.8	6.5	2	Japan	122.6	9.7
3	France	81.9	6.3	3	Germany	116.3	9.2
4	Germany	72.3	5.6	4	United Kingdom	69.7	5.5
5	Italy	71.2	5.5	5	Italy	69.1	5.5
6	Japan	68.4	5.3	6	France	61.4	4.9
7	Netherlands	48.5	3.7	7	Netherlands	43.4	3.4
8	Spain	43.6	3.4	8	Canada	35.7	2.8
9	Hong Kong	37.4	2.9	9	Korea	33.4	2.6
10	Belgium-Luxembourg	33.3	2.6	10	Belgium-Luxembourg	32.2	2.5

Source: World Trade Organization

25 What Countries Are Global?
What Countries Are Not?

Globalization is the buzzword of the decade, but what exactly does the term mean? More important, how do you measure a country's level of participation in the world economy?

For starters, globalization represents the accelerating pace of international economic integration and interdependence through rising cross-border transactions in goods, capital, services, and labor. Like the first decade of this century, the last decade has seen a sharp rise in global trade and investment. In general, but not always, globalization confers many benefits on nations actively linked with the outside world, including better resource allocation, economies of scale, technology transfers, and greater availability of capital.

Measuring a nation's degree of integration or interdependence with the rest of the world is difficult, but two measures provide rough approximations. One measure is the ratio of trade (imports plus exports) to gross domestic product. This determines a nation's level of trade openness. The second measure is the level of foreign direct investment (FDI) as a percentage of gross fixed capital formation. This variable highlights the extent of participation by foreign companies in the local economy.

The countries of Central Europe and developing Asia have relatively high levels of trade openness, versus those of Latin America. Note the contrast between China and India—Asia's two dream markets. With the former as the more outward-looking of the two, China's level of trade openness stood at 40% in 1995, up from 25% in 1985 and just 9% in 1978. India, on the other hand, has been more reluctant to trade with the rest of the world, with a trade openness figure of 27% in 1995. One of the remarkable and important economic trends in Central Europe has been the region's rapid reorientation of trade from the communist bloc nations to the West, boosting the trade openness of many nations in the region.

Shifting to investment as a percentage of gross fixed capital formation, the nation with one of the highest ratios was none other than China (25.7%) in 1995, the last year of available data. Brazil and India, similarly with trade, have been less amenable to foreign investment in the past than their counterparts. Both nations, however, have become more receptive to investors as of late and have experienced a corresponding rise in foreign direct investment.

As a benchmark, the level of trade openness of the United States was 18.3% in 1996, above Japan's (15.2%) but well below Germany's (40.8%).

Global Integration

Country	Trade Openness*	Investment Openness†
Asia		
Hong Kong	297	8.4
Singapore	275	24.6
China	40	25.7
Philippines	80	9.0
Indonesia	53	6.5
Malaysia	194	17.9
Thailand	90	2.9
Korea	67	1.1
Taiwan	80	2.7
India	27	3.6
Latin America		
Mexico	48	17.1
Brazil	15	4.7
Argentina	16	11.7
Chile	54	10.8
Venezuela	49	7.6
Colombia	35	14.8
Peru	30	24.7
Central Europe		
Poland	53	18.1
Czech Republic	108	17.6
Hungary	67	59.7
Russia	44	0.9
Romania	60	8.7
United States	18.3	5.9
Japan	15.2	0.1
Germany	40.8	1.7

*Exports plus imports/GDP
†Share of inward FDI to gross fixed capital formation

Source: OECD; U.N., World Investment Report, 1997; World Bank

26 America and the World Economy

No country is an island economically, not even the United States. Even though the United States accounts for over one-fifth of world GDP and the domestic market is one of the largest and wealthiest in the world, America's prosperity is closely linked with the world economy. The accompanying charts make this clear.

In 1996, the United States depended more on exports of goods and services for output than Japan, with America's exports as a share of gross domestic product more than 11% in 1996, versus 9.4% in Japan. Among the "Big Three" (the United States, Japan, and Germany), the German economy (with exports as a percentage of GDP at 23.3%) is far more dependent on exports as an engine of growth, a function of Germany's tight trading ties with its European neighbors and the relative size of its economy.

U.S. exports as a percentage of GDP never climbed above 6% over the 1960s but surged to 10% by the start of 1980. Over the first half of the 1980s, the strong U.S. dollar, weak growth in Europe, and the onset of Latin America's debt crisis all converged to slow U.S. export growth and reduce the role of exports in aggregate output. The share of exports to GDP sunk to 6.9% in 1986. Since then, however, the share has steadily climbed, rising to roughly 11.3% in 1996, double the level of 1970.

From the vantage point of just trade, America's dependence and linkages with the world economy are rather shallow. But trade is just one conduit by which the United States interacts with the rest of the world. Even greater participation comes via investment, the principal means of U.S. global engagement.

The interdependence of the U.S. economy and the world economy is much higher when U.S. foreign direct investment is added into the equation. Exports, imports, and foreign investment receipts and payments cover the gamut in terms of U.S. interaction with the rest of the world. And on this basis, when all the variables are aggregated, they accounted for 29% of U.S. gross domestic product in 1996, up from 24% in 1992 and just 12.4% in 1970.

Against this backdrop, the United States is far more integrated with and inextricably linked to the world economy than most people realize. Protectionism and the disengagement of America from the world economy, as called for by some parties, would only be self-defeating. Besides, as one of the world's largest exporters, a global technology leader, and the largest recipient of foreign direct investment, the United States and American workers have everything to gain from an expanding and thriving global trading system.

Exports as a Percentage of GDP, 1996

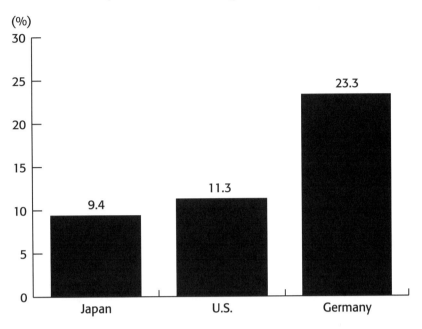

Source: IMF

Importance of Trade* to the U.S. Economy
(Total Trade as a % of GDP)

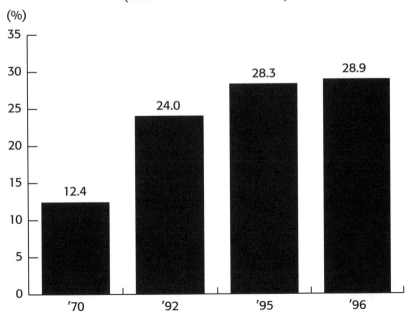

*Total exports and imports plus foreign investment receipts and payments

Source: U.S. Department of Commerce

27 Exports and Jobs—the Favorable Link

Almost nothing conjures up more debate and discord than the role of trade in the United States economy. The emotional issue is important not only to America but also to the world economy, given that the United States is the world's largest exporter and importer and, therefore, a linch-pin of the global trading system.

One frequently heard argument is that international trade does more harm than good, since imports destroy jobs, lead to lower wages, and, ultimately, undermine the standard of living of most Americans. Reality is different.

A large and growing share of the American workforce depends on exports for jobs, a fact highlighted in the first table. Jobs linked to the exports of goods and services rose by more than 60% over the 1986–94 period and now include more than 10 million workers. One in five jobs in the manufacturing sector is either directly or indirectly linked to exports. Farmers are closely linked as well, with one in six jobs in agri-culture somehow related to exports. In general, companies that are in the global market for the long haul experience faster, not slower, levels of employment growth over the long term.

These jobs, meanwhile, are not low-paying, hamburger-flipping jobs, but rather work that pays more than jobs at local companies. U.S. indus-tries producing products for the world markets require higher skill levels and thus pay higher wages than domestic producers. How much higher? According to various studies, salaries in export industries pay 5 to 15% more than salaries not linked to the global markets.

How can these higher wages be afforded, given that workers in many parts of the world work for far less money, many for as little as a dollar a day? Although wages in the United States are much higher relative to many other countries, notably those in the developing nations, American workers are among the most educated, trained, and therefore productive in the world. This makes them worth more in terms of higher wages and allows them to compete, in most industries, against low-wage countries.

By state, America's export growth over the 1990s has emanated from some unusual places. The second table tells the story. While such tradi-tional exporters as New York, California, and Texas remain America's top exporting states in dollar terms, in terms of export growth, some unlikely states have emerged as export leaders. Indeed, of the 10 states that achieved the fastest rates of growth from 1992 to 1996, seven are land-locked and predominantly located in the mountains or plains regions. Key exports from the interior include wheat, semiconductors, aerospace components, mining equipment, pasta, and chickens.

The bottom line: It is certainly undeniable that many U.S. workers and U.S. companies have been adversely affected by the harsh winds of foreign competition. Going global is not easy. But global competition bestows many rewards on countries and companies. Across a broad swath of American industry, ranging from the exterior to the interior, exports increasingly play a constructive and favorable role in the well-being of U.S. workers.

U.S. Jobs and Exports
(Share of Total Jobs Supported Directly
or Indirectly by Exports)

All civilian jobs	1 in 9
In manufacturing	1 in 5
In agriculture	1 in 6
In services	1 in 12

Source: U.S. Department of Commerce

Fastest Growing Exporters by State
(Merchandise Exports)

Rank	State	Average Growth, 1992–96 (%)
1	New Mexico	38.2
2	Nebraska	34.2
3	South Carolina	20.7
4	Wyoming	20.6
5	Arkansas	19.4
6	South Dakota	18.0
7	Arizona	17.1
8	Montana	16.3
9	Michigan	16.1
10	Connecticut	16.1

Source: U.S. Department of Commerce

28 America's Top Trading Partners

The United States maintains trade relations with virtually every country in the world, although just a handful of nations weigh heavily in America's trade performance. As the tables show, the most prominent are Canada, Mexico, and Japan, which, collectively, took roughly 42% of America's total exports of goods in 1997 and accounted for 43% of total U.S. goods imports.

Trade between the United States and Canada is unique in some ways, given that Canada's economy is just one-thirteenth the size of America's, while the nation's total population of 30 million is less than California's. What underpins this trade relationship, the largest in the world by a wide measure, are intense manufacturing and investment linkages between the two nations. Most trade between the United States and Canada is done intraindustry or intracompany, with the automobile industry the linchpin. Intrafirm trade also plays a major role in trade between the United States and Japan.

Given the persistence of America's trade deficit with Japan, many people do not realize that Japan is our third largest export market after Canada and Mexico. The problem lies in the fact that U.S. exports to Japan, $64.7 billion in 1997, were roughly half of what the United States bought from Japan, $121.6 billion, leaving a sizable trade deficit of $57 billion in goods.

Mexico is among America's largest export markets, as well as one of the largest sources of imports. Similar to trade between the United States and Canada, a large percentage of America's trade with Mexico is tied to cross-border manufacturing and investment linkages. Above all else, the North American Free Trade Agreement (NAFTA) has helped solidify and promote bilateral trade between Mexico and the United States. In total, America's NAFTA partners (Mexico and Canada) accounted for more than 32% of total U.S. exports in 1997 and supplied nearly 30% of America's total imports.

Across the Atlantic, the United Kingdom is the top export market for the United States, accounting for 5% of America's total exports in 1997, but 20% of total U.S. exports to the 15-member European Union. In the Pacific Rim, South Korea is the largest Asian market for American goods after Japan.

On the side of imports, China and Germany round out the top five suppliers of the United States. From the European Union, the United States imports the most from Germany, with machinery and transport equipment and chemicals the leading imports. Imports from China run the gamut and include such products as sneakers, toys, sports equipment, consumer electronic goods, furniture, and other consumer-related products.

Over the 1970s and early 1980s, many of these same light-manufactured goods were assembled in and exported from such countries as South Korea, Hong Kong, and Taiwan. However, the shift in manufacturing production from Asia's smaller economies to mainland China has altered trade flows over the past decade. What America once imported from Taiwan, for instance, is now bought from China, a trend that has raised China's profile in terms of U.S. imports. Indeed, in 1983, U.S. imports from China totaled only $2.3 billion and accounted for less than 1% of total imports. Today the picture is radically different, and given its low-cost manufacturing capabilities, China is likely to remain a top source of U.S. imports well into the future.

Top Five U.S. Export Markets, 1997

Rank	Country	US$ Billions	% of Total Exports
1	Canada	151.8	22.4
2	Mexico	71.2	10.5
3	Japan	64.7	9.5
4	United Kingdom	35.9	5.3
5	South Korea	24.6	3.6

Top Five U.S. Import Markets, 1997

Rank	Country	US$ Billions	% of Total Imports
1	Canada	170.8	19.2
2	Japan	121.6	13.9
3	Mexico	86.7	9.9
4	China	62.6	7.1
5	Germany	43.1	4.9

Source: U.S. Department of Commerce

29 America's Top Exporters and Importers

There are two common ways to measure trade. The most frequent way is to express trade in terms of value, or in U.S. dollars (which is the case for many nations around the world), German marks, or Japanese yen. Another way to measure trade is in volume, which is the basis of the accompanying table. The companies are ranked according to the number of waterborne containers they exported or imported in 1996, which gives a different perspective (volume-based versus value-based) on America's top traders.

Note that America's premier exporting firms are concentrated in industries that manufacture industrial materials—paper, agricultural products, chemicals, plastics, metals. Indeed, out of America's top 10 exporters, 4 are lumber or paper companies. Philip Morris, thanks to rising cigarette exports, in addition to strong global demand for its food products, ranks as the third largest U.S. exporter.

Chemicals and related products dominate America's export picture as well. Du Pont is one of the largest exporters of chemicals not only in the United States but also in the world. So too are Eastman Chemical, Union Carbide, and Dow Chemical. Capital machinery exporters are limited to Chrysler Corporation and Caterpillar Tractor.

On the import side, America's largest importer is a banana company, Chiquita Brands, which has large holdings throughout Central America. Dole Food, with extensive holdings in such nations as the Philippines, also ranks as a premier U.S. importer.

Some of America's largest importers are none other than your common retail outlet—Wal-Mart was the second largest U.S. importer in 1996. Target Stores ranked fifth, JCPenney seventh, and Payless Shoes eighth. Just how much these companies source from abroad is underscored by their ranking among America's largest importers.

Many of America's top importers are foreign firms with large production facilities or extensive distribution networks in the United States. Sumitomo America, a large Japanese trading company, is the third largest importer in America. Honda (sixth) and Canon (ninth) also rank in the top 10.

Thus, trade measured in terms of volume gives a slightly different picture of America's top exporters and importers. Companies such as Boeing, General Electric, Motorola, and IBM that export high-value-added goods rank as some of America's top exporters in terms of dollars. In terms of volume, the picture changes, and some unlikely companies emerge as America's top traders.

Top U.S. Exporters and Importers, 1996*

Rank	Exporter	Commodity
1	Weyerhaeuser	Paper, lumber
2	Du Pont	Chemicals, plastics
3	Philip Morris	Food, agricultural
4	America Chung Nam	Paper, lumber
5	Westvaco	Paper, lumber
6	Pacific Forest Resources	Paper, lumber
7	IBP	Food, agricultural
8	Eastman Chemical	Chemicals, plastics
9	Chrysler	Vehicles, parts
10	Union Carbide	Chemicals, plastics
11	Dow Chemical	Chemicals, plastics
12	Rayonier	Paper, lumber
13	Caterpillar Tractor	Vehicles, parts
14	Dole Food	Food, agricultural
15	Engelhard	Metals, minerals

Rank	Importer	Commodity
1	Chiquita Brands	Food, agricultural
2	Wal-Mart Stores	Household goods
3	Sumitomo America	Unclassified
4	Dole Food	Food, agricultural
5	Target Stores	Household goods
6	Honda Motor	Vehicles, parts
7	JC Penney	Household goods
8	Payless Shoe Store	Clothing, textiles
9	Canon	Electronics, machinery
10	Ford Motor	Vehicles, parts
11	Bridgestone/Firestone	Chemicals, plastics
12	Michelin Tire	Chemicals, plastics
13	Mattel	Household goods
14	Nissan Motor	Vehicles, parts
15	Pier One Imports	Household goods

*Via water, containerized cargo only, based on number of 20-foot containers

Source: The Journal of Commerce-Piers

30 Export Breadth—the United States Stands Alone in the World

Some nations export grain and other primary commodities. Some nations export industrial inputs, such as chemicals and steel. Some nations export automobiles and related parts, as well as electronics goods, including computers. The United States, for its part, exports all these commodities.

America's breadth of exports, or more specifically, the nation's ability to sell either apples or aircraft to the world, is one compelling reason why the United States is the globe's export leader. The physical and strategic endowments of the United States are unparalleled and range from the highly skilled worker in Silicon Valley to the world's most efficient farmer in Iowa.

The accompanying graph highlights the six broad categories of U.S. exports. Capital goods, composed of such products as computers and their peripherals, telecommunications equipment, electrical machinery, and aircraft, is the largest U.S. export category, accounting for 42.7% of total U.S. exports in 1997. Over the 1987–97 period, capital goods exports rose by over 12% on a compound annual average rate, reaching $294 billion in 1997. That figure is greater than the total exports of most nations, including Canada, the Netherlands, and China.

In terms of exports of goods, industrial supplies rank behind capital goods as the second largest category of U.S. exports. Industrial supplies represent an amalgam of products ranging from paper products to textiles. The bulk of the category is composed of chemicals and metals. In the aggregate, exports of industrial supplies rose by about 9% on average over the 1987–97 period and accounted for 23% of total U.S. exports in 1997. Like capital goods exports, what the U.S. exports in just industrial supplies in one year is greater than the total exports of such nations as South Korea and Taiwan.

America's automotive trade accounts for just 10.7% of total exports. Exports totaled $73.4 billion in 1997, having expanded by more than 10% during the 1987–97 period. Most of this trade is between the United States and its NAFTA neighbors, Canada and Mexico. Given the importance of in-country sales, citing total U.S. automotive exports is somewhat misleading; American automobile manufacturers produce more cars and components in-country than they export.

Down on the farm, U.S. agricultural exports are unmatched on a global basis. American farmers are among the most efficient and productive in the world and sell everything from apples to oranges to the world. U.S. farm exports hit a record of $61.5 billion in 1996, but fell back to $58.4 billion in 1997, with the combination of Asia's financial crisis and increased global supplies accounting for the downturn. However, since 1990, U.S. farm exports have doubled. Behind this blistering pace of growth are a number of secular trends that should help maintain robust growth in farm exports well into the future.

One key global trend in favor of U.S. farmers is growing demand in the emerging markets, where falling trade barriers and shifts in diets are fueling demand for U.S. goods ranging from coarse grains to beef.

Private commercial services round out the top categories of U.S. exports, and a more in-depth look at America's top ranking in global services is presented in another entry.

In summary, America's ability to offer the world what it desires or needs—whether potato chips or computer chips—is one of the chief underlying competitive strengths of the country. The nation's export breadth is unmatched on a global basis.

U.S. Exports by Category, 1997

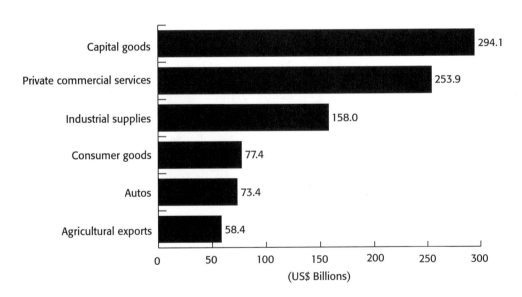

Source: U.S. Department of Commerce

31 | Services–One Area in Which the United States Enjoys a Trade Surplus with Japan

For decades, the United States has posted annual trade deficits with Japan in goods, with the merchandise trade deficit rising from $1.2 billion in 1970 to a peak of over $65 billion in 1994. Even the massive yen appreciation, with the yen rising from 200.5¥/$ at the end of 1985 to a peak of 79.5¥/$ in April 1995, hardly put a dent in the deficit. America's trade deficit in goods with Japan has remained in excess of $40 billion for over a decade (see the first graph).

The good news is that America's trade deficit with Japan is not as bad as the widely quoted trade figures suggest. Using 1997 as a base year, the $55.7 billion deficit with Japan reflects the difference in U.S. exports and imports of *goods* to Japan. As everyone knows, Japan sells more cars, computers, and Walkmans to the United States than America sells oranges and hay cubes to Japan. The United States sold $65.7 billion of exports to Japan in 1997; imports from Japan totaled $121.4 billion. The result was another deficit and continued pressure from Washington on Tokyo to "do something" about the trade imbalance.

However, trade in services yields a different picture. The United States, the world's premier service exporter, enjoys a sizable trade surplus in services with Japan. U.S. service exports to Japan totaled $38.1 billion in 1997, while imports amounted to roughly $14.1 billion, leaving a $24 billion surplus, up from $22 billion in 1996 and $10.7 billion in 1990. The widening surplus in services reflects two key variables: one is the large and expanding role of trade and investment between the U.S. and Japan, a relationship that brings Japanese goods to America's ports and Japanese businesspeople to America in general. These activities count as U.S. service exports. Travel and transportation (freight and port services) account for more than 50% of U.S. service exports to Japan.

The second variable reflects the competitiveness of America in many knowledge-intensive industries such as health care, financial services, professional services, education, and entertainment. More than 20% of U.S. service exports are in these types of high-value services.

As the second graph illustrates, when trade in services is added to the U.S.-Japan trade equation, the widely reported trade deficit of $55.7 billion in 1997 declines to $31.7 billion, or by over 40%. The silver lining to America's trade with Japan, then, lies with rising service exports.

Services Tell a Different Story in U.S.-Japan Trade

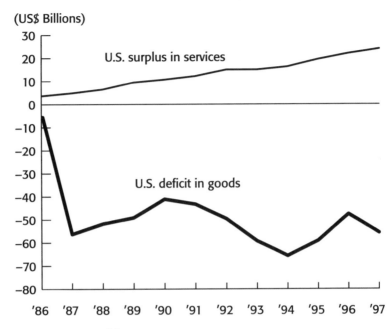

Source: U.S. Bureau of the Census

U.S. Trade with Japan, 1997

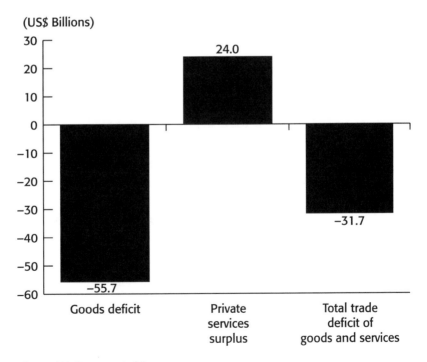

Source: U.S. Department of Commerce

32 The United States—What Trade Deficit?

As every first-year economics student knows, the United States runs a trade deficit with the rest of the world. This has been an ongoing annual trend since 1976, when the U.S. trade balance in goods and services swung to a $6.1 billion deficit. The deficit hit a peak of $152 billion in 1987, and tallied $113.7 billion in 1997. Over the 1990–97 period, America's average annual trade deficit in goods and services was $81 billion, versus an annual average of $84.5 billion over the 1980s.

Thus, the difference in what America exports to the world versus what it imports remains sizable. However, that is not the end of the story. Exports alone are not a very good representation of what America sells to the world. Long-term success in the global markets requires an in-country presence, thereby giving a company a number of competitive advantages, ranging from the ability to adapt products to local tastes, to overcoming currency swings.

Accordingly, in-country sales of U.S. affiliates (e.g., what General Motors Germany assembles or produces in Germany and then sells in the country or exports) should be added to the trade equation. When they are, the global commercial image of the United States changes drastically, as shown in the first graph.

Tallied by the Commerce Department, though with a significant lag, sales of overseas affiliates of U.S. companies totaled over $2.1 trillion in 1995, almost three times larger than the total exports of U.S. goods and services in the same year ($794 billion). In other words, foreign affiliates of American firms sell far more in-country than what the parent company exports from America's shores.

Similarly, what American affiliates of foreign companies sell right here in the United States easily exceeds total U.S. imports. In 1995, as a base year, U.S. imports of goods and services totaled $896.5 billion; however, sales of foreign affiliates in the United States were more than $1.5 trillion. Like U.S. multinationals, foreign companies have long recognized that success in penetrating the American market requires not just imports, but also a local presence. Hence the role and predominance of in-country sales.

The second graph shows that the aggregate of U.S. exports and sales of overseas affiliates of U.S. companies was almost $3 trillion in 1995. Meanwhile, U.S. imports and the in-country sales of foreign affiliates in America totaled $2.4 trillion, leaving the United States with none other than a $477 billion surplus with the rest of the world.

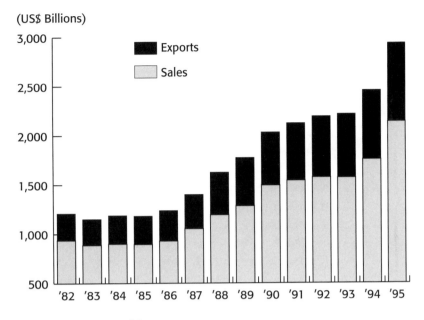

Sales by U.S. Foreign Affiliates Versus U.S. Exports

(US$ Billions)

Source: U.S. Department of Commerce

What Trade Deficit?

(US$ Billions)

MNC = Multinational company

Source: U.S. Department of Commerce

33 | Some Different Perspectives on the U.S. Trade Deficit

Nothing evokes more outcry in Washington than America's chronic trade deficit with the world. The last year the United States posted a trade surplus in goods and services was in 1975, or over 20 years ago.

Over the second half of the 1970s, America's trade balance swung into a deficit, and it has remained there ever since. Two sharp increases in world oil prices, stiffer global competition from not only Japan but also developing Asia, and the strong U.S. dollar culminated with the U.S. trade deficit in goods and services reaching a record $152 billion in 1987. The deficit in goods and services approached $114 billion in 1997, and continued to widen over 1998 as a result of Asia's economic downturn. Predictably, as the deficit grows, so do calls for trade protectionism.

Amid the demands for Washington to "do something," investors should realize a few particulars regarding America's chronic trade deficit. First, the trade deficit is more about how much this country saves and invests in a given year, rather than about America's overall ability to compete in the world markets. As a chronic undersaver, the United States must borrow from abroad in order to finance new investments. But in order for other countries to lend money to the United States, they must first sell more goods and services than they buy, thereby generating the extra savings to loan to America. In short, the U.S. trade deficit reflects the difference in America's domestic savings and investment rates.

Second, even though the trade deficit has widened over the 1990s, the deficit's overall impact on the U.S. economy is less today than in the past (see the bar graph). As a share of gross domestic product, the trade deficit averaged roughly 1.5% of GDP annually over the 1994–97 period, significantly below prevailing levels racked up over the second half of the 1980s.

Finally, investors would do well to understand the role U.S. foreign affiliates play in U.S. imports. It's hardly inconsequential. Indeed, in any given year, almost one-fifth of total U.S. imports of goods are imports from the foreign affiliates of U.S. companies. Part of the trade deficit, in other words, is homegrown. As shown in the following table, a significant share of what the United States imports from such nations as Singapore, Ireland, and Mexico are in fact imports from the affiliates of American parent companies.

The bottom line is that the trade deficit is all too often associated with foreign companies unfairly selling more goods to the United States than they buy. Reality is slightly different—America's trade deficit reflects the nation's low level of savings, as well as the role of U.S. foreign affiliates.

U.S. Trade Deficit as a Share of GDP

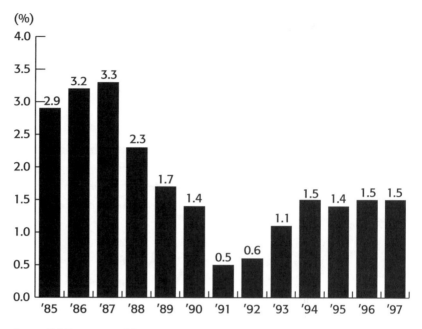

Source: U.S. Department of Commerce

U.S. Affiliate Imports as a % of Total
U.S. Imports from Individual Countries, 1995

Country	%	Country	%
Singapore	80.5	Belgium	17.6
Hong Kong	52.1	France	15.6
Ireland	46.2	Indonesia	13.8
Canada	39.9	Germany	10.8
United Kingdom	29.8	Italy	9.2
Mexico	25.5	Taiwan	5.0
Thailand	19.4	South Korea	2.5
Brazil	19.3	Japan	2.4
Malaysia	18.1	China	1.9

Source: Bureau of Economic Analysis

34 U.S. Global Exposure—the Complete Picture

Trend 28 highlighted America's top trading partners. Entry 32, meanwhile, put the spotlight on the role of in-country sales of U.S. affiliates. This entry combines the two to uncover the markets that are the most important to U.S. business. As a starting point, it is important to realize that American multinationals sell nearly three times as much overseas through their affiliates than the United States exports to the world.

With this as a backdrop, the critical point for investors to realize is this: How one measures America's global engagement—either through exports or in-country sales—determines which foreign markets are the most important to U.S. business. The accompanying table tells two different stories.

The first column shows America's top export markets. Canada ranks as the number one market for U.S. goods, while Asia (Japan and the rest of Asia) clearly ranks as the top region for U.S. goods, representing nearly 30% of total U.S. exports. Hence, when Asia slipped into recession in 1997–98, there were mounting concerns that Asia's problems would wreak havoc on the United States.

Looked at from the perspective of in-country sales of affiliates (the second column), Asia's importance is significantly diminished. Indeed, exports reveal one story, in-country sales quite another. Based on the latter measurement, America's top foreign market in 1995 was the United Kingdom by a wide margin. While the country accounted for only 4.9% of total U.S. exports, a relatively minor share, the United Kingdom accounted for over 22% of total in-country sales of U.S. affiliates in 1995. Taken together—exports plus in-country sales (the third column)—the United Kingdom emerges as the most important foreign market for U.S. firms, with a 16.4% share of total U.S. global commerce in 1995. The country holds this unique position because sales of U.S. overseas affiliates in the United Kingdom were 12 times the value of U.S. exports to the country.

Note that Europe, based on the third column, is overwhelmingly the most important region of the world for the United States. That is impossible to discern from just looking at export statistics. Conversely, note that America's global exposure to Asia (excluding Japan) is less than the export figures suggest. The region accounts for nearly one-fifth of total U.S. exports, but for less than 8% of total in-country sales and just 11.5% of the two variables combined.

The bottom line: By analyzing only trade, investors are missing the big picture as it relates to America's global exposure and participation. Exports are indeed important, although in-country sales of affiliates largely drive and determine U.S. profits from the rest of the world.

U.S. Global Exposure: The Complete Picture, 1995

Region/Country	U.S. Exports (% of Total)	In-Country Sales (% of Total)	Exports + In-Country Sales (% of Total)
Europe	**22.4**	**58.2**	**46.2**
United Kingdom	4.9	22.2	16.4
Germany	3.8	10.9	8.5
Belgium	2.1	1.7	1.9
France	2.4	6.9	5.4
Italy	1.4	3.9	3.1
Netherlands	2.7	3.2	3.1
Canada	**22.0**	**11.8**	**15.2**
Japan	**10.8**	**8.4**	**9.2**
Australia	**1.9**	**3.1**	**2.7**
Subtotal	**57.1**	**81.5**	**73.3**
Latin America	**17.8**	**8.2**	**11.4**
Argentina	0.7	0.9	0.8
Brazil	2.1	2.9	2.6
Mexico	9.3	1.9	4.3
Chile	0.7	0.4	0.5
Colombia	0.8	0.5	0.6
Venezuela	0.8	0.5	0.6
Asia	**18.6**	**7.9**	**11.5**
China	1.9	0.4	0.9
Hong Kong	2.3	1.8	2.0
Indonesia	0.7	0.3	0.4
Korea	4.3	0.6	1.8
Malaysia	1.4	0.7	0.9
Singapore	2.7	1.9	2.2
Philippines	1.0	0.4	0.6
Taiwan	3.0	1.1	1.8
Thailand	1.2	0.8	0.9
Other	**6.5**	**2.4**	**3.8**
Total	**100.0**	**100.0**	**100.0**

Source: Bureau of Economic Analysis

35 The "Sucking Sound" Revisited: Import Demand in the Developing Nations

It is all too common to associate the developing nations with low wages, barriers to trade, and unscrupulous business practices, variables that harm the welfare and livelihood of American companies and, more important, American workers. This image is widespread in the United States and one that was effectively driven home by presidential candidate Ross Perot in 1992, when he warned that the "sucking sound" was American jobs being lost to Mexico.

In many respects Mr. Perot was right—numerous developing nations, including Mexico, have inherited jobs from the United States and other developed nations for decades, an ongoing process that is not likely to be reversed anytime soon. However, it is hardly a one-way street, with the developing nations accruing all the benefits. Rather, with their massive infrastructure needs, burgeoning middle classes, and more open and receptive trade and investment regimes, the developing nations represent something of a new frontier for many companies in the United States, Europe, and Japan. Emerging-market opportunities in nations as diverse as Turkey and China are critical to most Western multinationals who confront mature, oversupplied, and stagnant markets at home.

As the accompanying graph highlights, the developing nations over this decade have bought more goods from the industrialized nations than they have sold in return, resulting in sizable trade deficits. Since the collapse of the Berlin Wall and the demise of communism, free-market reforms, including trade liberalization measures, have become the norm in such nations as Russia, Poland, Argentina, Mexico, South Africa, Vietnam, and other countries once sealed off from the rest of the world. Asia's current problems aside, millions of new consumers are emerging in such nations as China, Indonesia, and Thailand. Infrastructure investment, as many countries rebuild after years of neglect and a rush to modernize, is soaring across the developing world, creating demand for capital goods imports.

As a result of these circumstances, import demand in the developing nations has soared over the past decade, with the industrialized nations supplying the bulk of their needs. While the developing nations bought $348 billion worth of goods from the industrialized nations in 1986, the annual import bill rose to $573 billion in 1990 and hit almost $1.2 trillion in 1997, a 232% increase from the level of 1986. In return, the industrialized nations bought $1 trillion in goods from the developing nations in 1997, resulting in a sizable trade deficit ($122 billion) for the developing nations. In the prior year, 1996, the deficit was even larger, reaching $148.9 billion.

This shift in the balance of trade, with the developing nations running sizable trade deficits with the industrialized nations, has been remarkable. During the 1980s the developing nations posted an aggregate trade deficit of just $16 billion; however, this swung to a massive cumulative deficit of over $740 billion in the 1990s. Asia's economic slowdown will no doubt lead to a deceleration in import growth to the developing nations over the short term. However, the fundamental and secular forces remain in place in the developing nations, which have emerged as significant sources of global import demand. The developing nations' share of total world imports now stands at around one-third, up from 24.9% in 1986. Asia notwithstanding, the share will continue to rise over the long term.

All of this is good news for the United States, which has come to increasingly rely on the developing nations for export growth. A little more than a decade ago, in 1986, the developing nations accounted for 36.2% of total U.S. exports. However, the share has steadily increased over the past decade, rising to over 43% in 1997. In the end, the "sucking sound" really reflects the voracious appetite of the developing nations for Western goods.

Developing Nations' Trade with the Industrialized Nations

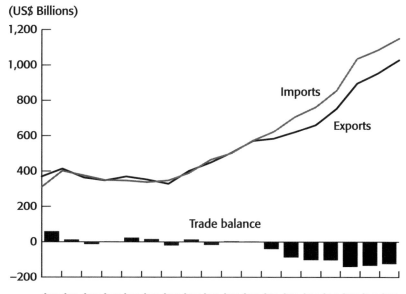

Source: IMF

36 Supplying the Goods to the Developing Nations

The developing nations are ripe and attractive markets for Western goods, sparking an intense rivalry among the United States, Japan, and Germany to be the main suppliers to these growth markets. Of the roughly $1.1 trillion in goods that the developing nations imported from the industrialized nations in 1996, America, Japan, and Germany accounted for 62.4%.

More than half of Japan's exports went to the developing nations in 1996, while 43.5% of U.S. exports went to these countries. U.S. exports to the developing nations have grown by 11.5% on an annual average basis over the 1990–96 period versus growth of 8% for total exports. Germany is not as reliant on the emerging markets as either the United States or Japan; the bulk of Germany's exports (56.4% in 1996) are sold to the nations of the European Union, although more and more German companies are turning toward the emerging markets in the hope of new sales.

Geographic proximity and, by extension, historical and traditional commercial ties play a clear role in who among the United States, Japan, and Germany supplies the developing nations. As the "Top Suppliers" table shows, each country has its own sphere of influence. America is the top supplier to most of Latin America. Japan dominates developing Asia. And following the collapse of communism, the traditional trade ties between Germany and the smaller countries of Central Europe have been reestablished over the 1990s. There are some notable exceptions, however.

In Asia, thanks to the weak dollar and a determined effort by South Korea to reduce its import dependence on Japan, the United States emerged as South Korea's number-one supplier in 1996 and again in 1997. The integration of China and Hong Kong is clearly reflected in the trade figures. Panama is used by Japan as a regional distribution center, which accounts for Japan being the number-one supplier to the pivotal Central American nation.

In summary, the export performance of the United States, Japan, and Germany is increasingly intertwined with the emerging markets. In turn, what transpires close to home or in the region is important. The United States benefits from a thriving and stable Latin America. Asia's economic problems have been keenly felt by Japan. The commercial windfall from the opening of Central Europe has gone largely to German companies.

Top Suppliers to the Developing Nations

	1985	1990	1997*
Asia			
China	Japan	Hong Kong	Japan
Indonesia	Japan	Japan	Japan
South Korea	Japan	Japan	United States
Malaysia	Japan	Japan	Japan
Pakistan	United States	United States	United States
Philippines	United States	United States	Japan
Singapore	Japan	Japan	Japan
Thailand	Japan	Japan	Japan
Taiwan	Japan	Japan	Japan
India	United States	United States	United States
Hong Kong	China	China	China
Western Hemisphere			
Argentina	United States	United States	Brazil
Brazil	United States	United States	United States
Chile	United States	United States	United States
Colombia	United States	United States	United States
Costa Rica	United States	United States	United States
Ecuador	United States	United States	United States
Mexico	United States	United States	United States
Peru	United States	United States	United States
Venezuela	United States	United States	United States
Russia/Central Europe			
Russia	CMEA	NA	Germany
Czech Republic	CMEA	NA	Germany
Hungary	CMEA	Former USSR	Germany
Poland	CMEA	Germany	Germany
Romania	CMEA	Former USSR	Germany
Turkey	CMEA	Germany	Germany

NA = Not available

CMEA = Council for Mutual Economic Assistance

*Based on the first nine months of 1997

Source: *IMF: Direction of Trade*

37 Albeit Slowly, Japan Warms Up to Manufactured Imports

Change comes slowly to Japan, notably on the trade front. For decades, the United States and Japan have been at loggerheads over Japan's trade practices, particularly the country's bias against manufactured imports.

Since Japan is an island-state devoid of most natural resources, its imports have historically been dominated by primary commodities, including oil and food.

Early on, during Japan's post-war industrialization in the 1950s and 1960s, import barriers were erected to protect local industry. Since then, and contrary to conventional wisdom, formal import barriers have been removed. Informal barriers, however, have remained. They include the following: traditional long-term relationships between Japanese manufacturers and their suppliers; a strong, deep-rooted preference for domestic goods; the critical role played by Japanese trading companies, which handle a large share of both imports and exports; and informal coordinated interests within loose conglomerate business groups (Keiretsu) or industry associations. These variables do make Japan relatively unique.

As far back as the early 1970s, manufactured imports have accounted for more than half of the total imports of the United States and Europe. Of North America's (United States and Canada) total imports in 1973, 65% were in the form of manufactured imports, up from 47.4% in 1963. Europe was not far behind, with manufactured imports accounting for 59% of total imports, versus 46.6% a decade earlier (see the accompanying table).

In contrast, Japan's share of manufactured imports (25.8%) was much lower than its counterparts not only in 1973, but also in 1983 (21.4%) and 1993 (46.2%). Indeed, it was not until 1995, long after Japan had emerged as one of the most vibrant economies in the world, that manufactured imports as a percentage of the total topped 50%.

The good news is that Japan is now more receptive to manufactured imports out of necessity than anything else. The 1990s has been a particularly painful decade for Corporate Japan, which has seen its global competitiveness undermined by the steep rise in the yen, higher operating and labor costs at home, and greater competition from developing Asia. The nation has also had to cope with greater demands from Japanese consumers for cheaper imports and incessant threats of trade retaliation from the United States and other principal trading partners. To escape rising costs at home, Japan invested roughly $500 billion abroad between 1986 and 1997. The end result has been a rise in Japan's manufactured imports since the intention of the investment is not only to serve the local market but also to export cheaper products back to Japan.

On balance, the second largest economy in the world is warming to imports, albeit gradually. A number of forces of change are converging, ranging from domestic calls for cheaper imports to external pressures, that will increase, over the long term, Japan's propensity to import manufactured products.

Imports of Manufactured Goods
(As a % of Total Imports)

	1963	1973	1983	1993	1995	1996
North America	47.4	64.9	63.6	78.0	79.5	78.2
Western Europe	46.6	58.9	56.0	72.4	74.2	72.7
Japan	22.6	25.8	21.4	46.2	53.0	54.3

Source: World Trade Organization

Japan's Imports of Manufactured Goods
(As a % of Total Imports)

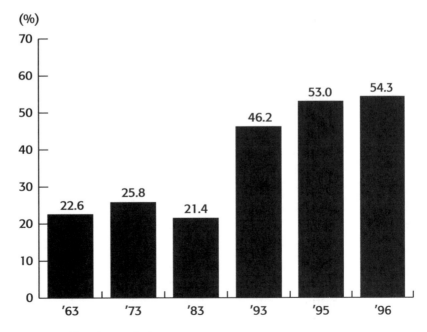

Source: World Trade Organization

38 | Trade: It's All in the Family

A basic assumption of international trade is that countries manufacture products based on their resource endowments and exchange those goods with other nations that have a different set of endowments. However, as is often the case with classical economic principles, theory does not quite reflect reality.

Contemporary trade is increasingly driven and determined by the strategic goals of multinationals. Where these global giants decide to outsource functions, relocate production facilities, or enter new markets affects the flow of trade. Intrafirm trade—the goods traded among the branches and subsidiaries of multinational corporations—rarely stirs any discussions in trade circles, yet it accounts for a major share of U.S. international transactions in goods. Trade within firms is critical in controlling the costs and supplies of global operations; it helps distribute goods more efficiently and helps to acquire inputs from abroad more effectively. In addition, multinationals with production facilities in various countries are better able to adjust to sudden shifts in exchange rates. The fact that roughly one-third of world trade represents intrafirm trade attests to the role of multinationals in affecting trade flows.

Intrafirm trade represents a major share of America's international trade in goods (see the graph). Transactions between multinationals (both American and foreign) and their overseas affiliates accounted for 40% of total U.S.trade in 1995, the latest year for which data are available. In other words, multinationals are a critical vehicle of U.S. trade. Likewise, the ultimate market for traded goods is often among the firms themselves rather than traditional customers.

Intrafirm exports of the United States totaled $209 billion in 1995, or roughly 36% of total merchandise exports for that year. The bulk of intrafirm exports is trade conducted between U.S. parent companies (e.g., General Electric of the United States) and their foreign affiliates (e.g., GE Hungary). More than a quarter of U.S. trade in exports is conducted in this fashion. In addition, exports between U.S. affiliates (e.g., Honda America) and their foreign parents (Honda Japan) accounted for another 10% of total U.S. exports in 1995.

U.S. intrafirm imports account for an even greater share of total U.S. imports. Out of the $743 billion of goods the United States imported in 1995, 43.2% represented intrafirm imports. Transactions between American parent companies (e.g., IBM USA) and their foreign affiliates (e.g., IBM Singapore) accounted for 17% of total imports; another 26.3% of U.S. imports represented trade between U.S. affiliates (e.g., Mercedes-Benz USA) and their foreign parent (Mercedes Germany).

Intrafirm trade is a unique feature of America's trade with Japan. Over 80% of all U.S. imports from Japan in 1995 were shipped intrafirm from Japanese parent companies to their affiliates in the United States. More striking is the extent to which Japanese multinationals control U.S. exports to Japan. More than half of what the United States exports to Japan are intracompany shipments from trading companies and manufacturing affiliates in the United States to their Japanese parents. In other words, Japanese-owned subsidiaries are the largest U.S. exporters to Japan.

In summary, international trade in goods increasingly reflects the complex strategies of multinationals, rather than the strict resource-based comparative advantages of nations. To a significant degree, trade remains all in the family.

Multinationals' Role in U.S. Trade Flows
(Intrafirm Trade as a % of Total U.S. Trade, 1995)

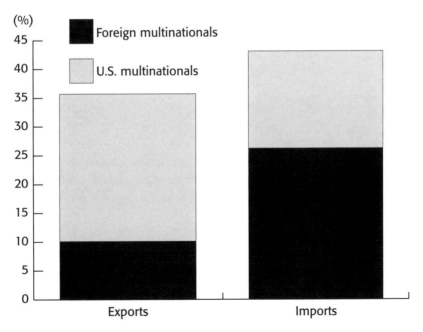

Source: Bureau of Economic Analysis

39 | A World Full of Trading Blocs

Regionalism, or the creation of preferential trade agreements among nations, has become one of the most pronounced trends of the world economy over this decade. Although trading blocs are not new, the first half of the nineties saw a sharp increase in the number of new agreements, as the accompanying graph illustrates.

Why the sudden jump? The goal of most agreements is to improve the welfare of participating nations. Toward this end, regional agreements generally aim to phase out or eliminate restrictions on trade and on the cross-border flow of goods, which, in theory, should promote economies of scale, lead to better resource allocation, increase competition, foster technology change, and generate a host of other favorable spillover effects. The gain to consumers comes in the way of lower prices and an increase in the variety of available goods.

There are costs associated with the creation of trading blocs, however. Lower trade barriers entail heightened regional competition, and as the rancorous U.S. debate over the creation of NAFTA showed, not all industries and companies are enamored with these trade agreements. An even greater danger to the world economy lies with the potential of regionalism to undercut the global multilateral trade system, a pillar of world growth over the last 50 years. Whether the proliferation of regional trading agreements yields building blocs or stumbling blocs remains a key question.

More than 100 regional trading blocs exist today, and the number continues to fluctuate, given that new agreements are being created, existing arrangements are being extended, and old groupings are being merged. Two prominent regional trading blocs are the European Union (E.U.) and the North American Free Trade Agreement (NAFTA). Each accounts for roughly one-fifth of world GDP.

In the Pacific Rim, two other trading blocs stand out. One is the sweeping trade alliance called the Asia-Pacific Economic Cooperation (APEC) forum, which incorporates countries that lie along the Pacific Rim, including the United States, Mexico, and Chile. The second key regional bloc is the Association of Southeast Asian Nations (ASEAN), a group geographically centered around Singapore, Malaysia, Indonesia, the Philippines, and Thailand but also now extending into Indo-China.

Mercosur, the Andean Group, and the Central American Common Market are the three major trading unions in South and Central America. Mercosur is the youngest (established in 1991) and largest of the three and includes Argentina, Brazil, Paraguay, and Uruguay. Other nations, such as Chile, have joined or are considering joining. The Andean Group includes Bolivia, Colombia, Ecuador, Peru, and Venezuela.

Beyond Europe, North and South America, and the Pacific Rim, there are numerous other regional trading groups in operation. Africa, for example, has been carved up into numerous trading blocs, ranging from the Mano River Union to the Southern Africa Customs Union. The Gulf Cooperation Council and the Arab Common Market are two central regional groups of the Middle East.

One noteworthy consequence or trend from the proliferation of trading blocs is the rise in intraregional trade. Roughly half of all global trade is now considered intraregional, with the greatest concentration in Western Europe, where nearly 70% of total trade is classified as intraregional. Other regions of the world lag but are growing, with intraregional trade in North America, Latin America, and Asia accounting for 36%, 20.8%, and 50.9%, respectively, of total trade in 1995.

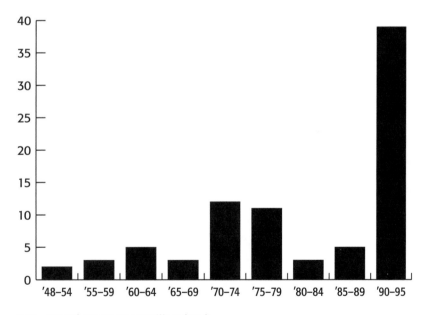

Number of Regional Integration Agreements Notified to GATT, 1948–95

GATT = General Agreement on Tariffs and Trade

Source: World Trade Organization

40 The World Trade Organization—What Nations Are Waiting to Join?

Global trade confers a number of benefits on nations, including lower-priced products, increased competition, better resource allocation, and rising living standards. Trade is one of the most dynamic aspects of the global economy, and in general, those nations that embrace trade benefit from trade.

However, in order to fully reap the rewards of global commerce, nations must abide by rules and regulations spelled out and enforced by the World Trade Organization (WTO). The WTO serves as a framework and forum in resolving trade disputes between countries. The WTO, in effect, is the referee of international trade, enforcing the rules agreed upon by all member nations. These rules, in turn, provide the basis for global trade and ensure that members' interests are protected in the global marketplace.

Not all nations, however, are willing to conduct trade within the confines of the World Trade Organization, since accession into the WTO entails that nations adopt and accept a number of regulations governing import practices, government procurement policies, export subsidies, intellectual property rights, and anticompetitive initiatives. For some nations, this is just too high a price to pay, at least for now.

The accompanying table highlights the nations that, for various reasons, are not yet members of the WTO. The most prominent member of this group is China, which has been negotiating to enter the global trading organization for years. At China's insistence, Taiwan is not allowed to be a full-fledged member of the WTO.

Other excluded notables include Russia, the largest economy in Central Europe and one of the largest traders in the world. Ukraine is not a member; neither are the Baltic states of Latvia, Lithuania, and Estonia, which need trade contacts to thrive and survive. Many other nations that were once a part of the Soviet Union—Moldova, Uzbekistan, Armenia, Belarus—have yet to become a member of the WTO. In the Middle East, Jordan and Saudi Arabia are particular exceptions to the WTO membership roster.

Most of the nations listed are currently negotiating their entry into the WTO. As a footnote, 1998 marks the 50th anniversary of the multilateral trading organization, a key pillar of growth over the past half-century.

Countries That Have Applied to Join the WTO*

Country	Working Party† Established
Albania	Dec. '92
Algeria	Jun. '87
Armenia	Dec. '93
Belarus	Oct. '93
Cambodia	Dec. '94
China	Mar. '87
Croatia	Oct. '93
Estonia	Mar. '94
Former Yugoslav Republic of Macedonia	Dec. '94
Georgia	Jul. '96
Jordan	Jan. '94
Kazakhstan	Jun. '96
Kyrgyzstan	Apr. '96
Latvia	Dec. '93
Lithuania	Feb. '94
Moldova	Dec. '93
Nepal	Jun. '89
Oman	Jun. '96
Panama	Oct. '91
Russian Federation	Jun. '93
Saudi Arabia	Jul. '93
Seychelles	Jul. '95
Sudan	Oct. '94
Taiwan	Sep. '92
Tonga	Nov. '95
Ukraine	Dec. '93
Uzbekistan	Dec. '94
Vanuatu	Jul. '95
Vietnam	Jan. '95

*As of August 1997
†GATT/WTO committee to consider accession

Source: World Trade Organization

CHAPTER 3

Investment

Overview

Chapter 3 highlights the key trends and trendsetters driving global investment flows. The first half of the chapter centers on global foreign direct investment, while the second half spotlights portfolio investment. It is important that investors understand the difference between the two:

- Foreign direct investment (FDI) is usually more strategic and long term in nature, and undertaken by multinationals or small and medium-sized companies setting up overseas operations. Foreign direct investment has long been a mainstay of the global economy, with some of the earliest forms of direct investment in the United States occurring at the turn of this century. At that time, foreign investors built railroads and electric power plants in the emerging market called America. Currently, foreign direct investment flows are the largest component of external resource flows to the developing countries.

- Cross-border portfolio investment, in contrast, is a relatively new phenomenon of the world economy. As the following pages highlight, just 25 years ago, the world equity markets were dominated by the United States and Europe. Since then, however, stock markets have proliferated in number around the world, with the most notable growth coming from Japan and the emerging markets. Portfolio investment, which is considered more fickle and footloose than foreign direct investment, is now one of the most powerful variables of the global economy. The trends behind this development are discussed in this chapter.

Also presented here are the countries and companies driving ever-rising levels of global investment. The United States figures prominently as both a host and recipient of foreign direct investment. The same is true of the United Kingdom, which has attracted more investment than any other nation in the European Union. Investment outflows from Japan over the past decade have been stunning, while China has exhibited an insatiable appetite for foreign direct investment.

We have listed some of the world's largest companies in this chapter, measured in different ways—by foreign assets as a percentage of total assets or by stock market capitalization—knowing full well that the rankings are subject to change. The goal is to give investors an indication of the world's global giants and a benchmark of the world's principal stock markets.

41 Going Global–the Foreign Direct Investment (FDI) Boom of the 1990s

Surging foreign direct investment (FDI) has been one of the most important trends of the global economy this decade. Indeed, at the core of globalization, or the rapid integration of the world economy, lie the multinationals—or transnationals, as the United Nations calls these global behemoths. These entities are reshaping the global competitive landscape, influencing international trade flows, and helping to decide the economic fate, to a significant degree, of many countries. The tidal wave of FDI is reflected in the fact that annual FDI outflows averaged nearly $260 billion over 1990–96, up from $136.4 billion in 1985–89 and less than $50 billion in 1980–84 (see the accompanying graph). By 1996, the FDI stock of the roughly 44,000 firms invested abroad reached $3.2 trillion. The sales of all foreign affiliates stood at $6.4 trillion in 1994, more than the level of world exports.

Many forces are behind the surge in outward investment, ranging from declining global transportation and communication costs to market deregulation and liberalization measures in numerous countries. The former has made it much easier and efficient for companies to deploy their assets and resources around the world. The latter entails a new attitude toward foreign companies among host governments, particularly those in the developing nations. Rather than being feared and scorned, transnationals are now courted and cajoled by governments hoping to gain jobs, technology, and export capabilities. Toward this end, the United Nations counted 599 regulatory changes affecting foreign investment worldwide over the 1991–96 period, with all but 27 of these directed at greater investment liberalization.

Besides a more receptive environment from host governments, the boom in FDI reflects the shifting strategies of many corporations that confront either rising global competition or stagnant markets at home, or both. As a result, finding new markets, moving closer to the customer, and understanding the strengths and weaknesses of the competition have become imperative and require a more active global presence. The spread of privatization in Europe, Latin America, and central Europe, and the proliferation of regional trading blocs have also converged as underlying trends. These structural variables have combined with cyclical forces such as expanding world output and low global interest rates to produce an unprecedented period of global FDI flows in the 1990s.

Building a global presence can be costly, which is why the preferred method of expanding overseas is through mergers and acquisitions; the latter accounted for roughly 80% of total global FDI in 1996. Total cross-border mergers and acquisitions were valued at $274.6 billion in 1996, with most of the activity centered in the developed nations. Key industries with the highest rates of mergers and acquisition activity over the past few years include energy, telecommunications, pharmaceuticals, and financial services.

By sector, the rapid increase in global foreign direct investment has shifted over the decades. Over the 1950s, foreign direct investment was concentrated in raw materials, primary products, and resource-based manufacturing. Today, the sector composition has shifted to services and technology-intensive manufacturing.

By expanding at a faster pace than either world output or world trade, foreign direct investment has moved to the forefront as one of the most powerful variables of the world economy. Between 1980 and 1994 the ratio of FDI stock to world GDP doubled. Accordingly, global trade as well as industry competitiveness and the economic well-being of nations are increasingly tied to FDI and the attendant strategies and actions of transnationals.

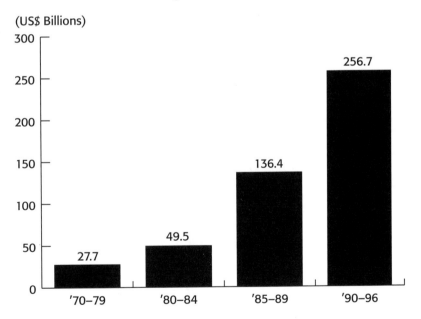

World Average Annual FDI Outflows

Source: United Nations

42 Who Is Leading the Surge in FDI?

The developed nations have long been the major source of global foreign direct-investment flows. That is hardly surprising given that the majority of the world's multinationals are based in the developed countries. In 1960, the United Kingdom and the United States accounted for 65.4% of total world outflows of investment stock, with the United States alone accounting for 49.2% of the world total. In 1996, five nations—the United States, the United Kingdom, Germany, France, and Japan— accounted for nearly two-thirds of all global outflows.

America's global share of outward foreign investment has declined over the past decades, although the United States is still, by an overwhelming margin, the largest source of FDI in the world, providing roughly 25 to 35% of the annual global total over the 1990s. U.S. overseas investment hit a record $119.4 billion in 1997. For the 1990–97 period, cumulative U.S. outward foreign direct investment topped $540 billion, more than triple the total amount for the entire 1980s—$162.4 billion. Many variables converged to trigger this boom, including robust levels of mergers and acquisitions between the United States and Britain; rising investment levels in both of America's NAFTA neighbors, Canada and Mexico; increased investment levels in developing Asia; and sustained investment flows to Europe, the prime location of U.S. overseas investment.

Just in excess of 70% of America's total overseas direct investment is in the developed nations, namely Europe, which accounts for 50.1% of the total. This reflects America's long-standing commercial relationship with Europe, which dates back to the last century. On a historic-cost basis, the United Kingdom is by far the most popular place for U.S investment, taking over one-third of the total U.S. investment in Europe.

Besides the surge of investment from the United States, rising investment outflows from Germany is another key trend that has emerged over the second half of this decade. Germany's annual level of FDI averaged just $10.4 billion over the 1985–89 period but rose to $24.5 billion over 1990–97 and reached a record $38.5 billion in 1995 before dropping back to $27.8 billion in 1996 and $29.7 billion in 1997 (see the accompanying graph).

Why the corporate exodus from Germany? The strength of the deutsche mark over the first half of the decade has certainly not helped Germany, driving the dollar-based cost of German industry sky-high. In 1996, hourly compensation costs for manufacturing workers in Germany were nearly double those of the United States. The shift in the currency, however, is not the only reason behind the migration of German industry out of Germany. Unfavorable local operating conditions, including rigid labor practices and high corporate and social security taxes, have contributed as well. This climate has sent many German companies packing for friendlier sites that include the United Kingdom, China, Central Europe, and above all else, the United States.

Interestingly, the United States, whose profit-driven shareholder focus has been resisted in Germany, emerged as the preferred destination of German investors in 1996 and again in 1997. The United States accounted for a quarter of all German investment in 1997, up from 21.3% in 1996 and just 6.3% in 1993.

Japan has also emerged as a key provider of overseas direct investment, which is the subject of another entry.

Foreign Direct Investment Outflows

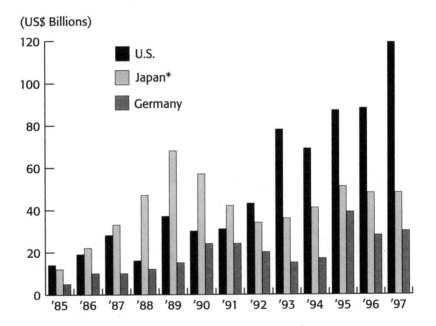

(US$ Billions)

*Fiscal year ending in March

Source: National sources

43 The United States—the Preferred Location of Multinationals

Nothing conjures up more domestic opposition and hostility than news of another U.S. company closing a plant and shifting production abroad. Yet, what is often overlooked is that while U.S. companies do invest a great deal of capital abroad (nearly $550 billion in foreign direct investment over 1990–97), foreigners put nearly just as much money back into the United States. In fact, no other nation in the world attracts as much foreign direct investment in a given year as the United States, not even China. What the United States received in overseas direct investment in 1997 (see the accompanying graph), $108 billion, was roughly triple the amount garnered by China.

What is so attractive about the United States? A number of factors make America a good investment, ranging from political stability to the depth of our capital markets to a first-class infrastructure. A prolonged economic expansion, a large and wealthy consumer market, and a respectable rate of return have helped as well.

The economic benefits from this external flow of investment are enormous. Nearly 5 million people, or roughly 5% of the American labor force, now work for U.S. subsidiaries of foreign parent companies. In some states, the figure is well above 5%—Hawaii (11.3%), South Carolina (8.1%), and North Carolina (7.5%). Moreover, these are not low-paying jobs, but rather jobs that pay 22% above average U.S. wages.

Despite some widely publicized investments of the Japanese in the United States over the past decade, the British are the single largest foreign investors in America. Japan ranks behind the United Kingdom, with some $118 billion invested in the United States at the end of 1996. On an annual basis, Japan was the largest investor in the United States in 1992, although sluggish activity in Japan, huge losses in U.S. real estate, and weak profits from some U.S. operations have slowed the pace and level of Japanese overseas investment in the United States over most of this decade.

In sum, the United States has not only experienced a boom in its equity markets over most of this decade but has also enjoyed a boom in overseas foreign direct investment, a development that has been highly beneficial to the country. Foreign investment flows in such nations as Germany and Japan have been largely one-way—outbound. U.S. outflows of investment have been strong as well, but matched, to a significant degree, by robust levels of inbound investment.

U.S. Foreign Direct Investment

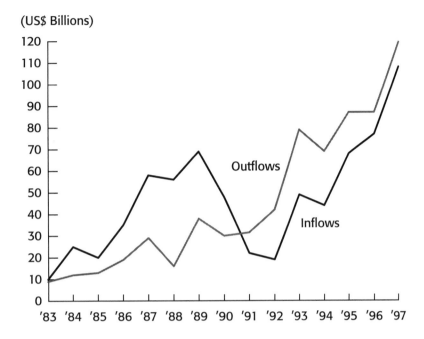

Source: U.S. Department of Commerce

Top Foreign Investors in the United States*

Rank	Country	US$ Billions	% of Total
1	United Kingdom	142.6	22.6
2	Japan	118.1	18.7
3	Netherlands	73.8	11.7
4	Germany	62.2	9.9
5	Canada	53.8	8.5
6	France	49.3	7.8
7	Switzerland	35.1	5.6
8	Luxembourg	10.3	1.6
9	Ireland	9.8	1.6
10	Australia	9.7	1.5

*Based on FDI position in the United States on a historical-cost basis at year-end 1996

Source: U.S. Department of Commerce

44 Foreign Direct Investment to the Developing Nations—Only a Few Need to Apply

The good news is that foreign direct-investment flows to the developing nations have soared this decade, rising from $23.7 billion in 1990 to $120.4 billion in 1997. The comparable figure for 1980 was just $4.4 billion. Behind this surge are many factors, including free-market reforms in the developing nations, as well as falling transportation and communication costs. The latter have greatly enabled multinationals to spread their reach to far-flung corners of the world.

The discouraging news is that the investment flows have been highly skewed toward just a handful of countries. In 1997, over 70% of net foreign investment flows to the developing countries went to just 10 nations (see the accompanying table). In other words, the tide of foreign direct investment to the developing nations has not lifted all countries, just a few.

As the dream market of virtually every multinational, China has easily attracted more foreign investment than any other developing nation in the 1990s, raking in over $190 billion over the 1990–97 period. Not surprisingly, total foreign direct-investment inflows to Asia fell in 1997 to $53.2 billion, down from $58.7 billion in 1996. Investment flows to China fell 10%, while those to Indonesia fell by over 25%. The most significant trend in Asia centers on India, which has slowly, but gradually, become more receptive to multinationals. Foreign companies, in turn, have become more confident of India, investing over $3 billion in the nation in 1997 versus an annual average of just $403 million during the first half of the decade.

Investor confidence in Latin America has improved over the 1990s as well. The Latin American and Caribbean nations attracted a record $42 billion in foreign direct investment last year, more than three times the amount of 1993. Of the top 10 recipient developing countries of foreign investment in 1997, five nations—Brazil, Mexico, Argentina, Chile, and Venezuela—were from Latin America. The downside is that these five nations capture the bulk of investment inflows in a region with over two dozen nations.

The sudden and sharp rise in foreign direct investment to Eastern Europe and Central Asia is one of the most important trends regarding investment flows to the developing nations. During the Cold War era, this part of the world was largely off limits to multinationals. Yet when the

Berlin Wall came down, foreign direct investment went up as Western firms rushed to build a stake in one of the world's last frontiers. In 1990, one year after the collapse of the Berlin Wall, the region attracted just $1.1 billion in foreign investment, less than 5% of the total investment to the developing nations. In 1997, in contrast, multinationals invested over $15 billion in Eastern Europe and Central Asia, or nearly 13% of the total. Poland, one of the largest market economies in the region, has been at the forefront in attracting foreign direct investment.

At the bottom of the investment league are sub-Saharan Africa, the Middle East and North Africa, and South Asia. Endemic problems—ethnic conflicts, massive poverty, weak growth, poor infrastructure—have kept multinationals at bay for years, with the three regions combined attracting just 8% of total investment inflows to the developing nations in 1997. More encouraging is that investment inflows are gradually accelerating, with combined total inflows into the three regions reaching nearly $10 billion in 1997, the highest of the decade.

FDI Flows to the Top 10 Recipient Developing Countries, 1990, 1994, and 1997
(US$ Billions)

Country	1990	Country	1994	Country	1997*
China	3.5	China	33.8	China	37.0
Mexico	2.6	Mexico	11.0	Brazil	15.8
Thailand	2.4	Malaysia	4.3	Mexico	8.1
Malaysia	2.3	Peru	3.1	Indonesia	5.8
Argentina	1.8	Brazil	3.1	Poland	4.5
Indonesia	1.1	Argentina	3.1	Malaysia	4.1
Brazil	1.0	Indonesia	2.1	Argentina	3.8
Egypt	0.7	Nigeria	1.9	Chile	3.5
Turkey	0.7	Poland	1.9	India	3.1
Chile	0.6	Chile	1.8	Venezuela	2.9
Top Ten's Share of Total FDI to All Developing Countries	70.5%		76.1%		72.3%

*Preliminary

Source: World Bank

45 | Corporate Japan Goes Global

Japan is one of the largest economies in the world—a top global exporter and home to one of the largest pools of capital on earth. Yet, despite its formidable attributes, Japan has only recently—in the past decade—gone global.

In 1985, Japan's stock of foreign direct investment was only $44 billion, half the level of the United Kingdom's. Over the intervening years, though, Japan's stock of outward FDI soared to $204.7 billion in 1990, $284.2 billion in 1994, and $330.2 billion in 1996. By the middle of the 1990s, only the United States, with $794 billion in foreign outward stock in 1996, and the United Kingdom ($356 billion) held larger overseas positions.

Prior to 1985, most of Japan's foreign direct investment was directed at resource-rich nations such as Indonesia, where the objective was straightforward: to obtain the necessary raw materials to keep Japan's economy running. Over the late 1970s and early 1980s, Japan also began to build an investment stake in the newly industrialized nations of Asia, attracted by the region's low wages and expanding markets. Despite this investment thrust, exporting was the preferred and main strategy by which Japan interacted with the world up through the mid-1980s.

Over the second half of the 1980s, the world economic landscape changed radically for Japan. The yen appreciated dramatically. U.S. threats of trade protectionism grew louder and more ominous. At home, rising wage costs, coupled with a costly domestic operating environment, weighed heavily on companies trying to compete in the international arena. The upshot? Japan was forced to go global, or shift to investment-led growth abroad versus export-led growth.

From a level of just $12.2 billion in 1985, as the accompanying graph portrays, Japan's foreign direct investment soared to $33.4 billion in 1987 and hit a peak of $67.5 billion in 1989. Foreign investment fell off in the early 1990s, reaching a trough of $34.1 billion in 1992, a downturn triggered by the collapse of Japan's stock market, deflationary pressures, the economic slowdown, and weak corporate profits.

Despite the ebb and flow of foreign direct investment and shift in exchange rates, the general global thrust of Japan has not changed. Investment-led growth overseas is the preferred strategy of large and medium-sized companies. Accordingly, notwithstanding economic difficulties, Japan's overseas investment averaged roughly $50 billion over the 1995–97 period. During the 1986–97 period, Japan invested over $525 billion overseas.

Where has the majority of Japan's investment gone? By an overwhelming margin, the bulk has been directed at North America, including the United States and Canada. Over the past decade, roughly 40 to 48% of Japan's annual total foreign investment has been sunk in North America.

Beyond North America, Japan's investment drive into Asia stands out. At the beginning of this decade, roughly 10% of Japan's total overseas investment went to Asia; the percentage has since risen to roughly one-quarter. The most striking feature in Asia has been Japan's soaring investment presence in Southeast Asia and China. The mainland accounted for less than 1% of Japan's total foreign investment in 1990, although the share has since risen to nearly 6% as more and more Japanese companies turn to China as a low-cost production site and a budding emerging consumer market.

The bottom line? Over the past few years, Japan has reaped the benefits of a weaker yen, stirring resentment in many quarters of the United States. The cheap currency has been a boost, though investors would do well to remember the following: (1) the benefits of a weak currency are unsustainable, and (2) Japan increasingly competes through investment, not trade. Corporate Japan has gone global.

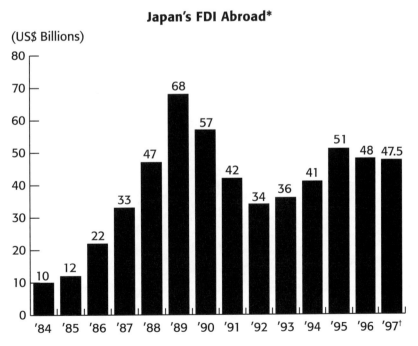

Japan's FDI Abroad*

(US$ Billions)

*Fiscal-year data (April–March)
†Estimate

Source: Japanese Ministry of Finance

46 Foreign Direct Investment—a Critical Competitive Edge Japan Has over the United States

Over the decades, many people in America have challenged and questioned Japan's global trade practices. U.S. presidents—whether Democrat or Republican—have all felt local pressure to "do something" about America's chronic trade deficit with Japan.

But trade is not the only avenue in which Japan and the United States compete. An even more important contest is being waged via foreign investment, and on this score, Japan has a commanding edge over the United States.

As the first graph highlights, Japan's foreign direct-investment position in the United States has soared over the past 15 years and is now nearly three times larger than America's investment position in Japan. U.S. direct investment in Japan reached a cumulative value of $39.6 billion in 1996, while Japan's totaled $118 billion. This flow of capital from Japan doubtless has been beneficial to America, notably to many midwestern states that have attracted new investment from Japan's large automobile manufacturers. However, the skewed investment flows confer a number of strategic advantages to Japan that U.S. companies and others do not have in Japan.

Given the commanding investment position of Japan in the United States, sales of U.S. affiliates of Japanese companies ($419 billion) were almost two times greater than comparable sales of Japanese affiliates of U.S. companies in Japan ($212 billion) in 1995. Accordingly, not only does Japan enjoy a sizable trade surplus, but also a sizable in-country sales surplus, as shown in the second graph.

Why has so little U.S. direct investment penetrated the Japanese economy? America's own short-sighted strategies and tactical mistakes in Japan are part of the explanation. Yet, other forces are at work. Government policies, a bias against majority holdings by foreign companies, and cross-share holdings among large Japanese firms have all contributed to the paltry level of foreign direct investment in Japan. The good news is that Japan is becoming more receptive to foreign direct investment, with investment flows rising to $7 billion in 1996, a record high. The bad news is that Japan will maintain an investment edge over the United States for some time to come.

United States Versus Japan: Foreign Direct Investment*

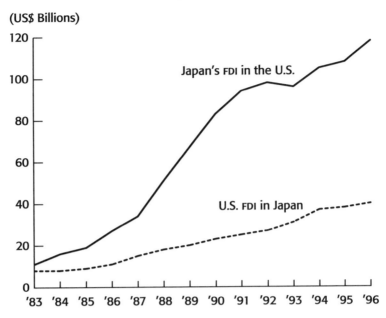

(US$ Billions)

Japan's FDI in the U.S.

U.S. FDI in Japan

*Historical-cost basis

Source: U.S. Department of Commerce

Japan's Twin Surplus with the United States

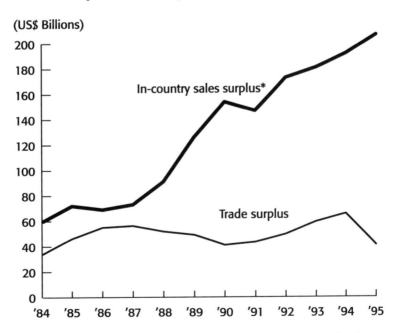

(US$ Billions)

In-country sales surplus*

Trade surplus

*In-country sales of U.S. affiliates of Japanese companies minus in-country sales of Japanese affiliates of U.S. companies

Source: U.S. Department of Commerce

47 The Role of Foreign Direct Investment in the Rise of China

One of the great economic success stories of the past decade has been the rise of China. Largely impoverished, underdeveloped, and isolated from the world for three decades after the 1949 revolution, China turned decisively toward the West in the latter years of the 1970s. At that time, foreign trade and investment played only a minor role in the economy, since external contacts were kept to a minimum.

Over the past decade and a half, however, China has embraced the world, and the world has embraced China. No other developing nation has attracted as much foreign direct investment (FDI), with the mainland taking in nearly $200 billion in foreign direct investment (actual FDI utilized) over the 1990–97 period. In 1996, China attracted a record $42.3 billion in foreign direct investment, and another $37 billion in 1997.

Foreign direct investment, and its attendant benefits ranging from rising exports to job creation, has been a critical variable to China's economic rise. Just how significant and important foreign direct investment is to China is demonstrated in the accompanying table.

Note first the stunning rise in foreign direct investment over the 1990s, with the annual level rising from $4.4 billion in 1991 to over $30 billion by 1994. This massive surge, in turn, has greatly raised the profile of foreign companies in China's overall level of gross fixed capital formation. Indeed, in 1995, roughly one out of every four dollars invested in China came from a foreign source.

The impact on trade has been just as significant. Exports by foreign affiliates operating in China reached an estimated $46.1 billion in 1995, which is nearly four times the level of 1991. As a percentage of total exports, exports of foreign affiliates accounted for more than 30% in 1995, up from 20.4% in 1992 and 17% in 1991. In other words, China's emergence as one of the world's premier exporters has been greatly underpinned by foreign firms who have turned to the mainland as a new and cheap export platform.

In terms of industrial output, foreign affiliates accounted for 13% of total industrial production in 1995, up from a level of 9% in 1993 and just 5% in 1991. Meanwhile, foreign companies have become critical sources of employment for China, with foreign companies employing some 16 million people in China in 1995, a near fourfold increase from the level of 1991. As a comparison to the United States, foreign firms (nonfinancial) employ roughly five million workers in the United States. As a significant source of tax revenue, foreign affiliates accounted for 10% of China's total taxes in 1995.

Who are the top foreign investors in the mainland? It is neither the United States nor Japan, two of the world's largest sources of foreign investment. Rather the bulk (well over half) of China's FDI is sourced locally, with overseas Chinese firms based in Hong Kong and Taiwan the primary providers of capital to the mainland. As discussed further in trend 94 ("The Overseas Chinese—the Silent Force of Asia"), Asia's overseas Chinese have played a pivotal role in the industrial rise of China.

On balance, China is now more integrated and dependent on the world economy than ever before. But it is worth remembering that notwithstanding the mainland's attributes, ranging from industrious workers to high levels of savings, foreign direct investment has been critical to China's rise and global integration. The role of foreign investment is notably important to realize given the decline in inflows in 1998. Any prolonged slowdown in foreign investment carries significant consequences for China.

China's Dependence on Foreign Trade and Investment

	1991	1992	1993	1994	1995
Actual FDI inflows (US$ Billions)	4.4	11.2	27.5	33.8	35.8
Share of inward FDI to gross fixed capital formation (%)	3.3	7.8	20.0	24.5	25.7
Volume of exports by foreign affiliates (US$ billions)	12.1	17.4	25.2	34.7	46.1
Exports of foreign affiliates as % of total exports	17.0	20.4	27.5	28.7	31.3
Exports as % of GDP	15.9	16.7	14.0	19.8	25.9
Imports as % of GDP	13.5	15.4	16.0	18.4	22.4
Trade openness (exports + imports/GDP)	29.4	32.1	30.0	38.2	48.3
Industrial output by foreign affiliates as % of total industrial output	5.0	6.0	9.0	11.0	13.0
Number of employees in FDI projects (millions)	4.8	6.0	10.0	14.0	16.0
Tax contribution as share of total (%)	NA	NA	NA	NA	10.0

NA = Not available

Source: U.N., World Investment Report, 1996

48 The World's Top Transnationals—Who They Are and Why It Matters

Which companies are truly global players? How can an investor measure a company's level of global participation or involvement? Why is any of this relevant?

To take the last question first, investors should recognize the world's top transnationals, since they represent, to a large degree, the very companies that are well positioned to derive the most benefit from rapid and profound shifts in the world economy. Their expanding global reach promotes global economies of scale in production, distribution, marketing, and management. With complex corporate strategies and intricate network structures, these companies are global agents of change. They have the wherewithal to seize the opportunities presented by globalization.

Measuring a firm's level of global commitment or participation is not easy. But one measure lies with a company's foreign assets as a percentage of total assets. This relationship provides a benchmark as to whether or not a multinational is a global player with a local presence. This is a proxy for "glocality," in other words. The world's leading global multinationals, based on this definition, are presented in the accompanying table.

Only 25 companies are listed, but out of the 100 companies singled out by the United Nations, the United States accounted for 33 in 1995; 16 companies were from Japan. Both Germany and the United Kingdom placed 12 companies on the list, while 9 firms were from France.

By industry, notice the predominance of companies from the petroleum, automobile, and electronics sectors, which are among the most global industries in the world. Petroleum companies, by their very nature, must be global as they search the world for new oil deposits and reserves. In the automobile sector, the bulk of foreign assets held by Ford and General Motors is concentrated in Canada, the European Union, Mexico, and, lately, Brazil. For the industry at large, international partnerships and distribution arrangements have become the norm. The production facilities of the world's top electronics manufacturers are dispersed all over the globe as well, boosting the foreign assets of such companies as General Electric, Sony, IBM, and Philips. Rapid changes in technology and intense competition from the developing nations have forced these companies to step up their global push. Food giants such as Nestlé and Unilever are based in small markets but have long relied on the global markets for growth.

Top 25 Transnationals Ranked by Foreign Assets, 1995

Rank	Company	Country	Industry	Foreign Assets in US$ Billions	Foreign Assets as % of Total	Foreign Sales as % of Total	Foreign Employment as % of Total
1	Royal Dutch/ Shell	UK/ Netherlands	Oil & Gas	79.7	67.8	73.3	77.9
2	Ford	United States	Automotive	69.2	29.0	30.6	29.8
3	General Electric	United States	Electronics	69.2	30.4	24.4	32.4
4	Exxon	United States	Oil & Gas	66.7	73.1	79.6	53.7
5	General Motors	United States	Automotive	54.1	24.9	29.2	33.9
6	Volkswagen	Germany	Automotive	49.8	84.8	60.8	44.4
7	IBM	United States	Computers	41.7	51.9	62.7	50.1
8	Toyota	Japan	Automotive	36.0	30.5	45.1	23.0
9	Nestlé	Switzerland	Food	33.2	86.9	98.2	97.0
10	Mitsubishi	Japan	Diversified	NA	NA	40.8	41.8
11	Bayer	Germany	Chemicals	28.1	89.8	63.3	54.6
12	ABB Asea Brown Boveri	Switzerland	Electrical Equipment	27.2	84.7	87.2	93.9
13	Nissan Motor	Japan	Automotive	26.9	42.7	44.2	43.5
14	Elf Aquitaine	France	Oil & Gas	26.9	54.5	65.4	47.5
15	Mobil	United States	Oil & Gas	26.0	61.8	65.9	52.2
16	Daimler Benz	Germany	Automotive	26.0	39.2	63.2	22.2
17	Unilever	UK/Netherlands	Food	25.8	85.7	85.9	89.9
18	Philips Electronics	Netherlands	Electronics	25.2	77.1	95.8	83.4
19	Roche Holdings	Switzerland	Pharmaceuticals	24.5	79.3	96.0	80.0
20	Fiat	Italy	Automotive	24.4	41.3	64.8	38.7
21	Siemens	Germany	Electronics	24.0	41.6	57.3	43.4
22	Sony	Japan	Electronics	NA	NA	70.0	59.6
23	Alcatel Alsthom	France	Electronics	22.7	44.3	75.4	61.2
24	Hoechst	Germany	Chemicals	21.9	59.7	36.9	61.9
25	Renault	France	Automotive	21.2	47.5	51.9	28.6

Note: Where data for foreign assets were not available, the United Nations made estimates on the basis of the ratio of foreign to total employment, foreign to total sales, and other similar ratios.

NA = Not available

Source: U.N. World Investment Report, 1997

49 The Global Giants of the Developing Nations

The number of transnationals among the developing nations is small but growing. While 85% of the total FDI outflows emanated from the industrialized nations in 1996, investment flows from the developing nations rose to $51.5 billion in the same year, up from $40.7 billion in 1994 and an average of just $10.6 billion over the 1985–90 period.

Similar to transnationals based in the industrialized nations, more and more companies in the developing nations confront rising operating costs at home and intense competition in their own markets. They also require a steady supply of foreign resources, whether it is cheap labor or leading-edge technology. For these companies to survive, exporting is becoming less of a strategic option. Going global is increasingly becoming a necessity.

The leading transnationals in the developing nations, based on total foreign assets, are highlighted in the accompanying table. In 1995, the last year of available data, 15 out of the top 25 nations were from Asia, with the remaining from Latin America.

Among the most aggressive foreign investors are none other than the mainland Chinese which, combined with Hong Kong firms, account for 8 of the 25 transnationals listed. South Korea ranks second among nations with the most transnationals.

Looking to the future, the level of foreign direct investment from the developing nations, while small, is expected to continue rising. The demands of globalization permeate almost every corner of the world. Consequently, as General Motors and Kodak roam the globe for cheap labor, new markets, advanced technology, and more profit, they are increasingly likely to cross paths with companies from South Korea, Taiwan, Brazil, and Mexico.

Top 25 Transnationals in the Developing Nations Ranked by Foreign Assets, 1995

Rank	Company	Country	Industry	Foreign Assets in US$ Billions	Foreign Assets as % of Total	Foreign Sales as % of Total	Foreign Employment as % of Total
1	Daewoo	South Korea	Diversified/ trading	11.9	41.3	31.5	72.3
2	Petroleos de Venezuela S.A.	Venezuela	Oil & Gas	6.8	16.8	94.0	22.4
3	Cemex S.A.	Mexico	Construction	4.3	50.3	55.7	42.4
4	First Pacific Company	Hong Kong, China	Electronics parts	3.8	55.4	89.4	72.9

Rank	Company	Country	Industry	Foreign Assets in US$ Billions	Foreign Assets as % of Total	Foreign Sales as % of Total	Foreign Employment as % of Total
5	LG Electronics	South Korea	Electronics	NA	NA	58.2	40.4
6	Jardine Matheson Holdings	Bermuda	Diversified	3.1	26.7	69.7	70.0
7	Hutchinson Whampoa	Hong Kong, China	Diversified/ retailer	2.9	24.8	36.0	55.3
8	YPF Sociedad Anonima	Argentina	Oil & Gas	2.6	22.0	39.4	24.6
9	China State Construction Engineering Corp.	China	Diversified/ construction	2.4	NA	NA	NA
10	Sunkyong Group	South Korea	Energy/trading/ chemicals	2.3	8.1	23.9	8.2
11	Cathay Pacifica Airways	Hong Kong, China	Transportation	2.2	34.0	48.6	26.3
12	Samsung Electronics	South Korea	Electronics	NA	NA	20.0	12.8
13	China Chemicals Import/Export Co.	China	Diversified/ trading	2.1	24.2	NA	NA
14	Petroleo Brasileiro S.A., Petrobras	Brazil	Oil & Gas	1.9	5.9	5.4	0.0
15	Singapore Telecommuni-cations Ltd.	Singapore	Utilities	1.5	27.3	2.3	14.8
16	Hyundai Corporation	South Korea	Diversified/ machinery	1.5	12.9	16.1	2.1
17	Companhia Vale Do Rio Doce	Brazil	Mining	1.5	10.1	27.0	0.6
18	Grupo Televisa	Mexico	Media	1.4	43.1	24.4	33.7
19	New World Development Co. Ltd.	Hong Kong, China	Diversified/ construction	1.2	9.4	21.8	74.6
20	Citic Pacific	Hong Kong, China	Diversified/ automotive	1.1	21.0	49.5	68.7
21	Panamerican Beverages	Mexico	Beverages	1.0	73.1	76.9	75.0
22	Gruma S.A. de C.V.	Mexico	Food	1.0	90.6	54.0	72.3
23	Dairy Farm International Holdings Ltd.	Hong Kong, China	Retailing	0.9	32.9	63.8	48.4
24	Companhia Cervejaria Brahma	Brazil	Beverages	0.9	29.1	7.5	6.4
25	Fraser & Neave Ltd.	Singapore	Beverages	0.9	29.9	58.9	81.4

Note: Where data for foreign assets were not available, the United Nations made estimates on the basis of the ratio of foreign to total employment, foreign to total sales, and other similiar ratios.

NA = Not available

Source: U.N. World Investment Report, 1997

50 Global Stock Market Capitalization–Greater Diversity, but the United States Remains Number One

Just over 25 years ago, the U.S. equity market was the gorilla of the world markets, accounting for two-thirds of total global equity market capitalization. Consequently, many American investors were not compelled to venture far from home; neither did many European investors, whose markets accounted for nearly a quarter of the aggregate global equity pie. Combined, the United States and Europe accounted for nearly 90% of the world equity pie in 1970 (see the first graph).

Today there is greater market diversity, although by a significant margin the United States remains the largest global equity market in the world, accounting for nearly half the world total in 1997. Japan ranked second at the end of 1997, but fell to third behind the United Kingdom in early 1998. Japan's decline has been stunning and reflects a decade of sluggish or little economic growth. At the apex of Japan's financial prowess, Japan accounted for over 40% of the world equity total in 1988 and 37.5% in 1989.

Europe's share has remained relatively stable over the past 25 years. By a comfortable margin, the United Kingdom was home to the largest equity market in Europe in 1997, with a market capitalization of nearly $2 trillion, more than double second-ranked Germany.

Owing to Asia's financial crisis of 1997, which wiped out billions of dollars in wealth, the global equity share of the emerging markets fell last year to 9% from 11% in 1996. At its peak in 1994, the emerging markets accounted for 12.7% of the world equity market.

Total world market capitalization topped $23.5 trillion in 1997, more than double the level ($9.4 trillion) of 1990. Behind the global bull market of the 1990s are many variables, with financial-sector reform in both the developed and emerging markets and advances in information technology two key catalysts to growth. The former has helped roll back the barriers to global capital flows, while the latter (information technology) has made it much easier and efficient to transmit data, ideas, and above all else—money—around the world. The upshot? A broad menu of choices for global investors.

Global Equity Market Capitalization, 1970

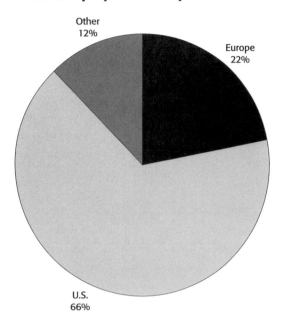

Other
12%

Europe
22%

U.S.
66%

Global Equity Market Capitalization, 1997

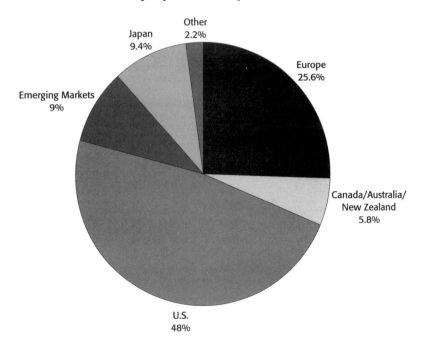

Japan
9.4%

Other
2.2%

Europe
25.6%

Emerging Markets
9%

Canada/Australia/
New Zealand
5.8%

U.S.
48%

Source: International Finance Corporation, Emerging Markets Factbook, 1998

51 Going Global–the Surge in World Equity Markets

The global equity markets today are far larger than they were a decade ago. Indeed, the world stock market capitalization topped $20 trillion at the end of 1996, and despite turmoil in Asia, reached $23.5 trillion in 1997. The figure was just $9.4 trillion in 1990.

Behind the surge are many variables, both secular and cyclical. The latter, in general, include a global environment characterized by modest growth, low inflation, and therefore low interest rates since 1992. More important are the secular forces at work, with market liberalization a primary impetus not only in the developing nations but also in many developed countries. These measures include privatization of state enterprises, the removal of capital controls, and financial-sector reform. The rapid diffusion of information technology in various parts of the world has also been a key underpin of global equity growth.

Significant advances in the world equity markets have come from the developed nations, bolstered primarily by the long-running bull market in the United States. As the bar graph shows, the total market capitalization of the developed nations rose from $8.8 trillion at the start of the decade to over $21 trillion at the end of 1997. This represented roughly 91% of total world market capitalization. In the emerging markets, the general trend has been upward, with 1997 a notable exception. Owing to Asia's financial crisis, the region's main equity markets declined sharply, lowering the overall market capitalization of the emerging markets to $2.229 trillion in 1997, down from $2.293 trillion in 1996. The emerging markets accounted for 11% of the world equity markets in 1996, but only 9% in 1997.

The market capitalization of the world's leading stock markets is presented in the accompanying table of rankings. Among the industrialized nations, the United States easily outdistanced every other country in 1997. Japan was second at the end of 1997 but was surpassed by the United Kingdom in early 1998.

Among the emerging markets, 7 of the top 10 largest markets in 1996 were in Asia. That figure, however, dropped to 4 last year given the steep markdowns in Asia over 1997. As one example, Malaysia had a market capitalization of over $300 billion in 1996, but lost over two-thirds of its market capitalization in 1997. Notice that the combined equity markets of China, Hong Kong, and Taiwan (or "Greater China") totaled $907 billion, making it the fourth largest in the world in 1997.

World Market Capitalization, 1987–97

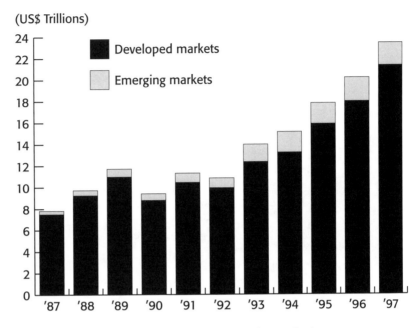

Source: International Finance Corporation, Emerging Markets Factbook, 1998

World Stock Market Rankings, 1997

Rank	Developed Markets	Total Market Capitalization (US$ Billions)	Rank	Developing Markets	Total Market Capitalization (US$ Billions)
1	United States	11,308.0	1	Taiwan	287.8
2	Japan	2,216.0	2	Brazil	255.5
3	United Kingdom	1,996.0	3	South Africa	232.1
4	Germany	825.2	4	China	206.4
5	Australia	696.7	5	Mexico	156.6
6	France	674.4	6	India	128.5
7	Switzerland	575.4	7	Russia	128.2
8	Canada	567.6	8	Malaysia	93.6
9	Netherlands	468.7	9	Chile	72.0
10	Hong Kong	413.3	10	Turkey	61.1

Source: International Finance Corporation, Emerging Markets Factbook, 1998

52 Investment Flows to the Developing Nations—Private Capital Now Calls the Tune

The good news is that capital flows to the developing nations have grown rapidly over this decade, with aggregate net long-term capital flows rising more than threefold over 1990–97, from $98.3 billion in 1990 to $300 billion in 1996. Behind the surge are many variables, including low global interest rates, better economic management in many nations, privatization initiatives, and higher-yielding investment instruments. These have been the main lures enticing capital to the emerging markets.

The bad news, however, is twofold. One, a massive gulf separates the countries that are receiving the capital, "the haves," and those nations that are not, or the "have-nots." The second point relates to the first: while private capital flows continue to increase to the emerging markets, official development aid and assistance continues to decline. The divergence between the two—rising private capital flows and declining official flows—has characterized the 1990s and has contributed to the uneven distribution of capital to the developing nations.

One of the most significant trends of the world economy, as represented in the accompanying graph, is that aggregate capital flows to the developing nations are now overwhelmingly from the private sector. Private capital flows (consisting of three main components—private lending, foreign direct investment, and portfolio equity flows) totaled just $42 billion in 1990 and accounted for just 42.6% of aggregate flows to the developing nations. Yet, by 1997, and notwithstanding volatile year-to-year flows in portfolio capital and commercial lending, total private capital flows had increased to $256 billion, more than a sixfold increase from 1990. Foreign direct investment has been the key component behind the surge. The share of private capital flow in aggregate flows rose to 85.2% in 1997, versus less than 50% at the start of the decade.

Meanwhile, official development assistance (which includes official grants and government loans) made up roughly 57% of total flows at the start of the decade. Its share has since plunged, falling to 25.7% in 1993 and 12.3% in 1996. Owing to the Asian crisis and attendant need for official financial assistance, development finance jumped 27.4% in 1997 to $44.2 billion. Despite this rise, official development assistance represented only 14.7% of net resource flows in 1997.

Development assistance for the poor nations has shrunk as fiscal austerity has taken hold in the industrialized countries. The end of the Cold War and significant reductions in military spending have led to sharp cuts in aid budgets around the world. The lack of domestic constituencies to protect, let alone promote, aid funding has contributed to less official assistance as well. More important, not only has the amount of aid dollars declined over the 1990s, but also what official assistance has been doled out has not gone toward long-term development programs and poverty reduction schemes, traditional areas of spending. Rather, a greater share of assistance has been spent on emergency relief funding and peace-keeping activities in such places as Central Europe and Africa.

The declining trend in official aid, coupled with the emergence of private capital as the primary source of funding for the developing nations, puts many poor countries at a disadvantage. Private capital is far more discriminating than official aid and flows only to those nations with attractive attributes. As a result, only a few countries, mainly middle-income nations, are attracting the bulk of private capital, while many low-income countries go without. Indeed, sub-Saharan Africa, South Asia and the Middle East, and North Africa are home to some of the poorest people in the world yet attracted less than 18% of net capital flows to the developing nations in 1997. In summary, private capital now calls the tune, but is it the right tune?

Net Long-Term Resource Flows to Developing Nations

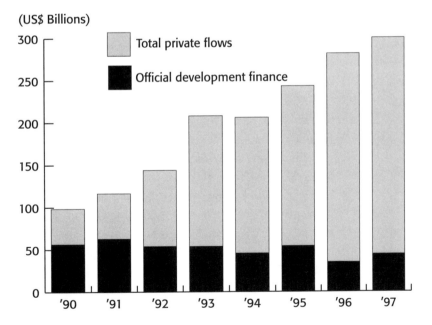

Source: World Bank, Global Development Finance, 1998

53 Portfolio Flows to the Developing Nations— Upward with Plenty of Volatility

Portfolio flows have grown tremendously as a source of capital for the developing nations over this decade. Now the bad news: growth in portfolio flows has been anything but linear. Year-to-year volatility is a key characteristic versus the steady upward rise in foreign direct investment, another key source of private finance for the developing nations.

From a level of just $3.2 billion in 1990, portfolio flows soared to $45 billion in 1993, sparking the first bull market in the emerging markets. The bottom fell out of many emerging stock markets the next year courtesy of rising U.S. interest rates, which reversed the flow of capital to the developing nations. Portfolio flows plunged by over 28% in 1994 to $32.6 billion. Next came the Mexican peso crisis, which triggered a loss of confidence in the emerging markets over 1995. Portfolio flows rebounded strongly in 1996. Asia's financial crisis in 1997, however, led to another exodus from the emerging markets, with portfolio flows dropping to $32.5 billion in 1997, or by nearly 30%.

Investors' on-again, off-again love affair with the emerging markets is likely to characterize portfolio flows to the developing nations over the medium-term. Notwithstanding periodic bouts of instability and volatility, the general direction of flows is upward due in large part to the following: better macroeconomic management in many emerging economies; financial-sector reform, with a particular emphasis on greater transparency; greater depth and breadth of capital markets; state privatization; political reform measures; and trade and investment liberalization. The potential for higher returns relative to the United States and Europe remains a critical lure as well.

Note from the accompanying graph that while portfolio flows to the developing nations have exhibited wide swings over this decade, foreign direct-investment flows have continued rising each year, supporting the contention that the latter are more strategic and therefore less volatile in nature. Why? Because foreign direct-investment flows reflect the long-term plans of multinationals, many of which assume a degree of political and economic risk before making an investment. Portfolio flows, in contrast, are more "footloose," responding more to short-term factors, such as shifts in exchange rates, interest rates, or unexpected political events. In the wake of the Asian crisis, many governments are considering imposing capital controls on portfolio flows to prevent wild swings in their respective money supply and stock markets.

Given the different determinants and attributes of portfolio flows versus foreign direct investment, it is imperative that investors in the emerging markets realize the composition of private flows to a particular nation. Both types of flows are important to the health of any economy, but many countries encourage one (foreign direct investment) while trying to control the other (portfolio). China, for instance, has long welcomed foreign direct investment given the nation's employment demands but has moved relatively slowly in opening its markets to Wall Street. The composition of private capital flows for 1997 is presented in the accompanying table.

Net Private Capital Flows to the Developing Nations
(Portfolio Investment Versus Foreign Direct Investment)

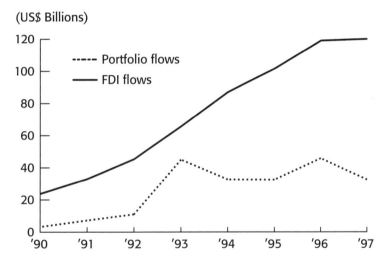

Source: World Bank, Global Development Finance, 1998

Composition of Private Flows, 1997
(% of Total)

	FDI	Portfolio Equity	Bonds	Private Debt
East Asia	60	2	17	21
Latin America	44	16	28	12
Eastern Europe/Central Asia	38	21	24	17
Middle East	18	11	14	57

Source: World Bank, Global Development Finance, 1998

54 Global Privatization—Out with the State, In with Private Ownership

One of the most pronounced trends of the 1990s is the surge in global privatization—the sale or transfer of state-owned enterprises to private investors, through stock flotations, auctions, or voucher and coupon schemes. Worldwide privatizations totaled $29.8 billion in 1990 but more than doubled to $73 billion in 1993 and approached $100 billion in 1997 (see the graph). Between 1990 and 1997, cumulative global privatization proceeds topped $500 billion.

What is behind the boom? The surge in privatization reflects the global sweep of free-market reforms, and the corresponding notion that the best government is the least government. The theory is that companies should thrive or wither on the basis of unfettered competition. The way to more jobs, stronger growth, and greater competitiveness lies not with coddled state-owned companies, but rather with private-sector firms that compete within the framework of the global economy.

Rolling back the presence of the state, and the attendant rise in privatization, has induced a number of positive changes. First, by providing more liquidity to the equity markets, the selling off of state firms has assisted in the development and growth of equity markets in both the developed and developing nations. Second, privatization has helped increase share ownership and spawned a "shareholder" mentality in countries that have long shunned equities. Third, hiving off companies has become an important source of revenue for many debt-ridden governments. Finally, with the placing of key sectors such as telecommunications, energy, railroads, and financial services in the hands of the private sector, the efficiency and growth prospects of many nations have been enhanced. The sectoral distribution of privatization varies across regions and countries, although in general, privatization has been dominated by offerings in the telecommunications, public utilities, financial services, transportation, and petrochemicals sectors.

Of total recorded privatization proceeds over 1990–96, roughly 71% ($292 billion) came from the OECD (Organization for Economic Cooperation and Development) nations, notably those in the European Union. Through the end of 1996, one of the largest transactions was the initial public offering of Deutsche Telekom, the German telecommunications giant. As far as being among the most aggressive in Europe in terms of privatization, Italy, France, and the United Kingdom stand out, generating privatization proceeds of $22.4 billion, $26.9 billion, and $56.6 billion, respectively, over the 1990–96 period.

Among the developing nations, Latin America has set the pace in hiving off state companies, with privatization proceeds totaling $64.2 billion over 1990–95. That is more than double the amount of Asia ($24.5 billion) and Europe and Central Asia ($24.4 billion) in the same period. It is not surprising that the speed and scope of privatization have varied across nations. Mexico and Argentina have been pacesetters in Latin America, while Brazil, with the largest economy in Latin America, has lagged until recently. In Asia, Malaysia and China have been notably aggressive, while Hungary also was very active in selling off state enterprises over the first half of this decade. By sector, privatization in the developing nations has been directed at telecommunications, banking, petroleum, and energy.

In summary, privatization has emerged as one of the most significant trends of this decade and marks a distinct shift in global corporate ownership. More and more governments are getting out of business and getting back to governing. To be sure, many sectors remain under the control of the state, but privatization continues to grow as free-market reforms take root around the world.

Global Privatization
(Gross Proceeds from Privatization)

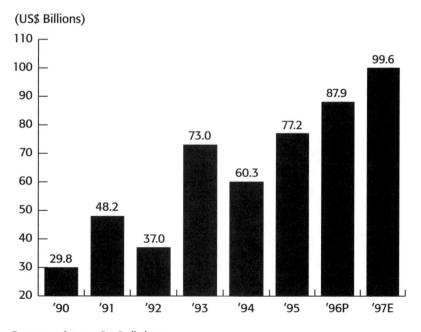

E = OECD estimate   P = Preliminary

Source: © OECD, 1997, Financial Market Trends, No. 66. Reproduced by permission of the OECD.

55 Global Investing—the Best Returns Are Usually in Some Unusual Places

Despite the great U.S. bull market of the 1990s, greater returns have been posted outside the United States in every year of this decade. Only once in the 1990s, in 1995, did the United States rank in the top five markets in terms of dollar-based performance.

Note from the table that the top performers, with 1995 the exception, are predominantly from the emerging markets. Russia took the top spot in 1996 and again in 1997. In a surprising performance, Nigeria topped all other markets in 1994.

That was the last time, however, that Nigeria made the top 10, which highlights a key fact of the world equity markets: life at the top is often precarious. Venezuela, ranked number 1 in 1990 among major developed and developing markets, crashed to number 52 two years later. Argentina was number 1 in 1991 but plunged to number 46 the following year. Turkey ranked second in 1993, plunged to number 68 in 1994, but rebounded to number 8 in 1996.

Then there is Russia, which has experienced a sharp fall from grace among investors in 1998, giving back most of the stellar gains of 1996 and 1997. The plight of Russia and others underscores one of the chief fundamentals of investing in the emerging markets: the rewards are great, but so too are the risks. Volatility is a fact of life, with a top-performing market one year becoming a nightmare for investors the next year.

Why so much volatility in these markets? High levels of foreign debt, shifting capital outflows and inflows, political instability, an overriding dependence on exports, wide and sudden currency fluctuations— all of these forces can converge to either lift a particular market in a particular year or collide to precipitate a major downturn at virtually any moment.

On many occasions, problems in one emerging market spill over to other emerging markets, a trend that underscores the fact that emerging markets are still thought of as a homogeneous investment class by investors. Consequently, when Thailand suffered a currency crisis in 1997, the Thai stock exchange declined, and other regional markets did likewise. This is known as "contagion." Take particular note of the accompanying graph and Asia's loss of paper wealth over 1997.

Top-Performing Equity Markets, 1992–97
(US$-Based Returns)

Rank	1992	1993	1994	1995	1996	1997
1	Peru	Poland	Nigeria	Switzerland	Russia	Russia
2	China	Turkey	Brazil	Sweden	Venezuela	Oman
3	Israel	Philippines	Peru	United States	Hungary	New Zealand
4	Colombia	Zimbabwe	Finland	Netherlands	China	Turkey
5	Thailand	Hong Kong	Chile	Spain	Poland	Botswana
6	Hong Kong	Indonesia	South Africa	Belgium	Zimbabwe	Ireland
7	Malaysia	Malaysia	Colombia	Ireland	Nigeria	Latvia
8	India	Luxembourg	Zimbabwe	Hong Kong	Turkey	Hungary
9	Jordan	Thailand	Norway	United Kingdom	Spain	Panama
10	Mexico	Brazil	Taiwan	South Africa	Taiwan	Mexico
	U.S. #15	U.S. #46	U.S. #28	U.S. #3	U.S. #22	U.S. #21

Source: International Finance Corporation, Emerging Markets Factbook, 1998

Asia's Implosion
(Market Capitalization, US$ Billions)

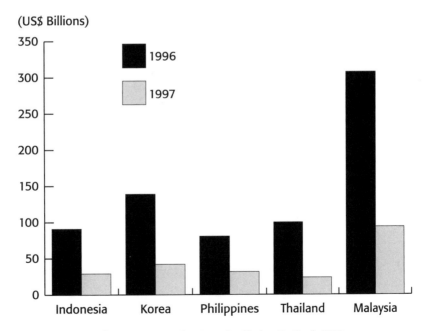

Source: International Finance Corporation, Emerging Markets Factbook, 1998

56 Assessing the Debt Levels of the Developing Nations

As the previous entry highlighted, the best returns are usually found outside the United States. Yet, in many of the high-yielding emerging markets, the risks can be just as great as the rewards in any given year. Investors, accordingly, should pay particular attention to debt levels and key indebtedness ratios.

Two popular indebtedness measures are presented in the accompanying table. One indicator is the value of total debt to exports. Exports are the means by which countries earn foreign exchange to service their debt, so the debt/export ratio reveals the capability of a country to service its debt. The second indicator—the ratio of total debt to gross national product—gives the investor an idea of how much debt is owed relative to the total output of the economy. According to the World Bank, if either ratio exceeds a key value—220% for the former and 80% for the latter—the country is classified as severely indebted. Making the list are some nations with large emerging equity markets, including Brazil, Argentina, and Indonesia. The latter fell into this category courtesy of the financial crisis of 1997.

Moreover, the most significant changes over the past year has been the inclusion of Malaysia and Thailand as moderately indebted countries. Both nations experienced a general deterioration in their debt indicators owing to the Asian crisis and the corresponding increase in debt to gross national product.

As a footnote, the World Bank further classifies nations by income. Low-income nations are nations with a per-capita GNP of $785 or less; middle-income nations are those with a per-capita GNP of more than $785 but less than $9,636. The last column, debt classification, combines the relative debt and income levels.

Note that China and many countries in Eastern Europe (the Czech Republic, Poland, and even Russia) are classified as less-indebted nations. In fact, China's debt to GNP ratio (17%) is the lowest of the countries listed in the table. As for Central Europe, their foreign debt exposure remains low since most of these nations were cut off from Western finance until only recently. Russia experienced its own brand of currency turmoil in 1998 and saw its level of foreign debt rise accordingly.

In terms of debt to exports, notice the debt burden of Argentina and Brazil, two of Latin America's most promising economies. Exports are not only important to these nations in terms of growth and employment, but also in servicing debt. This represents a significant burden and puts both nations at the risk of a sharp and sudden slowdown in export growth. Many other nations in the region—Colombia, Peru, Chile, Venezuela, and Mexico—face similar challenges that should be recognizable to investors.

Key Indebtedness Ratios, 1994–96

Country	Indicators (%)		Debt Classification
	Debt/Export	Debt/GNP	
Argentina	323	31	Severely indebted, middle income
Brazil	293	26	Severely indebted, middle income
Chile	166	48	Moderately indebted, middle income
China	76	17	Less indebted, low income
Colombia	206	40	Moderately indebted, middle income
Czech Republic	70	42	Less indebted, middle income
Hungary	158	62	Moderately indebted, middle income
India	152	22	Moderately indebted, low income
Indonesia	236	64	Severely indebted, middle income
Malaysia	50	52	Moderately indebted, middle income
Mexico	154	44	Moderately indebted, middle income
Pakistan	206	39	Moderately indebted, low income
Peru	318	43	Severely indebted, middle income
Philippines	116	51	Moderately indebted, middle income
Poland	102	31	Less indebted, middle income
Russia	97	25	Less indebted, middle income
Slovak Republic	66	41	Less indebted, middle income
South Africa	67	18	Less indebted, middle income
Thailand	131	56	Moderately indebted, middle income
Turkey	184	47	Moderately indebted, middle income
Ukraine	48	18	Less indebted, middle income
Venezuela	147	51	Moderately indebted, middle income
Vietnam	322	123	Severely indebted, low income

Source: World Bank, Global Development Finance, 1998

57 | Investing in American Depositary Receipts (ADRs)

There are several ways to invest globally, with American Depositary Receipts (ADRs) one popular avenue. An ADR is a negotiable receipt issued in certificate form that represents the equity share of a non-U.S. company. ADRs are issued and administered by U.S. depository banks and quoted in U.S. dollars. They clear and settle like U.S. shares and trade freely on U.S. exchanges, namely the Nasdaq and the American and New York stock exchanges. Legally, ADRs are considered U.S. securities and are treated in the same manner as American stock certificates for transfer and ownership purposes.

ADRs offer benefits to both U.S. investors and the foreign company that issues them. The benefit to the latter lies with the fact that a listing on a U.S. stock exchange brings visibility, prestige, and, above all else, access to U.S. capital. For investors, ADRs help add to a globally diversified portfolio with less of the hassle and risk associated with international investing. ADRs obviate the need for a foreign custodian, which in turn lowers carrying costs compared with direct investing. In addition, they eliminate the need for transporting or shipping foreign certificates to and from home markets; they provide dividends that are usually paid in U.S. dollars; their related reports and shareholder information are issued in English; and they reduce the complexities of dealing with foreign withholding taxes.

On the downside, a key risk of ADRs lies with sudden and unfavorable shifts in exchange rates, the bane of all global investors.

Despite the advantages to both investors and foreign companies, ADRs have only recently surged in popularity. The first ADRs were created in the 1920s to satisfy U.S. demands for foreign securities and to assist non-U.S. companies wanting to raise capital in America. Yet, as the graph shows, one of the strongest periods of growth has occurred over the 1990s, with the total number of ADRs rising from 836 in 1990 to more than 1,350 in 1997. Total trading volume in ADRs was just $75 billion in 1990 but rose to over $500 billion in 1997.

Behind this surge in popularity are a number of variables. Rising demand for international shares among U.S. individual investors and large institutions has been one central factor. Cross-border investing by both groups has become more common as investors look to diversify their portfolios and obtain higher returns outside the United States. On the issuance side, privatization in the developing nations has been one of the largest forces driving growth in depositary receipts. To obtain capital, non-U.S. companies in such fast-growing sectors as telecommunications, banking, and utilities have turned to the United States to fund their expansion. U.S. investors, for their part, have been more or less obliging, with some ADRs, such as Telemex of Mexico and Telebras of Brazil, now more actively traded in the United States than in their home markets.

For many companies in the developed nations, namely from the United Kingdom and Continental Europe, creating an ADR provides access to U.S. capital markets, which in turn is used to fund, in many cases, their expansion in the U.S. market.

ADRs thus have emerged as one of the simplest ways for investors to build a global portfolio and for non-U.S. companies to tap the capital markets of the United States. Looking forward, and given the pace of global privatization, the universe of ADRs, particularly from the emerging markets, is only expected to expand in the future.

Total Number of Depositary Receipt Programs

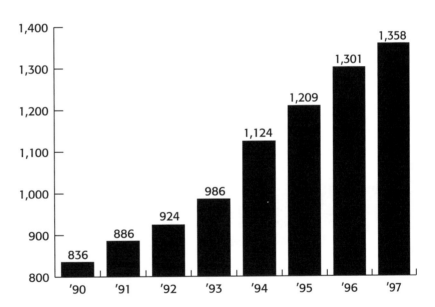

Source: Bank of New York, "Depositary Receipts, 1997 Year-End Summary"

58 Cross-Border Portfolio Flows—the Global Links Are Becoming Tighter and Tighter

It is a commonplace that in an era of rapid globalization, money knows no fatherland. Capital is attracted to markets offering the highest rate of return or to nations that offer the best opportunities to investors. This borderless world of capital is a result of financial-sector reform, including the elimination of capital controls in many nations, along with the rapid diffusion of information technology.

Cyclical factors play a part in determining global capital flows as well. Indeed, attracted by a modest-growth-cum-low-inflation environment, foreign investors purchased some $385.6 billion in U.S. securities in 1997, up slightly from the record set in 1996. As the first graph in this section highlights, the bulk of foreign purchases centered on U.S. Treasuries, with foreign purchases of U.S. fixed-income instruments reaching $183.6 billion in 1997. Over the 1984–97 period, net foreign purchases of U.S. Treasuries totaled $628 billion, a critical source of financing for a low-saving country like the United States.

In general, foreigners have long preferred U.S. bonds to U.S. stocks, notwithstanding the performance of the U.S. equity markets over most of this decade. However, thanks to heavy buying by European investors, net foreign purchases of U.S. equities soared to a record $66 billion last year, or about as much as the total of all the stock they purchased in the prior decade.

U.S. investors bought more foreign bonds than foreign stocks in 1997, although net purchases in both asset classes were down from the prior year. America's own stellar stock market performance, coupled with Asia's financial meltdown, compelled many U.S. investors to stay at home or bring money back from overseas. U.S. net purchases of foreign securities totaled $84.3 billion in 1997, down from 1996 and well off the record total of 1993. Asia's problems notwithstanding, America's appetite for foreign stocks has increased sharply over the 1990s relative to the 1980s (see the second graph). Between 1990 and 1997, U.S. investors purchased over $300 billion in foreign equities, with the bulk of the purchases directed at Europe. Over the 1980s, in contrast, total purchases came to just $28.3 billion.

On balance, global portfolio flows are highly cyclical, responding to year-to-year shifts in growth, interest rates, or currency movements. On a secular basis, however, the trend is toward greater and larger global capital flows, with the United States among the largest investors and recipients of capital.

Net Foreign Purchases of U.S. Securities

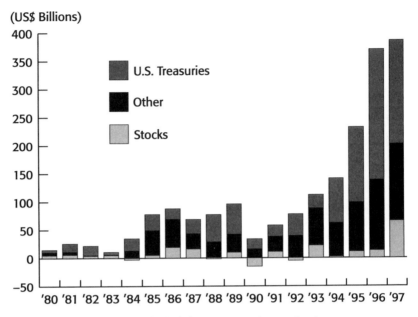

Net = purchases minus sales; Other includes corporate and agency bonds

Source: U.S. Department of Treasury

Net U.S. Purchases of Foreign Securities

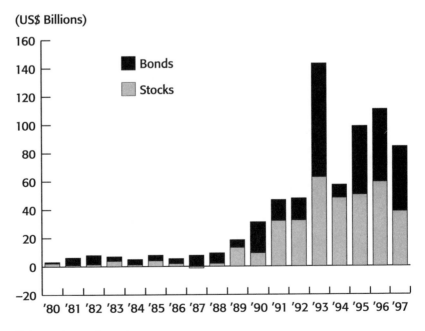

Net = purchases minus sales

Source: U.S. Department of Treasury

59 The Global Giants Based on Market Capitalization

There are many ways for investors to size up and compare companies. Annual sales, the total value of assets, market share, the number of employees—all of these are common benchmarks for corporate comparisons. Market capitalization, the market value of a company based on the price and number of shares outstanding, is another factor to consider. One caveat: market capitalization is driven (directly and indirectly) by a number of fluid variables, including earnings momentum, interest rates, investor confidence, industry cycles, mergers and acquisitions, and currency swings. The measure is therefore somewhat of a moving target. With that aside, the accompanying table lists some of the world's largest companies in mid-1998 based on market capitalization.

Given the U.S. bull market of the 1990s, it is hardly surprisingly that the table is dominated by U.S. multinationals. Led by General Electric, American firms accounted for 7 of the top 10 slots and 19 of the top 30 companies listed. Notice that only two companies from Japan (Nippon Telephone & Telegraph and Toyota) made the list, manifestation of Japan's struggling stock market over most of this decade.

The top spot belonged to General Electric in mid-1998, an "old-timer" relative to the newcomer Microsoft, ranked number 2. The growth in Microsoft's market capitalization has been nothing short of explosive. The company's market value rose from under $5 billion at the end of 1989 versus over $200 billion in 1998. Other technology leaders on the list include Intel, IBM, and Lucent.

By sector, the world's largest companies are generally found in industries that are global in scope or on the cutting edge of technological change. The oil sector is represented by Exxon, Royal Dutch/Shell, and British Petroleum. Consumer product companies also dominate the list and include General Electric, Coca-Cola, Procter & Gamble, Philip Morris, Unilever, Nestlé, and others. Following a wave of mergers and acquisitions, the pharmaceutical industry now has some giants in terms of market capitalization, including Merck, Pfizer, Novartis, Bristol-Meyers, Roche, Glaxo Wellcome, and Johnson & Johnson. Notice that Toyota of Japan was the only automobile company to make the list. Wal-Mart is among the least global of the companies listed, but ranked seventh in terms of global market capitalization. Walt Disney is the sole entertainment company to make the list.

The World's Top 30 Companies by Market Capitalization*
(US$ Billions)

Rank	Company	Country	Market Capitalization
1	General Electric	United States	270.0
2	Microsoft	United States	205.5
3	Coca-Cola	United States	196.4
4	Exxon	United States	172.8
5	Merck	United States	139.3
6	Pfizer	United States	135.6
7	Wal-Mart Stores	United States	126.6
8	Nippon Telephone & Telegraph	Japan	126.5
9	Royal Dutch Petroleum	United Kingdom/Netherlands	122.2
10	Aegon NV	Netherlands	116.3
11	Novartis AG	Switzerland	116.2
12	Intel	United States	115.3
13	Procter & Gamble	United States	114.7
14	IBM	United States	111.7
15	Bristol-Myers Squibb	United States	107.5
16	Roche	Switzerland	99.0
17	AT&T	United States	95.9
18	Glaxo Wellcome	United Kingdom	95.9
19	Johnson & Johnson	United States	92.7
20	Philip Morris	United States	91.5
21	Toyota Motor	Japan	91.2
22	Lucent Technologies	United States	90.3
23	Unilever	United Kingdom/Netherlands	89.3
24	Berkshire Hathaway	United States	87.5
25	American International Group	United States	85.8
26	Du Pont (EI) De Nemours	United States	85.1
27	Nestlé SA	Switzerland	84.5
28	British Petroleum	United Kingdom	83.8
29	Lloyds TSB	United Kingdom	78.4
30	Disney Company	United States	75.2

*As of June 1, 1998

Source: Company data

60 Market Concentration–a Key Risk in the Emerging Markets

As Asia proved in 1997, the emerging markets are fertile, yet volatile, markets for investors. The returns or rewards in any given year can be far greater than returns in the United States. But greater returns usually go hand in hand with greater risks, and so it is with the emerging markets.

The risks that accompany the emerging markets range from unpredictable currency swings to above-average and unexpected transaction costs. Others involve political risks, the lack of transparency, and local business practices that are not at all investor friendly.

Another recurrent risk of the emerging markets is the market concentration of many stock exchanges. All too often, equity markets in the developing nations beat to the tune of a handful of companies or to the rhythms of one or two key sectors of the economy. In the Philippines, for instance, nearly 50% of the Manila equity market is made up of companies in the real estate and financial sector. Thailand, Taiwan, and Poland are other markets in which the influence and the performance of the real estate/financial sector plays a pivotal role. In many developing nations in Asia, the financial sector is the weakest link of the economy but the mainstay of the stock market. Asia's financial crisis of 1997 exposed this flaw.

In Argentina, meanwhile, 45% of the main exchange is associated with companies in the mining sector. Transportation, communication, and utilities companies dominate Brazil's main stock market.

Given these characteristics, the first step for investors venturing into the emerging markets is to understand what sectors—telecommunications, mining, real estate—dominate the local stock exchanges.

Another related task is to ascertain the dominance of the market's top 10 companies. This is less of an issue in the more mature and developed stock markets. However market concentration among a few companies is common in many emerging markets, which is not altogether surprising given the underdevelopment of many stock markets. The risks lie in the fact that a few companies can have a disproportionate impact on the performance of the market.

The table presents the market concentration of some of the world's key emerging markets. As a benchmark, the top 10 companies of the S&P 500 accounted for about 20% of total market capitalization in mid-1997.

Market Concentration in the Emerging Markets

	1994	**1995**	**1996**
Argentina			
Number of companies listed	168	149	149
Top 10 stocks as a % of market cap	41.7	47.5	50.0
Brazil			
Number of companies listed	544	543	550
Top 10 stocks as a % of market cap	34.5	37.1	37.4
Mexico			
Number of companies listed	206	185	193
Top 10 stocks as a % of market cap	33.8	36.5	33.3
Venezuela			
Number of companies listed	93	90	87
Top 10 stocks as a % of market cap	73.8	63.0	70.7
China			
Number of companies listed	291	323	540
Top 10 stocks as a % of market cap	17.3	20.2	18.7
Indonesia			
Number of companies listed	216	238	253
Top 10 stocks as a % of market cap	29.8	41.3	51.1
Malaysia			
Number of companies listed	478	529	621
Top 10 stocks as a % of market cap	29.6	29.4	27.9
Philippines			
Number of companies listed	189	205	216
Top 10 stocks as a % of market cap	44.3	39.1	35.3
South Korea			
Number of companies listed	189	205	216
Top 10 stocks as a % of market cap	44.3	39.1	29.1
Czech Republic			
Number of companies listed	29	1,635	1,588
Top 10 stocks as a % of market cap	NA	46.4	54.4
Hungary			
Number of companies listed	40	42	45
Top 10 stocks as a % of market cap	43.9	30.9	80.8
Poland			
Number of companies listed	44	65	83
Top 10 stocks as a % of market cap	46.8	37.2	53.1

NA = Not available

Source: National sources

61 Whither the Central Banks?

Which party has more clout to influence global capital flows—central bankers, given their wherewithal to set monetary policies, or the world's currency traders, who trade billions of dollars each day and are more interested in profits than policies?

In the past, the answer was easy. It was the central bankers, the global keepers of capital and directors of monetary policies. However, as the accompanying graph vividly highlights, the power of the central bankers today is being challenged, if not reduced, by the staggering sums that are moved around each day by global traders. Some analysts have gone so far as to claim that the markets now rule—that nation-states have effectively lost control over the monetary policies and have only marginal roles to play in the new world economy.

The daily average turnover of foreign exchange now dwarfs the reserves of the central banks. In 1983, while the average volume on the major exchanges totaled $39 billion, the combined central bank foreign exchange reserves of the United States, the United Kingdom, Japan, Germany, and Switzerland were roughly $140 billion. By 1986, the positions were reversed, and the gap has only become larger with time. Indeed, against a daily average trading amount of $623 billion in 1992, aggregate central bank reserves of these five nations totaled just $278 billion, or less than half of the daily turnover in foreign exchange.

For the entire world, the daily average foreign exchange turnover rose to $820 billion by 1992 and soared to more than $1 trillion in 1995, the last year of available data. The bulk of the trading takes place in a small number of financial centers—namely, the United Kingdom (ranked number one), the United States, and Japan. Behind these three nations are Singapore, Hong Kong, Switzerland, and Germany.

A number of factors are behind the surge in global foreign exchange trading. One lies with the mobility of capital, thanks to the spread and diffusion of information technology. Technologies now allow massive flows of capital to traverse the world in seconds, allowing traders to move into and out of various markets. Financial reform, a general reduction in capital controls in numerous markets, and rapid globalization in numerous industries have also converged to put traders in the forefront of global capital flows.

Governments, or more specifically, central bankers, are increasingly overwhelmed by the sheer speed and size of global capital flows. Technology and information mobility are significantly encroaching on the capacity of central bankers to effectively manage their monetary policies. As demonstrated by the Mexican peso crisis in late 1994, and again in Asia in 1997, difficulties in one market can rapidly spread to other markets, thanks to the actions of traders. These events underscore the fact that policy makers now confront a new global force, a force that has increasingly become a source of reward for nations that maintain the confidence of global traders or punishment for those nations that do not. Not surprisingly, many governments and policy makers have warmed to the idea of capital controls, notably in light of Asia's financial meltdown in 1997. This possibility has yet to gain much support but could emerge as an alternative or weapon for central bankers if the world economy experiences another financial calamity such as occurred in Asia.

Central Banks Versus Foreign Exchange Markets

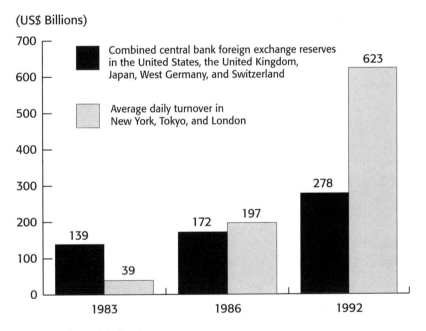

Source: McKinsey Global Institute

62 Savers and Investors in the Developing Nations

The economic prospects of any nation, developed or developing, are influenced by the rate of savings and investment. A country's savings rate signals the general amount of capital available for investment. The latter, in turn, is the foundation and building block of all economies.

A chief concern related to the developing nations (and the United States for that matter) lies with the gap between domestic savings and investment. This generally leaves a country with two options. One option is to curtail investment, with the downside being slower growth and delayed development. Option number two is to finance the gap via external borrowing. This option can turn out to be dangerous and has come back to haunt many developing nations who have seen their ability to service foreign debt levels impaired by currency devaluations, falling commodity prices, rising international interest rates, or all three.

History has shown that nations with relatively high rates of savings and investment enjoy many benefits, with faster rates of economic growth chief among them. The Asian financial crisis of 1997, however, also shows that too much investment can turn a virtue into a vice.

On an aggregate basis, the savings and investment ratios of the developing nations have improved over the 1990s. The overall average, though, masks some significant regional differences. The savings and investment rates of Latin America and Africa, for instance, are well below the average for the developing nations. More encouraging, at least in parts of Latin America, is the trend toward financial sector reform and more policies geared toward mobilizing domestic savings. The unequivocal leader is Chile, a financial pioneer, with one of the largest savings pools in Latin America, owing to its successful pension program.

The highest rates of savings and investment are in Asia. The region's penchant for savings and investment has underpinned stellar rates of economic growth over the past few decades. Over this decade, though, many countries in Asia were investing beyond their domestic means or savings. For instance, savings as a percentage of GDP was more than 30% in Indonesia, Thailand, and Korea over 1993–96. Investment rates, though, were even higher. Compounding matters, a significant proportion of this excess investment went to risky, highly cyclical, low-productivity investments like real estate. In addition, high capital spending led to overcapacity in many industries. The upshot? In both the property markets and across many sectors, supply quickly came to outstrip demand, leaving many corporations and their respective banks vulnerable to a loss of confidence and an economic downturn. The amalgam of low-productivity investments, along with lax financial standards, weak financial underpins, mismanaged exchange rates, unhedged short-term debt, and poor corporate governance helped spark the great Asian financial crisis of 1997.

Savings and Investment in the Developing Nations
(As a % of GDP)

	1990	1991	1992	1993	1994	1995	1996	1997
Developing Countries								
Savings	25.3	24.0	24.5	24.7	26.3	26.6	26.5	26.5
Investment	25.8	25.7	26.4	28.3	27.9	28.6	28.0	27.5
Africa								
Savings	18.6	18.2	16.9	13.9	14.9	14.4	16.8	16.8
Investment	19.3	20.9	20.1	19.7	20.5	20.4	19.6	18.6
Asia								
Savings	29.9	29.9	30.3	31.9	33.2	32.9	32.4	32.2
Investment	30.4	30.3	30.8	34.6	34.0	34.7	33.9	32.4
Middle East and Europe								
Savings	21.5	16.3	21.3	18.2	21.4	23.0	20.7	20.2
Investment	22.9	23.9	24.8	24.0	21.1	22.6	20.8	21.1
Western Hemisphere								
Savings	19.9	18.7	17.7	16.9	17.5	18.1	18.4	18.5
Investment	20.2	19.8	20.4	20.2	20.4	20.0	20.3	21.6
United States								
Savings	15.7	15.8	14.5	14.5	15.5	16.0	16.6	17.1
Investment	17.4	15.8	16.0	16.5	17.5	17.2	17.6	18.2

Source: IMF

63 | Official Development Assistance—"Aid Fatigue" Sets In

Any developing nation waiting to receive more foreign aid from the wealthy countries is in for a long wait. The wealthy countries have not been in much of a giving mood this decade on account of prevailing political and budgetary pressures at home. Accordingly, private financial flows to the developing nations continue to outstrip official funds, leaving many poor nations, notably those lacking an attractive investment environment, out in the cold in terms of receiving a fair or decent share of external financing.

In the United States, the emphasis on cutting the budget and government downsizing has resulted in less and less money for the developing nations. As the table shows, U.S. official assistance totaled $11.7 billion in 1992, making the United States the most generous official aid donor (in dollars) among the industrialized nations. However, official disbursements from the U.S. fell to $9.9 billion in 1994 and to just $7.4 billion in 1995, when America ranked number four in terms of assistance. In 1996, the figure rebounded to $9.1 billion, although the increase resulted less from newfound generosity on the part of the United States than from back payments due in the prior year. Despite the rise in official assistance in 1996, the United States ranked last in terms of the ratio of official development assistance to gross national product. The number for the United States was just 0.12%, less than half the overall average for the developed nations (0.25%).

The most generous nation, in terms of aid disbursements as a percentage of total national output, was Denmark in 1996, with official aid commitments accounting for more than 1% of GNP. Other generous donors included the Netherlands (0.83%) and Sweden (0.82%).

Based on total dollar amount, Japan has superseded the United States as the largest official aid donor to the developing nations over this decade. However, given slow growth in Japan and an oversized government budget deficit, even Japan has become less generous over the past few years. Official aid disbursements from Japan dropped nearly 25% in 1996, to $9.4 billion, or 0.20% of GNP. After Japan and the United States, which, combined, accounted for more than 34% of total assistance in 1996, Germany, France, and the Netherlands anted up the most money for the developing nations.

Total official development assistance fell to $55.1 billion in 1996, off nearly 10% from the level of 1992. More ominously, the 1996 total aid package from the developed nations represented a mere 0.25% of the members' combined gross national product, down from 0.30% in 1994 and 0.34% in 1992. The level for 1996 was the lowest ratio recorded in nearly 30 years.

Looking forward, the prospects of more official aid flowing out of the industrialized nations are not promising. Fiscal austerity is the general norm among the major aid donors. In addition, the end of the Cold War has lowered the strategic imperative of official development assistance. Both variables represent unfavorable omens for many nations, particularly those countries that are unable to attract capital from private sources.

Official Development Assistance (ODA)
(US$ Billions)

Rank	Country	1992 Amount	1992 % of GNP	1994 Amount	1994 % of GNP	1996 Amount	1996 % of GNP
1	Japan	11.15	0.30	13.33	0.29	9.44	0.20
2	United States	11.71	0.20	9.93	0.14	9.06	0.12
3	Germany	7.58	0.38	6.82	0.34	7.52	0.32
4	France	8.27	0.63	8.47	0.64	7.43	0.48
5	Netherlands	2.76	0.86	2.53	0.76	3.30	0.83
6	United Kingdom	3.24	0.31	3.20	0.31	3.19	0.27
7	Italy	4.12	0.34	2.71	0.27	2.40	0.20
8	Sweden	2.46	1.03	1.31	0.28	1.97	0.82
9	Canada	2.52	0.46	2.25	0.43	1.78	0.31
10	Denmark	1.39	1.02	1.45	1.03	1.77	1.04
	DAC countries*	60.85	0.34	59.16	0.30	55.11	0.25

Notes: 1996 data are preliminary; the 1992 figure for the United States includes military debt forgiveness; data for France include all of its overseas departments and territories but exclude forgiveness of non-ODA debt for 1992 and 1993.

*DAC = Development Assistance Committee

Source: © OECD, 1997, Aid and other financial flows in 1996. *Reproduced by permission of the OECD.*

CHAPTER 4

Trends in Global Competitiveness

Overview

What countries are globally competitive? What countries are not? What variables determine a nation's competitiveness? Why does any of this matter? These are just some of the questions that are answered in the following chapter on global competitiveness.

A country's ability to compete is critical for a number of reasons. Competitiveness influences real rates of growth, national living standards, and future development prospects. It is no coincidence that some of the world's most competitive nations enjoy higher standards of living relative to other nations. Conversely, the countries that struggle to compete also struggle to grow and advance in the global economy.

One notable trend of global competitiveness lies with the renaissance of U.S. industry over the past decade. Through cost-cutting measures, a razorlike focus on improving quality techniques, restructuring efforts, and heavy investment in information technology, American companies are among the most competitive entities on earth.

While America's competitiveness has improved, the comparable positions of Germany and Japan have deteriorated over the past 10 years. German industry remains burdened by inflexible labor practices and high corporate taxes. The lack of innovation and dearth of entrepreneurship are two pitfalls of corporate Japan. Both countries are committed to improving their level of competitiveness, as are a number of rising industrial stars such as South Korea, Taiwan, China, Brazil, and Poland.

These issues are highlighted in the chapter. Also discussed are comparable global wage rates, productivity levels, and research and development expenditures. We have included entries on global savings and education levels, since both variables are critical to a nation's level of competitiveness. On both accounts, the United States has its work cut out for it if the nation is to remain near the top of the global competitiveness charts. Also, a number of entries in this chapter highlight the plight of the world's workers.

In summary, sizing up a nation's level of global competitiveness is a crucial task for all investors. No economy operates or functions in isolation. Note as well that competitiveness is a moving target, and the nation on top today could fall tomorrow. This makes understanding the underlying forces of competitiveness all the more important.

64 Global Competitiveness–the Nineties Belong to the United States

Ranking and measuring the global competitiveness of a nation is more of an art than a science. For many years, a joint competitive ranking was released by the International Institute for Management Development (IMD) and the World Economic Forum (WEF). In 1996, however, the two organizations split, and now they each publish an annual competitiveness survey. The results from the IMD are listed in the table and one thing is clear: the United States has emerged as one of the most competitive economies in the world over the 1990s. More telling, perhaps, the competitive positions of both Japan and Germany have deteriorated sharply over the past decade.

As the table of rankings shows, Japan was ranked number 1 in terms of global competitiveness in 1990. However, the nation's share slipped modestly over the first half of the decade, before falling sharply to number 9 in 1997 and number 18 in 1998. Germany, Europe's largest economy, dropped from the number 4 slot in 1990 to number 10 in 1996 and number 14 in 1997. In 1998, Germany's position neither improved nor deteriorated, but held steady at number 14. For its part the United States again maintained its number one ranking in 1998.

A number of variables underpin America's top global ranking among its economic peers. They include the country's technological superiority relative to the rest of the world, world-class management skills, labor market flexibility, development of financial markets, quality of infrastructure, and role of the government. On all of these counts, and more, the United States ranked at or near the top of the league. Japan and Germany, in particular, do not.

What about the rest of the world? The first-world city-state of Singapore ranked number 2 in 1998, followed by Hong Kong. The future rankings of the latter remain in doubt, however, given its merger with mainland China in 1997.

Low on the list are nations such as China, ranked 24th, Israel (25th), Austria (22nd), Belgium (23rd), and France, ranked 21st. Not on the list, but part of the annual rankings of 46 nations, are such key emerging markets as Argentina, Thailand, Russia, and others. These are the key emerging markets multinationals are striving hard to penetrate, but as their low rankings imply, there is still a great deal of risk in these potentially promising markets.

On balance, the annual report on global competitiveness serves as a useful guide in measuring the relative standing of various nations. Year-to-year changes can be telling, but more important are the prevailing trends. In the 1990s, it has been the stellar ranking of the United States, while Japan and Germany have stumbled.

Rankings in Global Competitiveness

	1980	1985	1990	1995	1996	1997	1998
United States	2	1	3	1	1	1	1
Singapore	NA	NA	1	2	2	2	2
Hong Kong	NA	NA	3	3	3	3	3
Netherlands	6	8	10	8	7	6	4
Finland	NA	10	7	18	15	4	5
Norway	12	9	9	10	6	5	6
Switzerland	3	2	2	5	9	7	7
Denmark	11	5	8	7	5	8	8
Luxembourg	NA	12	15	17	8	12	9
Canada	5	7	5	13	12	10	10
Ireland	15	17	16	22	22	15	11
U.K.	9	13	12	15	19	11	12
New Zealand	NA	14	17	9	11	13	13
Germany	4	4	4	6	10	14	14
Australia	NA	15	13	16	21	18	15
Taiwan	NA	NA	2	14	18	23	16
Sweden	8	6	6	12	14	16	17
Japan	1	3	1	4	4	9	18
Iceland	NA	NA	NA	25	25	21	19
Malaysia	NA	NA	5	23	23	17	20
France	7	17	14	19	20	19	21
Austria	13	11	11	11	16	20	22
Belgium	10	12	15	21	17	22	23
China	NA	NA	NA	31	26	27	24
Israel	NA	NA	NA	24	24	26	25

Note: Prior to 1992, the IMD survey was presented in a slightly different format.

NA = Not available

Source: International Institute for Management Development (IMD)

65 The United States Leads the Global Technology Revolution

A new industrial order is emerging from the proliferation and utilization of the computer. As an agent of change, the computer ranks alongside the wheel, the printing press, the harness, and the steam engine as historic inventions that change how people work and play.

But the computer, like other historic inventions before it, has been slow to go global. As the first graph highlights, the share of global computers in use is heavily skewed toward the United States, which accounted for one-third of all computers deployed in 1997. Elsewhere, the role and penetration of the computer has been limited. Japan accounts for only a small fraction of the global computers in use, 8% in 1997, followed by Germany, 5.3%. The European Union accounted for roughly 25% of all computers in use in 1997. Clearly, then, the computer revolution has been contained to the industrialized nations, specifically the United States.

It is this embrace of the computer in particular, and information technology in general, that has led to what many call the technological revolution or productivity miracle in the American workplace. As a result of companies' investing heavily in information processing equipment (see the second graph) and computers over the past decade, U.S. manufacturing productivity growth rose from an annual rate of 2.4% over 1985–90 to 3.1% over 1990–95. This growth coincides with a surge in investment in computers, with the share of computers in total private nonresidential fixed investment rising from 1 percent in 1970 to 12.8% in 1995. In 1996, manufacturing productivity, measured as output per hour, rose 3.8% from the level of 1995.

However, productivity gains in the service sector have not been as dramatic. In fact, they have stagnated over the past decade, although we suspect, along with many others, that current data are faulty and have yet to pick up the improvements in service-sector productivity. Measuring and quantifying technological change is a difficult task, but the evidence suggests that America's large investment in computers and information technology has paid dividends and has helped boost the global competitiveness of the U.S. economy.

Finally, note the limited use of computers in the developing nations, home to roughly 80% of the world population and accounting for nearly half of world gross domestic product. China's share of worldwide computers in use, for instance, was less than 1.5% in 1996; the share of computers in use in India, a major world exporter of software, was even less. In short, the computer revolution has been very limited, leaving the United States as the world's top "cyber nation."

Computers in Use, 1997
(Share of Worldwide Computers in Use)

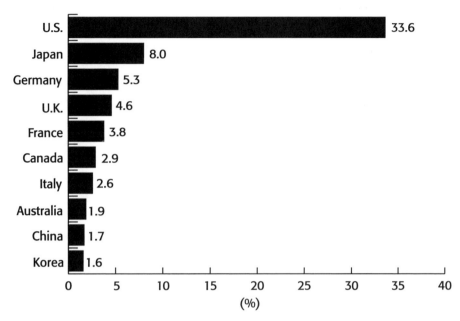

Source: IMD *World Competitiveness Yearbook, 1998*

U.S. Investment in Information Processing Equipment
(At 1992 Values)

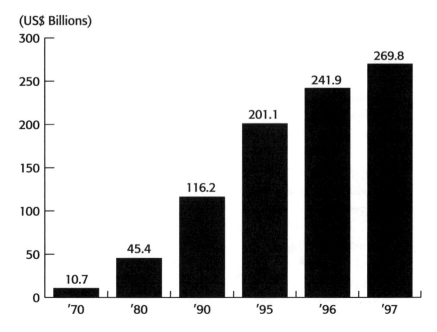

Source: *Federal Reserve Bank of St. Louis*

66 Global Wage Comparisons–the United States Gains the Edge, but for How Long?

One of the most significant trends of the 1990s has been the remarkable turnaround in the global competitiveness of the United States in conjunction with the corresponding deterioration of Japan and the European Union. From the mid-1970s to late 1980s, the United States was the high-cost producer among the industrialized nations, although Corporate America saw its competitive fortunes change along with the shift in exchange rates and the move toward a weaker dollar beginning in 1986. This is portrayed in the accompanying graph. The figures in both exhibits are based in U.S. dollars, an important point, since frequent and large changes in the value of the dollar can influence relative country compensation levels. Keep in mind, though, that a weak currency is just one variable of competitiveness.

Productivity gains, notably in the manufacturing sector, also contributed to America's turnaround of the last decade, as did restructuring measures, widespread mergers and acquisitions, and greater labor-market flexibility.

By the same token, not all of the competitive problems plaguing Japan and the nations of the European Union can be blamed on currency shifts. Europe's hourly compensation costs are more a result of strong unions, rigid labor practices, and widespread social welfare practices. Where the United States has invested in computers and information technology to boost its level of productivity, Europe and Japan have lagged and begun belatedly to make the type of capital investment needed to enhance their competitiveness.

The table illustrates where the workers were cheapest in 1997, and not surprisingly, some of the least expensive labor was in Asia. This reflects the region's extraordinary currency depreciations since mid-1997, which dramatically lowered dollar-based compensation costs.

Looking forward, the critical point to underscore is that international compensation costs are in constant fluctuation. The United States emerged as one of the world's largest low-cost producers in the 1990s. However, the dynamics of global competitiveness, while hard to discern, are once again shifting as the decade comes to a close. The continued strength of the U.S. dollar, Europe's accelerating pace of restructuring, and Asia's massive currency realignment have shifted the global dynamics once again. In short, global competitiveness is a game that never ends, while the stakes become larger and larger.

Hourly Compensation Costs for Manufacturing Workers

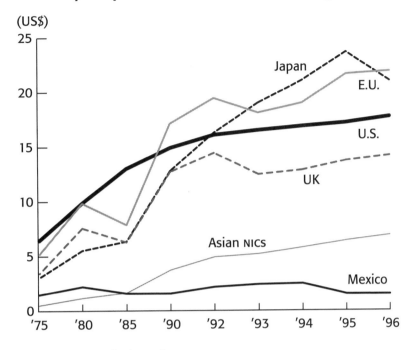

NICS = Newly industrialized countries

Source: Bureau of Labor Statistics

Where the Workers Were the Cheapest in 1997
(Total Hourly Compensation Costs for
Manufacturing Workers Based in US$)

Indonesia	0.06
Colombia	0.17
India	0.23
Venezuela	0.24
China	0.27
Turkey	0.53
Thailand	0.76
Malaysia	0.90
Russia	0.98
Mexico	1.39
United States	17.70

Source: IMD World Competitiveness Yearbook, 1998

67 | Measures of Global Productivity

Labor productivity—the ratio of output to inputs of labor and other resources—is a key determinant of a nation's income level and competitiveness. Productivity increases as output grows faster than the inputs used in the production process. This helps to boost real economic growth and the living standards of the workers. At a company level, productivity gains are fundamental to profitability and survival. Determinants of productivity include the utilization of technology, availability of skilled labor, investment in new plants and equipment, effective management, and quality-control processes. All of these variables, to one degree or another, influence productivity.

There are many ways to measure productivity, with the accompanying table offering two key measurements. The first one measures GDP per person engaged, or working. Based on this measure, the United States, Belgium, and Italy had high rates of labor productivity relative to the OECD and other member countries, notably Japan and Germany. On the basis of GDP per hour worked, the Netherlands was the most productive among the industrialized nations in 1994, followed by Italy, Belgium, and the United States. Notice that by both measures, Japan is among the least productive.

The graph in this section highlights manufacturing productivity over the past decade among the major industrialized nations. Owing to investment in new technology and corporate restructurings, U.S. manufacturing productivity grew at nearly a 3% compound annual rate over 1985–95, and by roughly 4.6% in 1996 and 1997.

Meanwhile, the level of national productivity for the U.S. economy as a whole is less encouraging. Notice that national productivity in the United States expanded by less than 1% on a compound annual basis over the 1985–95 period, one of the lowest rates among the industrialized nations.

What accounts for the difference in productivity rates in the manufacturing sector versus the overall economy? National productivity gauges productivity in both the manufacturing and service sectors. And while the U.S. has achieved gains in the former, improvements in the service sector have been harder to come by. This is critical to recognize, since the service sector is now an overwhelming percentage of U.S. total output. Until the United States achieves the same productivity gains in services as in the manufacturing sector, national productivity will continue to lag.

Labor Productivity Levels in OECD Countries, 1994

	GDP per Person Engaged (OECD = 100)	GDP per Hour Worked (OECD = 100)
United States	123.4	121.5
Japan	91.8	80.3
Germany	104.6	108.5
France	113.9	118.4
Italy	121.3	129.7
United Kingdom	92.0	97.4
Canada	102.5	97.0
Spain	103.5	86.3
Belgium	126.5	126.9
Netherlands	110.3	132.4
Switzerland	101.2	97.5
Norway	107.0	116.0
OECD	100.0	100.0

Source: © *OECD, 1997,* Labor Productivity Levels in OECD Countries: Estimates for Manufacturing and Selected Service Sectors. *Reproduced by permission of the OECD.*

Manufacturing Versus National Productivity
(Compound Annual Growth, 1985–95)

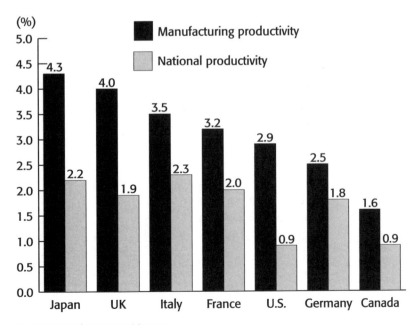

Source: Council on Competitiveness

68 | Global Leaders in Research and Development

Countries, like individuals, must invest in themselves, or they run the long-term risk of falling living standards, declining global competitiveness, and decreasing levels of economic growth. Investing in research and development is a principal way to avoid this fate, since R&D spending is one underpinning of a country's level of productivity.

The United States, by a wide margin, remains the world leader in research and development in absolute terms. Other nations spend more on R&D as a percentage of gross domestic product, although in dollar terms, the United States, along with Japan, easily outspends the rest of the world. Total expenditures on research and development in the United States rose to nearly $185 billion in 1996, equating to roughly 2 to 3% of gross domestic product. Combined, what Germany and France spent on R&D in 1996 ($89.5 billion) was still half the level of America.

Notice that of the top 20 countries listed in the accompanying table, 15 are from the industrialized nations, which have traditionally led the world in R&D investment. Standouts among the developing nations include South Korea, ranked 7th, Taiwan (13th), Brazil (16th), China (17th), and Russia (18th).

The accompanying graph, charting the number of Nobel Prize winners in physics, chemistry, physiology, medicine, and economics, complements the R&D expenditures table. By a staggering margin, the United States easily outdistances the rest of the world when it comes to winning Nobel Prizes. The United States has been awarded nearly 180 Nobels since 1950, more than the rest of the world combined. The United Kingdom was a distant second, Germany a distant third.

In summary, the United States is a global leader when it comes to investment in research and development. America's advantage lies in a highly skilled labor force, a strong technology base, and a large pool of private capital that has helped fund R&D. Another factor behind America's lead in R&D spending lies with expenditures from the public sector, notably defense spending.

Looking forward, one key trend centers on greater cross-border R&D between multinationals, which is gradually blurring the lines as to which nations actually benefit from greater expenditures on research.

Total Expenditures on R&D, 1996

Rank	Country	US$ Billions	Rank	Country	US$ Billions
1	United States	184.7	11	Switzerland	6.5
2	Japan	153.2	12	Australia	5.4
3	Germany	53.6	13	Taiwan	5.0
4	France	35.9	14	Spain	4.8
5	United Kingdom	22.6	15	Belgium	4.3
6	Italy	13.6	16	Brazil	4.1
7	South Korea	13.5	17	China	3.9
8	Canada	9.6	18	Russia	3.8
9	Sweden	8.3	19	Austria	3.4
10	Netherlands	8.2	20	Denmark	3.3

Source: IMD *World Competitiveness Yearbook, 1998*

Number of Nobel Prizes Awarded Since 1950*

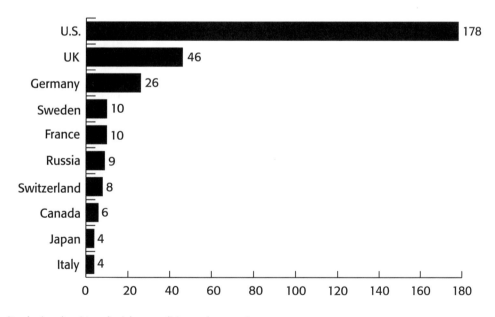

*In physics, chemistry, physiology, medicine, and economics

Source: IMD *World Competitiveness Yearbook, 1997*

69 The Tax Man Cometh–Global Tax Rates

Taxes are the bane of individuals, as well as corporations. Nearly all companies must bear some type of tax burden, and in general, the higher a nation's tax burden, the heavier the claim on profits. A big tax bite is a major disincentive to investors and consumers. Likewise, national tax rates are one of the factors that determine whether a multinational invests in country A or country B.

On this basis, many Scandinavian countries do not look that appealing relative to many other industrialized countries. Indeed, with direct and indirect taxes accounting for over 50% of GDP in some nations, many Nordic companies have decided to invest elsewhere. The level of investment outflow from Germany has soared over the past few years as well, due in part to Germany's high-tax structure. The latter reflects both Germany's attempt to lower the federal budget deficit and the country's burdensome social welfare system. In France, budgetary pressures led the government to boost corporate taxes for large companies from 36.6% to 41.6% in 1997.

In general, national taxes are wide ranging, as the table shows. Japan's tax claim was 28.8% of GDP in 1997, lower than Germany's but slightly higher than the level in the United States, which was 27.6%. The tax burden in the United Kingdom was 35.1% of GDP, slightly less attractive than the United States'. Relative to Germany and France, however, the tax bite in the United Kingdom is much lower, and a key factor, among others, that has helped the country attract more foreign direct investment than its counterparts in the European Union. Ireland's relatively low tax rate, 35.4%, has helped attract billions in new investment over the past few years as well. It should be noted that corporate tax rates can be offset to a degree by tax cuts or tax incentives doled out by individual states or local governments vying to attract the investment of companies.

In the developing nations, the tax bite varies. Notice the tax burden of Poland, where direct and indirect taxes accounted for 41.9% of GDP. The figure for the Czech Republic was 40.5%. Missing from the table are tax figures for Asia and Latin America. In general, most Latin American economies and many Southeast Asian nations collect less than 20% of GDP in taxes.

On balance, a country's tax onus can influence and determine its level of global competitiveness. A high tax rate usually implies a large role of the state in the economy, with tax revenue needed to pay for social welfare programs, large public-sector payrolls, and public capital-investment projects. These are critical considerations for multinationals. They are also relevant variables for individual investors to realize. A rising or large corporate tax burden can have adverse consequences on any company's level of profitability, a prospect that loomed large over many French companies in 1997, when the government decided to raise taxes. Wide-ranging capital gains taxes are another consideration for investors.

Total Tax Revenues
(Direct and Indirect Taxes, Including Social Security Contributions, as a % of GDP)

Rank	Country	Tax Rate/GDP
1	Denmark	51.9
2	Sweden	51.7
3	Finland	48.2
4	Belgium	45.9
5	France	45.6
6	Austria	44.0
7	Italy	43.5
8	Netherlands	43.5
9	Poland	41.9
10	Norway	41.4
11	Czech Republic	40.5
12	Luxembourg	39.5
13	Germany	38.2
14	Canada	36.3
15	New Zealand	36.2
16	Ireland	35.4
17	United Kingdom	35.1
18	Israel	34.8
26	Japan	28.8
27	United States	27.6

Source: IMD World Competitiveness Yearbook, 1998

70 | Global Savers—the United States Is Not One of Them

A nation's level of savings is important in that savings help determine a country's ability to invest in infrastructure, education, plants and equipment, and research and development. These are the building blocks of growth, and without them, no nation can expect to maintain a reasonable level of advancement and continued rise in its standard of living. Only by borrowing capital from abroad can a country offset a paltry level of national savings.

And America has had to do just that, given its own low level of savings. In terms of gross national savings as a percentage of GDP, the United States has long had one of the lowest rates among the industrialized nations. In 1996, as the first table of selected OECD countries shows, the U.S. gross national savings rate was 16.6%. This was up from 14.1% in 1992, the nadir of the past two decades, but significantly below its industrial counterparts. The United Kingdom had one of the lowest levels of national savings in 1996 (14.6%).

At the other end of the spectrum was Japan, whose level of national savings has hovered in the range of 30 to 35% over the past few decades. Switzerland followed Japan, with a savings rate of 27.1% in 1996. Germany's level of savings has hovered in the 20 to 24% range over the past decade.

At the household level, as the next table shows, the picture does not get any better for the United States. In general, Americans are consumers rather than savers, with the United States posting a household savings rate (as a percentage of disposable income) of just 4.4% in 1996 versus Japan's household savings rate of 13.8%. Germany, France, Italy, and many other European countries have household savings rates nearly triple that of the United States.

What determines national and household savings rates? The former is influenced by a variety of factors, including government spending, investment levels, and the extent and role of the public sector in the economy. Household savings rates are influenced by government policies that either encourage or discourage savings. Income growth, employment opportunities, and consumer confidence levels are three more variables that affect how much or how little households save. In general, the United States, at both the national and household level, is a nation lacking a strong commitment to savings, which is one chief reason why the United States is deep in debt to the rest of the world.

Gross National Savings
(As a % of Nominal GDP)

	1980	1985	1990	1995	1996
United States	19.4	17.2	15.2	15.8	16.6
Japan	31.1	31.7	33.6	30.9	31.4
Switzerland	28.5	30.4	32.3	28.4	27.1
Germany	21.7	22.0	24.9	20.8	20.0
France	23.6	18.9	21.5	19.8	18.7
Italy	24.7	21.5	19.5	20.6	20.5
Sweden	17.8	17.5	17.7	16.7	16.0
Finland	26.0	22.9	23.2	20.1	19.6
Ireland	15.2	15.0	21.1	20.7	21.7
United Kingdom	17.7	17.6	14.4	14.3	14.6
Canada	22.9	19.6	16.4	17.1	17.8

Source: © OECD, *1998,* OECD Economic Outlook, June 1998 No. 63. *Reproduced by permission of the* OECD.

Household Savings Rates[1]
(As a % of Disposable Household Income)

	1980	1985	1990	1996
United States[2]	8.8	7.4	5.5	4.4
Japan	17.9	15.6	12.1	13.8
Germany[2]	12.8	11.4	13.8	11.7
France[2]	17.6	14.0	12.5	12.7
Italy[2]	23.4	19.8	17.4	12.9
Belgium	18.3	13.1	16.3	16.5
Finland	5.4	3.8	0.4	0.9
Netherlands[3]	1.8	0.1	5.8	1.2
Sweden	6.7	2.3	−0.6	4.4
United Kingdom[2]	13.4	10.7	8.1	11.4
Canada[2]	13.6	13.3	11.5	5.9

[1]National definition except the United States
[2]Gross savings
[3]Excluding mandatory saving through occupational pension schemes

Source: © OECD, *1998,* OECD Economic Outlook, June 1998 No. 63. *Reproduced by permission of the* OECD.

71 Foreign Debt–America's Achilles' Heel

As the dust settles from the end of the Cold War, one fact stands out: the United States reigns as the world's sole military and economic superpower. Another fact stands out as well: America is number one in many categories, including the accumulation of foreign debt. As the accompanying graph highlights, the international credit position of the United States has deteriorated sharply over the past decade, while the investment position of America's competitors, notably Japan, has improved or at least stayed in a surplus.

In 1985, the United States was a net creditor nation. In 1996, though, America's total foreign debt rose by $194 billion, to a whopping $831 billion. This number is the difference between what Americans have invested abroad ($4.28 trillion) and what foreigners have invested in the United States ($5.12 trillion). Included in both numbers are investments in foreign currencies, government securities, stocks, and bonds, as well as foreign factories.

Many variables influence the net investment position of a nation, with shifts in capital flows and exchange rates two key factors that can result in year-to-year fluctuations. However, in the case of the United States, the tremendous shift from creditor to debtor nation status reflects more fundamental variables. Top on the list is America's low level of savings combined with its appetite and demand for capital. Net national savings in the United States dropped to roughly 5% of GNP in the 1980s and has remained relatively low since then. In contrast, other developed nations typically have savings rates that are two to three times larger than America's.

To make up for the shortfall in U.S. savings, America has increasingly borrowed capital from abroad, with a noticeable share of borrowing done through the sale of U.S. Treasuries.

The accompanying table details foreign holdings of U.S. Treasury securities. As of early 1998, foreign holdings totaled more than $1.2 trillion. The United Kingdom ($299.8 billion), Japan ($297.3 billion), and Germany ($92.0 billion) were the top three largest holders. China's presence in the U.S. Treasury markets has grown over the past few years, with the mainland now holding nearly $50 billion in U.S. Treasuries.

On balance, as the decade comes to a close, the United States basks in its hard-earned reputation as being one of the most dynamic industrialized nations in the world. But, America does have an Achilles' heel—it is the nation's increasing dependence on foreign capital.

Net External Financial Positions of Japan, Germany, and the United States, 1986–96

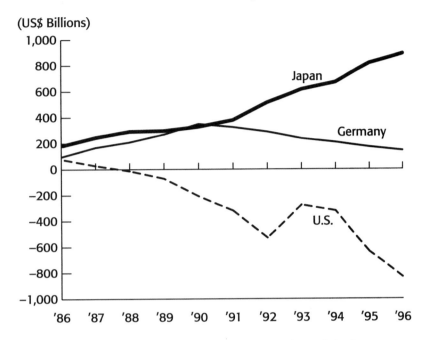

Source: U.S. Bureau of Economic Analysis; Bank of Japan; Deutsche Bundesbank

Top Foreign Holdings of U.S. Treasury Securities*

Rank	Country	$ Billions	% of Total
1	United Kingdom	299.8	23.3
2	Japan	297.3	23.1
3	Germany	92.0	7.1
4	Spain	48.3	3.8
5	China	47.5	3.7
6	Netherlands Antilles	46.3	3.6
7	Hong Kong	38.7	3.0
8	Singapore	35.4	2.8
9	Taiwan	29.9	2.3
10	Switzerland	25.9	2.0
	Total (including others)	**1,288.0**	**100.0**

*As of March 1998

Source: U.S. Bureau of Economic Analysis

72 | The Global Government-Debt Overhang

Large levels of public-sector debt in the industrialized nations are among the most worrisome elements of the world economy. After years of persistent budgetary shortfalls, the world's richest nations are deep in debt, a global fact of life every investor or businessperson should recognize. Onerous debt loads and the attendant servicing requirements can, and often do, adversely affect movements in interest rates, stunt capital investment, influence global capital flows, curtail government entitlements, and compromise the living standards of current and future generations.

Government budget deficits—the excess of spending over revenue—have been expanding as a percentage of GDP for the past 25 years in the industrialized nations. Large deficits emerged after the first oil crisis, although it was excess government spending over the 1980s that helped create today's mountain of debt.

The size of this mountain is evident from the accompanying table. For the entire OECD, the level of debt as a percentage of GDP rose to 71% in 1996, up from 54.5% in 1985 and 40.2% in 1980. In the United States, despite all the fanfare surrounding projections of a balanced budget, Washington remains deep in hock, with general government gross financial liabilities standing at 63.1% of gross domestic product in 1996. That is up from 55.5% in 1990, 49.5% in 1985, and 37% in 1980. On a more positive note, the debt level of the United States, based on government debt as a percentage of GDP, has remained below the OECD average and below many nations thought to be in better financial health than the United States.

Japan is a case in point. The combination of stagnant growth and numerous public stimulus packages to promote growth have dramatically upped Japan's debt burden in the 1990s. Japan's level of public debt to GDP soared from 62.6% in 1990 to 82.6% in 1996. Japan's government, in other words, is deeper in debt (based as a percentage of GDP) than Uncle Sam.

Debt levels are higher still in most of Europe, where sluggish growth and generous social welfare benefits have combined to significantly boost Europe's debt load. At a broad level, the European Union's debt as a percentage of GDP stood at 40.8% in 1980, not far from the level of the United States. The figure rose to 57.2 percent in 1985 and increased to just 59.5% in 1990. So far, so good. But between 1990 and 1996, Europe's debt load exploded, soaring to 78.3% in 1996, with weak real growth, record high unemployment rates, and rising social welfare payments converging to push many nations deeper into debt. As the table highlights, Europe's most indebted nations include Italy (125.2%), Belgium (126.9%), and

Greece (112.6%). Thanks to the free-market reform measures introduced by Margaret Thatcher, the United Kingdom has one of the lowest government debt levels in Europe. Similarly, Norway, compliments of steady oil income, had one of the lowest levels of debt among OECD nations in 1996.

Looking forward, the good news is that fiscal austerity has become the norm in Europe, a trend triggered by Europe's monetary union. The state, no doubt, remains a key economic player in Europe, although there is a growing recognition and acceptance for less government involvement across the region. Privatization—the shift from state-owned assets to the private sector—has become a hallmark of many European countries. Likewise, fiscal consolidation remains a priority in the United States, which is on its way toward a balanced budget. The bad news is that global fiscal consolidation, while welcomed, will have to remain in place for some time before the industrialized nations put a significant dent in their aggregate debt levels. The last point should not be forgotten or ignored by investors.

Government Debt as a Percentage of GDP

	1980	1985	1990	1996
Belgium	78.2	120.7	125.7	126.9
Italy	58.1	82.3	104.5	123.7
Greece	22.9	47.8	90.1	111.5
Canada	44.0	63.1	71.5	97.5
Japan	51.2	65.3	62.6	82.7
Sweden	44.3	66.7	44.3	77.5
Netherlands	46.9	71.5	78.8	76.6
Ireland	72.7	104.6	97.2	76.3
Spain	18.3	50.8	50.4	74.8
Germany	31.1	42.8	45.5	64.9
United States	37.0	49.5	55.5	63.1
France	30.9	38.6	40.2	63.0
United Kingdom	54.0	58.9	39.3	61.2
Norway	47.6	37.4	32.5	40.7
OECD average	40.2	54.5	56.7	71.0

Source: © OECD, 1998, OECD Economic Outlook, June 1998 No. 63. Reproduced by permission of the OECD.

73 Finding Work in the Global Economy

Creating jobs has been one of the most distinct features of the U.S. economy over the past decade. In contrast is Europe, whose inability to generate employment has been a characteristic and curse of the region for nearly the past two decades. The dichotomy is reflected in the fact that U.S. unemployment dipped below 5% in 1997–98, while the jobless rate in the European Union hovered around 11 to 12%. All totaled, more than 35 million workers in the OECD were without jobs at the start of 1998. Millions more were unemployed in the developing nations. All together, the International Labor Organization estimated that up to 1 billion workers were without jobs at mid-decade, or 30% of the global workforce.

Bucking the trend, total employment in the United States grew by almost 16%, or an annual average rate of 1.5%, in the decade ending in 1996, one of the fastest levels of growth among the major industrialized nations (see graph). Behind the relatively robust level of job growth are a number of factors, including labor market flexibility, fewer labor and social policies discouraging employment, rising demand for workers in the service sector, and a dynamic entrepreneurial class that has promoted growth in small companies, notably in the high-tech sector. All of these variables, in addition to the cyclical rebound of the U.S. economy, converged over this decade to generate employment growth. Critically, the bulk of the jobs were created in the private sector. On the downside, the United States has a much higher incidence of low-paying jobs than most other nations in the OECD.

In Japan, the annual average rate of job growth was 1.1% over the 1987–96 period. The unemployment rate remains among the lowest in the industrialized nations, although the country is not without its own job problems. Due to both cyclical (slow growth) and structural (a shift toward more overseas production) factors, Japan's unemployment rate rose to record highs in 1998, trending above 4%. Besides the general rise in unemployment, the jobless rate among women and university graduates is well above the national average. Underemployment, notably in large firms that hold on to their employees even during cyclical downturns, is also widely prevalent.

The greatest challenge on the job front lies in Europe, where the structural rate of unemployment has continued to ratchet up from cycle to cycle. Among the major nations, France and Germany created few jobs over the 1987–96 period, with many of the jobs created in the public sector. In Italy, total employment has actually declined over the past decade. Rigid labor practices, uncompetitive wages, burdensome social security taxes, and soaring nonwage costs have all contributed to Europe's employment woes. So too have Europe's lack of entrepreneurship and the region's lack of high-tech growth, with the United Kingdom, Ireland, Finland, and Norway notable exceptions. Technology both eliminates jobs and creates jobs, a creative/destructive process that has swept the United States. In Continental Europe, however, the process has been generally one-way—with rapid technological change destroying more jobs than creating new employment.

It is also worth noting that many of the same forces impacting job growth in the industrialized nations are also at work in the developing nations. China, for instance, has an itinerant workforce estimated at roughly 100 million people, as more laborers migrate from the countryside to the city in search of jobs. Finding jobs for these workers, and those in unprofitable state-run companies that should be shut down, is one of the most pressing challenges for the Chinese government. Asia's financial crisis translated into rising unemployment across the region in 1998. In Latin America, Central Europe, and Russia, creating the proper employment climate remains a critical challenge for all governments. The U.S. model has many positive attributes, although many governments find the American way just too ruthless to adopt.

Employment Growth Among the Major Industrialized Nations

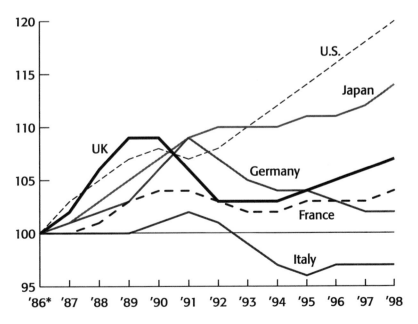

*1986 = 100

Source: © OECD, 1997, OECD Economic Outlook, June 1997 No. 61. *Reproduced by permission of the* OECD.

74 Work and Play Around the World

Intense global competition, the spread of information technology, corporate restructurings, rising unemployment, and heightened worker insecurity have converged this decade to take the sting out of union demands and to create a more acquiescent global workforce. As the table in this section highlights, the first half of the 1990s was relatively tranquil on the labor front, versus the second half of the 1980s. The number of annual working days lost to strikes in the OECD dropped to 100 days per 1,000 employees over the 1990–94 period from 145 days during 1985–89. Every country listed experienced a decline in the number of days lost to strikes in the first half of this decade, with the exception of two—Germany and Belgium.

Germany did not lose as many days to strikes as the United States in the first half of the decade, although traditional German labor practices have been severely tested and tried in the 1990s on account of German unification, the surge in outward foreign direct investment, sluggish German growth, rising unemployment, and fiscal austerity.

Note the dramatic improvement in the United Kingdom, which used to be one of the most vulnerable nations in Europe to labor strife. Strikes decreased substantially over the first half of the 1990s, due in part to strong growth, rising levels of foreign direct investment, and, above all else, labor reform under the conservative government of Margaret Thatcher. As in the United Kingdom, union power and influence in the United States have waned over this decade. Similar trends have materialized in Australia and New Zealand. Labor strife in Japan, meanwhile, remains almost nonexistent. The Mediterranean countries of Greece, Spain, and Italy are among the most strike-prone in the European Union.

With regard to play, the average number of vacation days a worker receives varies across nations, as shown in the graph. After only one year on the job in Austria and Brazil, workers are entitled to 30 days of vacation, three times the amount of play time in the United States. The average in most of Europe ranges from 20 days in countries such as the Netherlands to 25 days in France and Sweden.

In summary, the balance of power has tilted away from workers over this decade, a trend due to a number of factors, with globalization among the chief variables.

Annual Working Days Lost to Strikes per 1,000 Employees in Services and Industries

	1985–89	1990–94
Greece	3,976	3,500
Spain	647	492
Italy	300	240
Australia	227	157
Ireland	292	135
New Zealand	491	105
OECD average	145	100
Belgium	52	57
United States	86	43
United Kingdom	180	37
France	57	30
Germany	2	23
Japan	5	3

Source: OECD

Number of Vacation Days per Year

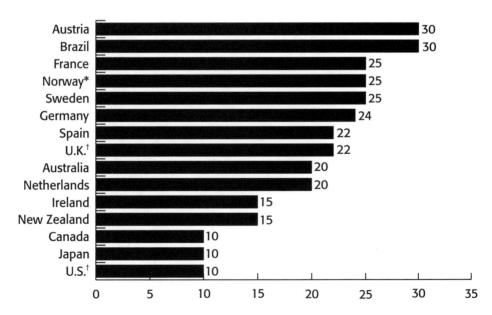

Austria	30
Brazil	30
France	25
Norway*	25
Sweden	25
Germany	24
Spain	22
U.K.†	22
Australia	20
Netherlands	20
Ireland	15
New Zealand	15
Canada	10
Japan	10
U.S.†	10

*Based on a six-day workweek
†No statutory minimum: United Kingdom—typically four or five weeks; United States—82% of employers provide two weeks

Source: Hewitt Associates, 1994 data

75 The World's Hardest Workers

The International Labor Organization estimates that some 1 billion workers were without jobs in 1995, equating to a global unemployment rate of roughly 30%. That is a relatively high and discomforting level, and one that poses all sorts of challenges to governments around the world.

But, what about workers with jobs? A previous entry outlined the fact that worker compensation levels vary by country, with a notable division existing between higher worker compensation levels in the industrialized nations and lower rates in the developing nations.

Another trend separates the worker in, say, the United States from the worker in India: the working day of the latter is likely to be much longer than the working day of the former. The accompanying table measures the average number of working hours per year by country. Hours worked are determined by many variables and vary according to industry.

In general, as the table shows, workers in the developing nations log more hours each year than workers in the industrialized nations. This does not, however, imply that the worker in India produces more than his or her American counterpart. Far from it. Labor is just one input of production. Technology, capital investment, and the availability of trained and skilled labor matter as well, and this is where workers in the industrialized nations have the advantage over their counterparts in the developing nations. In general, due to wide variations in productivity levels, workers in the developing nations work longer hours for less pay than workers in the United States, Japan, or Germany. Notice that out of the top 20 countries on the list, only the United States is from the developed nations.

Taiwan tops the list, with workers logging an average of 2,330 hours a year. That equates to a 46.6-hour workweek with two weeks off for vacation. Notice that the worker in Hong Kong works roughly 14% longer in a year than a worker in China. In the United States, the average number of working hours per year was 1,916 in 1997. This equates to roughly a 38-hour workweek, assuming two weeks for vacation. In Mexico, however, the average workweek in a year is roughly 46 hours (assuming two weeks' vacation), which is one reason why some American companies have found it cheaper to manufacture and produce goods in Mexico rather than the United States.

While a gulf separates the developing nations from the industrialized nations, another noticeable distinction exists between the number of hours worked per year in the United States versus its industrial counterparts in Japan and Germany. U.S. workers, for instance, spend 6.5%

more time at work each year than the average Japanese workers. Relative to Germany, the average number of working hours per year in the United States is 12.8% higher.

Notice that Germany ranks well down on the list (45th). On a comparative basis, workers in Taiwan work roughly 37% longer each year than workers in Germany, a differential that has prompted many German companies to invest in such places as Taiwan, as well as Mexico, India, and South Korea.

Average Number of Working Hours per Year, 1997

Rank	Country	Hours
1	Taiwan	2,330
2	Hong Kong	2,312
3	Mexico	2,302
4	Turkey	2,263
5	Chile	2,256
6	India	2,254
7	Korea	2,253
8	Thailand	2,245
9	Philippines	2,238
10	Colombia	2,187
11	Malaysia	2,157
12	Israel	2,128
13	Indonesia	2,121
14	Argentina	2,097
15	South Africa	2,033
16	Singapore	2,028
17	China	2,024
18	Venezuela	2,001
19	Czech Republic	1,976
20	United States	1,916
33	Japan	1,799
45	Germany	1,699

Source: IMD World Competitiveness Yearbook, 1998

76 Education–a Key Factor of Global Competitiveness Where America Lags

The skills and abilities of a national workforce begin with education. The latter determines the productivity levels and technological capabilities of all nations. The accompanying table, then, serves as a report card on global education levels. What is clear from the table is this: The United States hardly rates an *A* when it comes to math and science scores relative to the rest of the world. This carries significant implications for U.S. global competitiveness, and in particular, growth in U.S. high-tech industries.

The table gives the average math and science scores for 13-year-olds by nation. The four wealthiest Asian states claimed the first four places in math, with Singapore ranked number one, followed by South Korea, Japan, and Hong Kong.

Singapore also ranked first in science, followed by the Czech Republic, which has far less money to spend on education than many other nations. Along with the Czech Republic, Bulgaria, Slovenia, and Hungary ranked relatively high in both math and science scores, a positive omen for potential growth in these former communist nations.

As for the United States, the nation ranked in the bottom half on math scores (28th), below such countries as Russia, Thailand, and Hungary. In science, America's rank (17th) was somewhat better, but still lagging other nations such as Russia (14th), Slovakia (13th), and Bulgaria (5th). Given these numbers, it is not surprising that, among the industrialized nations, America maintains one of the lowest ratios of science and engineering degrees per total degrees awarded. This is critical to understand given the lack of skilled labor that has emerged in the U.S. high-tech sector.

Particularly troubling is this—the U.S. electronics and information technology sectors are at the forefront of America's economic resurgence. The high-tech sector has created millions of new jobs over the past decade, with these jobs, according to the U.S. government, paying 73% more than the average private sector wage. Yet, the high-tech manufacturing industry could be in for trouble given the growing shortage of high-tech workers. America's technical pool is not keeping up with industry demand due to the following: Between 1985 and 1997, the number of bachelor's degrees awarded in engineering fell 16%; between 1985 and 1995, the number of students receiving bachelor's degrees in mathematics/computer science dropped 29%; and over the same period (1985 to 1995), the number of degrees awarded in computer and information sciences plunged 42%, while those in electrical, electronics, and communications engineering decreased 37%. Making matters worse, a large percentage of the degrees awarded were to foreign nationals.

Against this backdrop, finding qualified workers is a key challenge before U.S. high-tech firms, which have been among the most dynamic stock performers of this decade. If there is a silver lining, it is this—the technology labor void has been partially offset by hiring non-U.S. workers with the appropriate skills. Nevertheless, the United States needs to step up its efforts in education, or risk a loss of global competitiveness.

Thirteen-Year-Olds' Average Score in TIMSS*

Rank	Math	Score	Science	Score
1	Singapore	643	Singapore	607
2	South Korea	607	Czech Republic	574
3	Japan	605	Japan	571
4	Hong Kong	588	South Korea	565
5	Belgium (F)	565	Bulgaria	565
6	Czech Republic	564	Netherlands	560
7	Slovakia	547	Slovenia	560
8	Switzerland	545	Austria	558
9	Netherlands	541	Hungary	554
10	Slovenia	541	England	552
11	Bulgaria	540	Belgium (F)	550
12	Austria	539	Australia	545
13	France	538	Slovakia	544
14	Hungary	537	Russia	538
15	Russia	535	Ireland	538
16	Australia	530	Sweden	535
17	Ireland	527	**United States**	**534**
18	Canada	527	Canada	531
19	Belgium (W)	526	Germany	531
20	Thailand	522	Norway	527
28	**United States**	**500**		

(F) = Flanders   (W) = Wallonia

*Third International Math and Science Study

Source: TIMSS

77 Getting the Basics Right–Global Illiteracy

The competitive advantage of any country begins with a skilled and educated workforce—the necessary building blocks of any economy. To be sure, physical endowments, such as natural resources and geographic location, to a large extent help determine the long-term growth and development of a nation. So does capital. However, no country has thrived over the long term or met its full economic potential without a labor force possessing basic literacy skills. And on this level, both the developed and developing countries have been relatively successful in eradicating illiteracy over the past few decades.

As is shown in the accompanying table, in the majority of the developed nations, the adult (population over 15 years) illiteracy rate hovers between 1 and 2%. Notable exceptions include Greece and Spain, whose adult illiteracy rates stood at 5% in 1995. Portugal's was even worse, and the highest among the industrialized nations at 15%. In the United States, less than 0.5% of adults are classified as illiterate.

The picture becomes a bit more interesting looking at the developing nations. The Czech Republic had the lowest rate of illiteracy, at 1%, among the developing nations in 1995. Not far behind the Czech Republic were South Korea, Hungary, Poland, and Russia, with illiteracy rates of just 2%. While Russia and the nations of central Europe are just beginning to become more integrated with the world economy following decades of communist rule, it's clear that the process is being facilitated by the presence of a literate workforce.

At the other extreme, India had one of the highest illiteracy rates among the major developing nations in 1995, a fact lost on many investors who view India as one of the most promising markets of the future. The nation's illiteracy rate among adults was a staggering 48% in 1995—off the charts, in other words, relative to other major countries. If India is to reach the economic status of its dynamic Asian neighbors, it must first get the basics right by educating its workforce.

Outside of India, a number of other key emerging markets confront high illiteracy rates. In China and South Africa, for instance, the adult illiteracy rates were 18.5% and 18.2%, respectively, in 1995. Brazil, Malaysia, Indonesia, and Mexico also posted double-digit levels in the same year. In Latin America, Argentina has the lowest illiteracy rate.

In general, adult illiteracy remains a basic development challenge in a number of emerging markets that have attracted a great amount of attention and capital from foreigners over the past decade.

Global Illiteracy
(Adult [over 15 years] Illiteracy Rate as % of Total Population, 1995)

Country	%
India	48.0
China	18.5
South Africa	18.2
Brazil	16.7
Malaysia	16.5
Indonesia	16.2
Portugal	15.0
Mexico	10.4
Venezuela	8.9
Singapore	8.9
Hong Kong	7.8
Thailand	6.2
Taiwan	6.0
Philippines	5.4
Spain	5.0
Greece	5.0
Chile	4.8
Argentina	3.8
Italy	3.0
Russia	2.0
Poland	2.0
Netherlands	2.0
South Korea	2.0
Hungary	2.0
United Kingdom	1.0
Germany	1.0
France	1.0
Czech Republic	1.0
United States	0.5
Japan	0.0

Source: IMD *World Competitiveness Yearbook, 1997*

78 Global Deindustrialization

One of the most pronounced trends in the industrialized nations, as well as in some developing nations, is the secular decline in manufacturing employment.

As shown in the "Employment in Manufacturing" graph, in the industrialized nations, the share of manufacturing employment has declined from roughly 28% in 1970 to roughly 18% in 1994. In the United States, the fall in manufacturing jobs has been the steepest, with manufacturing employment accounting for 16% of total civilian employment in 1994. In Europe, one in five workers holds a job in manufacturing. Even in Japan, the share of manufacturing employment is less than a quarter (23%) of total employment.

Why the steady decline in manufacturing jobs in the industrialized nations, which is referred to as *deindustrialization*?

Some argue that the loss of manufacturing jobs in the industrialized nations is due to rising competition from the developing nations. But even in some developing nations, the process of deindustrialization is becoming more evident. The share of manufacturing employment in Hong Kong, as one example, has been falling since the 1970s. Likewise, both South Korea and Taiwan, two of Asia's most dynamic exporters, have experienced a decline in the share of manufacturing employment over the past decade.

If manufacturing jobs are in a secular decline, even in some key developing nations, where are all the jobs being created? A larger share of employment is now in services. In the United States, for instance, nearly three-fourths of the civilian workforce is employed in service industries, the highest percentage among the industrialized nations. Services now account for more than 50% of gross domestic product in most industrialized nations and are expanding rapidly in a host of developing nations.

As part of this transition, productivity plays a major role. Rapid growth of labor productivity in the agricultural sector unleashed workers into the manufacturing sector over the first half of this century. The same process has been at work over the past few decades, only this time, productivity improvements in manufacturing have unleashed workers to the service side of the economy.

Despite fears that a loss in manufacturing jobs equates to declining living standards, global deindustrialization is associated more with economic success rather than economic failure.

Employment in Manufacturing as a Share of Total Civilian Employment

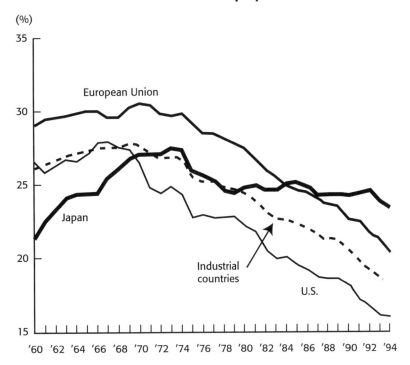

Source: IMF working paper, "Deindustrialization: Causes and Implications," by Robert Rowthorn and Ramana Ramaswamy, April 1997

Toward Service-Oriented Growth
(Services as a % of GDP)

Country	1980	1996
Hong Kong	68	82
Netherlands	64	70
France	62	71
United Kingdom	55	66
Italy	55	66
United States	64	66
Argentina	52	65
Mexico	59	64
Japan	54	58
Russia	37	55

Source: World Bank

79 Global Exchange Rates—on the Trail of the U.S. Dollar

Shortly after World War II, the United States held 70% of the international official gold reserves, and the U.S. dollar was the cornerstone of the international monetary system. Under the Bretton Woods system, a fixed exchange rate was in operation, whereby each member of the International Monetary Fund established a par value for its currency based on gold and the U.S. dollar. Currencies were allowed to vary within 1% of par value, depending on supply-and-demand conditions.

Under this arrangement, other countries could change the value of their currencies against gold and the dollar, but the value of the dollar remained fixed. The Bretton Woods system, however, started to show strains in the mid-1960s, when inflationary pressures began to build in the United States. In 1971, the United States ran its first merchandise trade deficit in decades, helping to doom the world's fixed-exchange-rate system. Following the devaluation of the dollar in 1971 and again in 1973, the world's major currencies began to float against each other instead of remaining relatively fixed against the dollar or gold. Flexible exchange rates became the norm and have been a key part of the global economy ever since. The bane of all investors, sudden and unexpected swings in exchange rates can have dramatic effects on dollar-based investments.

As the graph highlights, the trade-weighted value of the dollar remained relatively stable until the late 1970s. Then the dollar strengthened substantially against the world's major currencies, appreciating by more than 40% from late 1980 to early 1984. A number of factors were behind the strong dollar, notably high U.S. interest rates which help attract capital from abroad and create demand for dollars.

The strong-dollar period carried advantages and disadvantages for the United States. The strong currency was helpful in lowering inflation and made it more attractive for Americans to travel abroad. However, the downside was notably painful. The strong dollar hurt U.S. export growth and made it cheaper for foreigners to sell in the United States, undercutting the price competitiveness of many American industries (steel, autos, capital machinery). The strong dollar made it difficult to compete and emboldened many companies, notably the U.S. automakers, to lobby the government for trade sanctions or protectionist measures. The "hollowing out" of American industry became a rallying cry for many. In addition, the dollar's rise also hurt U.S. international earnings and reduced dollar-based returns of U.S. investors.

An international consensus emerged over the mid-1980s that the dollar had appreciated by too much. Following the September 1985 Plaza Accord Agreement and coordinated intervention from the world's central banks, the dollar reversed course and weakened over most of the second half of the decade. Indeed, the dollar ended the decade 30.4% below its peak in March 1985. For most of the early 1990s, the dollar remained relatively stable on a trade-weighted basis. However, since mid-1995 the dollar has gained strength, rising sharply against the world's major currencies, including the yen. Asia's financial crisis in 1997, coupled with Japan's recession in 1998, only made the dollar more attractive, driving the value of the dollar higher over 1998. Very few people, however, expect the dollar to scale the heights of the last decade.

Living with the ebb and flow of global exchange rates is a principal challenge for nearly all investors and businesses. A shift in exhange rates can influence trade flows, the international profitability of multinationals, and dollar-based returns for U.S. investors. Interest rate differentials, comparable rates of inflation, political events, capital flows, and trade performances all weigh heavily on any nation's exchange rate and should therefore be watched very closely by investors.

Trade-Weighted Value of the U.S. Dollar

Source: The Federal Reserve Bank of Atlanta

CHAPTER 5

Sizing Up Some Global Industries

Overview

The objective of this chapter is to present a handful of industries, along with the attendant corporate leaders, that are global in scope and scale. Our industry universe ranges from such high-tech sectors as computers and semiconductors to more traditional industries such as automobiles and energy. We have also included entries on telecommunications, pharmaceuticals, defense, food and beverages, tourism, and the media and entertainment industry. In each entry, we have tried to identify the relevant global trends of the industry, as well as the industry leaders.

The dynamics of each industry naturally vary. There are, however, many overarching characteristics of the sectors that we analyzed. One is industry consolidation, with one industry after another (pharmaceuticals, defense, food and beverages) facing intense global competition that has led to numerous sector-specific mergers and acquisitions. Where companies have not gone so far as to merge, they have brokered numerous strategic partnerships (automobiles, telecommunications, energy), a strategy that helps spread research and development costs or facilitates rapid market entry.

Technological change and industry deregulation are two other overlapping trends confronting most companies. New technology has reduced barriers to entry and created new competitors. Deregulation has replaced industry regulation, shaking the foundations of many global industries.

Another significant trend centers on the emerging markets and the race to provide goods and build brand awareness among the new consumers of the world economy. In virtually all of the industries we feature, the home markets of many multinationals—the United States, Europe, and Japan—present sluggish and stagnant growth prospects. These markets are relatively mature and saturated. In addition, the competition is well established, meaning that market-share gains are hard to come by and pressure on profit margins remains intense.

The emerging markets, in turn, are predominantly younger, more vibrant markets for the companies listed in this chapter. These are also more volatile, as Asia proved in 1997. Notwithstanding the current downturn in Asia, long-term growth prospects are promising in the developing nations. Incomes are rising. Consumerism is taking hold. A great deal of pent-up demand for Western goods and services exists. Market shares remain variable. It is this environment that has corporate leaders from the United States, Europe, and Japan scrambling to build a foothold in the developing nations.

80 The Global Outlook for Computers–Strong Demand amid Fierce Competition

The computer industry (both hardware and software) is among the most robust industries in the world. With the computer as the workhorse of the digital age, demand around the globe continues to swell, with double-digit growth for desktop computers, portables, and computer networks the norm for the 1990s. By most industry estimates, global demand and industry growth are expected to remain relatively strong for the remainder of the decade and beyond. Worldwide shipments of personal computers rose to more than 47 million units in 1994, increased to nearly 58 million in 1995, topped 70 million in 1996, and exceeded 81 million units in 1997. As the heaviest user of computers, the United States accounted for nearly 40% of total worldwide shipments in 1997. Europe ranked second.

Demand for computers has increasingly become cyclical, although a number of long-term secular trends portend continued strong growth. Chief among them are rising global Internet usage, the introduction of lower-cost units, and the ongoing transition to new Windows operating systems. Strong demand for portable units, global capital investment in computers and computer network systems, and the proliferation of multimedia technology are also drivers of growth. Finally, low global penetration of the computer is another critical factor to consider.

Robust demand from the developing nations, where the level of computer penetration is low but rising rapidly, will also fuel growth. Outside of Japan, China has emerged as one of the largest and fastest growing computer markets in not only Asia but also the world. Demand in Latin America and in the developing nations of Central Europe will continue to rise as well over the next decade. Yet, despite the promise of the emerging markets, the industry today remains highly concentrated in the OECD (Organization for Economic Cooperation and Development) nations, which account for close to 80% of production and 90% of world consumption at mid-decade.

On the downside, while global demand for computers remains strong, the competition is fierce. The result has been downward pricing pressures among software vendors and the increasing "commoditization" of the personal computer. Dominant firms (Compaq, Dell, IBM, Packard Bell NEC, Hewlett-Packard, Acer) increasingly confront competition from various new entrants, some of which have gained a competitive advantage by exploiting successive new waves of technological change.

Looking forward, one significant trend in the industry centers on the convergence of computing, telecommunications, and entertainment. From this mix will emerge the so-called information appliance and the advent of the multimedia industry. A second trend centers on the rapid commoditization of the computer, a prospect that could force weaker players into strategic alliances with stronger companies. In terms of software development, the industry is likely to remain concentrated in the OECD nations and in a few developing Asian states, such as India, South Korea, and Taiwan.

Global Personal Computer Penetration
(PCs per 1,000 People, 1996)

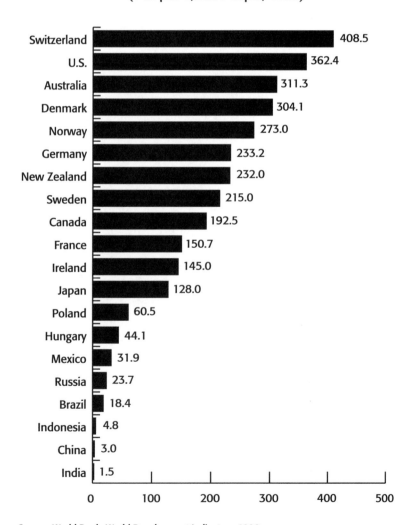

Country	PCs per 1,000
Switzerland	408.5
U.S.	362.4
Australia	311.3
Denmark	304.1
Norway	273.0
Germany	233.2
New Zealand	232.0
Sweden	215.0
Canada	192.5
France	150.7
Ireland	145.0
Japan	128.0
Poland	60.5
Hungary	44.1
Mexico	31.9
Russia	23.7
Brazil	18.4
Indonesia	4.8
China	3.0
India	1.5

Source: World Bank, World Development Indicators, 1998

81 The Global Semiconductor Industry

Think of semiconductors as "the crude oil of the information age." They process, store, and move information, which in turn has helped make technology cheaper and more adaptable to new uses. Semiconductors are already critical to the operation of most electronic goods, ranging from toasters to antilock brakes to computers. According to industry sources, the typical American interacts with more than 300 micro-controllers on a given day. Yet, the end-use applications of semiconductors continue to expand very rapidly. New products based on new technologies continue to drive growth. Telecommunications applications, digital broadcasting, Internet usage, and various multimedia applications all will help fuel future demand for semiconductors.

The dynamic nature of this industry is underscored by the accompanying graph, which shows that between 1990 and 1994, global semiconductor sales doubled from $50.5 billion in 1990 to $101.9 billion in 1994. World sales soared 47.1% in 1995 but fell 8.6% in 1996, the first annual decline since 1985. The downturn, however, was more cyclical than structural. Sales rebounded in 1997, and despite Asia's problems, are expected to continue rising over the long term. The largest markets are in the United States and Japan, although robust growth continues to emanate from developing Asia and Latin America.

On the downside, robust volume growth has not been able to offset falling prices lately, with the prices of DRAMs (dynamic random-access memory) falling by 75% in 1996 and by another 65% last year. The reason? Soaring new capacity has created more supply than demand in the industry.

The global semiconductor industry is dominated by Japanese and American firms (see the table), which account for roughly 80% of world production. U.S. companies are strong in the production of microprocessors. Japan's niche in the past has centered on the production of DRAMs, although Japan is moving into higher value-added production on account of increased competition from South Korea. The latter was just a minor player a decade ago but has since emerged as a significant global producer of chips. Lying in the wings are China and India, which will be major producers of semiconductors in the not-so-distant future.

Like many other global industries in which product life cycles have shortened and capital investment costs have increased, international alliances among semiconductor companies have become the norm. Competitors are becoming partners in many cases to help accelerate the pace of research and development, exploit economies of scale, share development costs, swap technology, and better respond to customers' needs. The sheer pace of technological change has forced many companies to work jointly.

The semiconductor industry is among the most explosive and dynamic industries of the world economy. It is also among the most influential. The development and application of smaller, faster, smarter chips will determine, to a very large degree, the pace of growth and development of many other sectors.

Worldwide Semiconductor Market Sales

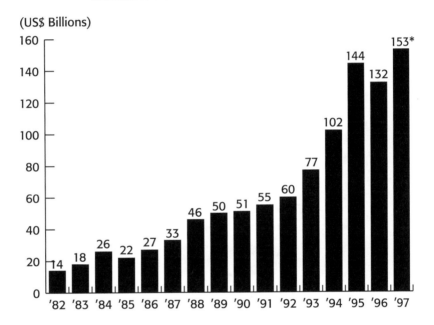

(US$ Billions)

*Industry estimate

Source: Semiconductor Industry Association, World Semiconductor Trade Statistics (WSTS)

Top Semiconductor Companies
(By Revenue, US$ Billions*)

Rank	Company	Country	Revenue
1	Intel	United States	21.1
2	NEC	Japan	10.7
3	Motorola	United States	8.1
4	Texas Instruments	United States	7.7
5	Toshiba	Japan	7.5

*1997 estimates

Source: Company sources

82 Global Telecommunications—Connecting the World

The international telecommunications market is among the most dynamic, fluid, and complex in the world. The industry has been radically energized and transformed over the past decade by the global sweep of privatization and deregulation. In 1998, the barriers that long insulated Europe's telecommunications companies were demolished. The same process is under way in Japan.

Meanwhile, soaring demand for telecommunication services in the developing nations, where the majority of the world's population has yet to make a phone call, represents an extremely positive growth trend for the industry going forward (see the accompanying graph). Regarding these untapped markets, the world telecommunications trade deal secured by the World Trade Organization in 1997 will open many of the world's telecommunications markets by 2000.

While demand for international telecommunications remains robust, global competition is fierce. The battle for customers has intensified as barriers to entry crumble around the globe, and as suppliers and carriers delve into each other's markets. Not content to miss out on the global telecommunications revolution, computer companies such as IBM and Microsoft, as well as some entertainment giants, have jumped into the fray. Given the high capital costs of the industry, many companies have adopted strategies that center on forming strategic alliances, securing joint ventures, or pursuing mergers.

The accompanying table lists the top five global telephone routes based on minutes of international traffic. Note that the United States is in four of the five routes, with telephone traffic between America and its NAFTA neighbors topping the list. Because the United States makes many calls abroad, it runs a "phone bill deficit" to the tune of roughly $4 billion a year. Trade in telecommunications (equipment and services combined) was valued at around $96 billion in 1995 and exceeded $100 billion in 1996.

Discerning the winners and losers from the coming global telecommunications revolution is not easy. Workers long employed by state monopolies are obviously at risk; so too are smaller state-owned companies that have neither the capital nor the technological wherewithal to compete in unfettered markets. Falling prices for phone services, a likely outcome of deregulation and greater competition, will undoubtably affect the profit margins of many phone carriers. Leading international telecommunication carriers include: AT&T (United States), Deutsche Telekom

(Germany), Nippon Telegraph & Telephone (Japan), MCI (United States), France Telecom (France), British Telecom (the United Kingdom), and Telecom Italia (Italy).

Two segments of the industry that should benefit, however, are cellular service providers and telecommunications equipment suppliers, companies that provide the hardware required to build the global information highway.

Wiring the World
(Telephone Mainlines per 1,000 People, 1996)

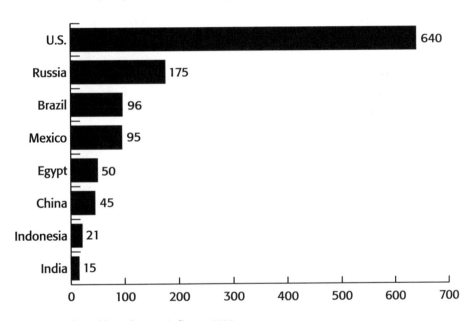

Source: World Bank, World Development Indicators 1998

Top Five International Routes
(Minutes of International Telephone Traffic)

Rank	Route		Total
1	United States	Canada	4,582
2	United States	Mexico	2,401
3	Hong Kong	China	1,528
4	United States	United Kingdom	1,488
5	United States	Germany	901

Source: International Telecommunications Union/TeleGeography Direction of Traffic database

83 The Global Auto Industry and the Rough Road Ahead

With more than 600 assembly plants spread across 60 countries, the automobile industry is among the most global sectors of the world economy. The industry employs more than 10 million people, and millions more indirectly in industries that supply parts and components to manufacturers. It is an industry that can be heavily influenced by politics, given that the automobile is a signature of industrial development as well as, on a practical level, a principal source of employment. Accordingly, barriers to trade, artificial incentives, and policies that favor "national" carmakers are part of the global scene.

"Build where you sell" is an overarching strategy of the industry and one that challenges companies to manage and operate complex supply chains across many geographic regions of the world. The paradox is that by manufacturing around the globe, automobile makers have gained economies of scale, leveraged their development resources, captured new markets, diversified their revenue base, and bolstered profits. But the downside is that in the rush to build new plants in Mexico, Brazil, Poland, China, and Thailand, a mountain of excess capacity is emerging. The industry's profitability is threatened by a global glut in cars. The latter triggered the industry's megamerger between Chrysler of the United States and Daimler-Benz of Germany in May 1998.

Worldwide vehicle capacity (including cars, trucks, and sport utility vehicles) was in the neighborhood of 68 million units in 1996, although only 50 million vehicles were actually produced, resulting in a profit-pinching capacity utilization rate of 73%. Based on various forecasts from the industry, the picture is not expected to improve anytime soon. If anything, it will get worse for the simple fact that demand is not expected to keep up with supply. The European Commission estimates that there are up to 7 million units of spare capacity in Europe alone, a dire state of affairs that is expected to lead to more mergers and acquisitions in Europe. Japan is also ripe for consolidation.

Prospects in the mature and, in many cases, stagnant markets of Europe, Japan, and the United States are anything but glowing. Future growth lies with the developing nations, where the consumer's ability to buy an automobile increases along with rising per-capita incomes. Yet, even in the promising growth markets of Asia and Latin America, making money is difficult for automakers. The competition is fierce. Moreover, these markets, while underpinned with solid long-term fundamentals, are not immune to cyclical forces. The crisis in Asia and slower growth in

Latin America will crimp demand over the near term. Capacity continues to run ahead of demand, notably in Asia, where U.S. companies face stiff competition not only from the Japanese, but also from new entrants such as Samsung and Daewoo of South Korea.

What about trends in China, which is universally accepted as the grandest auto market of them all? The demand side of the equation is very positive, given that the mainland has just in excess of 1 vehicle per 100 people, compared with 33 in Taiwan and 75 in the United States. On the negative side, per-capita incomes remain low, and high taxes make owning a car prohibitively expensive. In addition, China's auto market is still highly fragmented, and the distribution of production remains in the control of the government. Finally, excess capacity looms on the horizon if China's much-ballyhooed consumer market for autos does not develop or emerges slowly. Total vehicle sales of cars, vans, and trucks was roughly 1.6 million units in the country in 1996, although the government expects annual unit sales to rise to 2.7 million units in 2000 and to more than 6 million units in 2010. These projections imply that China will emerge as the fourth largest market in the world by 2010, after North America, Western Europe, and Japan.

The World's Top Automotive Companies
(By Unit Sales, Market Share, 1997)

Rank	Company	Country	Sales (Millions)	Share %
1	General Motors	United States	8.8	16.2
2	Ford	United States	6.9	12.9
3	Toyota	Japan	4.8	9.0
4	Volkswagen	Germany	4.6	7.9
5	Chrysler/Daimler-Benz	United States/Germany	4.0	7.4
6	Fiat	Italy	2.9	5.3
7	Nissan	Japan	2.8	5.2
8	Peugeot-Citroen	France	2.1	3.9
9	Honda	Japan	2.0	3.8
10	Mitsubishi	Japan	1.9	3.5
11	Renault	France	1.9	3.5
12	Suzuki	Japan	1.8	3.4
13	Hyundai	Korea	1.2	2.3
14	Bmw	Germany	1.2	2.2

Source: Automotive News

84 | Is the World Going Up in Smoke?

Smoking is a big global business. The World Health Organization (WHO) estimates that roughly one-third of the global population over the age of 15 smoke. As the accompanying table shows, that equates to roughly 1.1 billion puffers, who collectively consume 15 billion cigarettes every day. In the United States, an estimated 1 billion cigarettes are smoked daily.

The vast majority of the world's smokers (800 million) reside in the developing nations. Here, cigarette consumption remains buoyant, given rising per-capita incomes and shifting social norms. Smoking is not only tolerated in many developing nations, where antismoking campaigns are in their infancy, but it is also fashionable, notably among women and the young. Both represent the market of the future.

Women make up less than 20% of the global smoking population, yet in many nations where smoking was once taboo for women, female smokers are becoming more common and acceptable. This is particularly true in the developing nations, where women make up just 13% of the total smoking population, versus the 33% share of women smokers in the developed nations.

The most smoke emanates from China, home to 300 million smokers, roughly the same number as in all developed nations combined. In fact, there are more smokers in China than there are people in the United States. The Chinese buy 1.6 trillion cigarettes a year, which is a main reason why the world's leading tobacco companies covet China. With the help of the Marlboro Man, one of the most recognizable brands in China and the world, Philip Morris has been relatively successful in penetrating the Chinese market. Not to be outdone in the world's premier cigarette markets, R. J. Reynolds has been manufacturing in China since the late 1980s.

The accompanying graph illustrates that the highest rate of annual consumption per smoker occurs in Poland, followed by Greece and Hungary. Japan and South Korea round out the top five. The United States ranked number 3 in the world in per-capita cigarette consumption in 1972 but dropped to number 11 in the 1990–92 survey by the World Health Organization.

Among publicly held companies, Philip Morris earns more a year from tobacco sales than any other company in the world. Other large public tobacco companies include British American Tobacco (B.A.T.), American Brands, RJR Nabisco, Loews, and Brooke. The largest tobacco company in the world is the state-owned Chinese company, which has more than 30% of the world market. In terms of global production, the

United States, Japan, China, and Germany account for more than half of the world's total output.

There is a serious downside to all this smoke. As the World Bank warned in a 1993 report, "unless smoking behavior changes, three decades from now premature deaths caused by tobacco in the developing world will exceed the expected deaths from AIDs, tuberculosis, and complications of childbirth combined." By some private estimates, the annual worldwide death toll from tobacco-related illnesses will more than triple over the next 20 to 30 years, rising from roughly 3 million to 10 million deaths per annum. Not surprisingly, antismoking campaigns are becoming more common abroad, an ominous trend for the world's largest cigarette companies.

Estimated Number of Smokers in the World
(Early 1990s, Millions of People)

	Males	**Females**	**Total**
Developed countries	200	100	300
Developing countries	700	100	800
World total	**900**	**200**	**1,100**

Source: WHO estimates

Average Annual Cigarette Consumption per Adult by Country, 1990–92

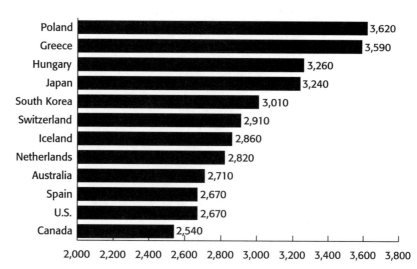

Source: WHO

85 Pharmaceuticals—Globalization and Consolidation

In some ways, the global pharmaceutical industry is unique among the industries included in this chapter. One distinguishing characteristic is that the industry is highly concentrated: in the early part of the decade, more than 70% of world production and consumption of pharmaceuticals was in the OECD nations. Second, although the industry sells products with universal appeal and usage, pharmaceutical markets remain highly segmented due to national health regulations, pricing practices, and certificate specifications. Third, at the firm level, the industry is significantly fragmented. In 1996, only three companies—Novartis, Glaxo Wellcome, and Merck—had more than 4% of the world market. The industry's top 10 companies held only 34% of the total world market share in 1996, notwithstanding a period of consolidation.

Consolidation and collaboration have become the norm, given ongoing attempts to lower costs, expand into new markets, spread research and development expenses, and increase product cycle times. All of these factors, in addition to health-care reform in the United States and other major markets, sparked a number of mergers, acquisitions, joint ventures, and strategic alliances over the first half of the decade. The principal aim of these deals is to boost productivity in manufacturing and marketing. Note that many of the world's top pharmaceutical firms spend more than $1 billion a year on research and development.

The global drug industry is also unique in that it is primarily dominated by large European and American companies, with only a secondary presence from Japan and the rest of Asia. All of the companies listed in the accompanying table are either European or American or, better stated, a combination of the two, given the numerous corporate marriages of the past few years. Most major European and American firms have Japanese subsidiaries.

In terms of trade, pharmaceuticals are not as trade intensive as many other products due to national market demands and the structure of the global industry. The largest exporters, measured by exports as a percentage of production, are in Europe's smallest nations: Switzerland, Denmark, the Netherlands, Sweden, and Austria. Based on total dollar amount, the five largest exporters of pharmaceuticals are Germany, Switzerland, the United States, the United Kingdom, and France. Trade is also highly concentrated, with the OECD nations accounting for 92% of world pharmaceutical exports in 1994 and 78% of world imports.

Looking forward, three main trends stand out: one centers on government cost-containment measures in the industrialized nations, which will most likely maintain pressure on the industry's profitability. A second trend lies with the escalating costs of developing new products, which supports the industry's move toward greater merger and acquisition activity over the past few years. The third development centers on rising demand in the developing nations as incomes rise, standards of living improve, and populations age.

Not unlike other global industries, growth rates in many emerging markets outpace those in the developed nations. Over the past five years, for instance, average annual growth rates in Europe and North America were 6% and 7%, respectively. In Latin America, in contrast, pharmaceutical sales rose by 15% annually. Despite the underlying potential of the emerging markets, many of the world's largest drug firms have enterd these markets only carefully and cautiously. Demand is strong, although price controls, unfavorable investment regulations, and the lack of intellectual property protection continue to pose as major problems and barriers to entry. Low health-care spending has not helped either.

Major Pharmaceutical Companies, 1996
(By Sales, US$ Billions*)

Rank	Company	Country	Pharmaceutical Sales
1	Glaxo Wellcome	United Kingdom	11.6
2	Merck	United States	11.4
3	Novartis	Switzerland	11.0
4	Bristol-Myers Squibb	United States	9.3
5	Johnson & Johnson	United States	8.7
6	American Home Products	United States	8.4
7	Pfizer	United States	8.4
8	Roche	Switzerland	8.0
9	Smithkline Beecham	United Kingdom	7.4
10	Hoechst Marion Roussel	Germany	7.4

*Twelve months ending September 1997

Source: Company sources

86 The Global Energy Market—Coping with Shifting Supply and Demand

Prospects for the world's largest energy companies remain variable and mixed. They depend on numerous factors, ranging from geopolitics to global energy supplies to prevailing global demand. For most of the 1990s, global supply and demand for oil were roughly in balance, resulting in relatively stable world prices. Nevertheless, the potential for rapid price movements (either down or up) makes the world energy market one of the most mercurial of global industries.

A more long-term focus centers on three variables: global oil reserves, production, and consumption. In terms of reserves, the chief point to underscore is that total proven oil reserves (estimated at 1 trillion barrels) remain dominated by Middle East producers, who account for 65% of the world total.

As for world oil production, the Organization of Petroleum Exporting Countries' (OPEC) world market share rose from 36% to 40% following the Gulf War, a share it has since maintained. Non-OPEC production continues to accelerate, with growth emanating from such countries as the United Kingdom, Norway, Argentina, Brazil, and Mexico. A key trend to watch is whether OPEC members and certain nations outside the group (e.g., Mexico) will work more closely in the future to control world oil supplies. Yet to reemerge onto the global scene are Russia and the oil-rich states of Central Asia, which have the potential to become significant global oil players.

In terms of consumption, most future growth will come from the developing nations, notably China and the rest of Asia. As shown in the graph, consumption in developing Asia is expected to rise by more than 4% a year, an above-trend rate of growth due to relatively stronger levels of industrialization, rapid urbanization, and greater automobile usage. In Latin America, annual consumption growth is projected to be more than double the level in the United States and Europe. On the assumption that the developing nations, over the long term, will continue to grow by a faster rate than the OECD nations, oil demand in the non-OECD nations is expected to surpass that of the OECD in the not-so-distant future.

The global industry is dominated by a few publicly traded companies and a handful of state-owned companies. Twelve of the world's 25 largest companies are wholly state-owned. The Saudi oil company, Saudi Aramco, is the largest oil company in the world. The largest privately owned oil firm is Royal Dutch/Shell. The top 10 largest oil companies are listed in the accompanying table.

Projected World Energy Consumption
(Annual % Change, 1995–2015)

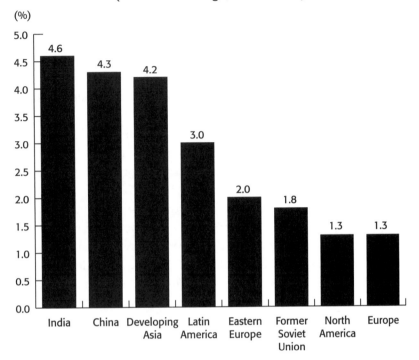

Source: Energy Information Administration

The World's Largest Oil Companies, 1996*

Rank	Company	Country	Millions of Barrels Produced per Day
1	Saudi Aramco	Saudi Arabia	8.8
2	Nioc	Iran	3.8
3	Pemex	Mexico	3.3
4	Pdvsa	Venezuela	3.0
5	Cnpc	China	2.8
6	Royal Dutch/Shell	Netherlands/United Kingdom	2.2
7	Kpc	Kuwait	2.1
8	Exxon	United States	1.6
9	Sonatrach	Algeria	1.3
10	British Petroleum	United Kingdom	1.2

*Ranked by various operational data such as oil reserves and output, gas reserves and output, refinery capacity, and product sales volumes

Source: Petroleum Intelligence Weekly, *December 22, 1997 (Publisher: Energy Intelligence Group)*

87 The Cold War May Be Over, but Global Arms Sales Remain Big Business

Global peace has helped trim global military expenditures, with military spending as a percentage of global gross domestic product falling from 3.5% in 1990 to 2.3% in 1996. Based on calculations from the International Monetary Fund (IMF), the "peace dividend"—defined as the difference between the expenditures that would have been spent in 1995 if the 1990 ratio of expenditures to GDP had been maintained and the actual dollar amount for 1995—totaled $324 billion over the 1990–95 period. (See the first table.)

The International Institute for Strategic Studies, meanwhile, estimates that military spending in 1996, $811 billion, was 40% below the peak of 1987 and the lowest since 1966. And like other global industries that have had to downsize and shed labor in order to stay competitive, or experienced a wave of mergers and acquisitions, the global weapons industry cashiered more than 6 million people directly (and indirectly many more) between 1987 and 1996.

Despite this consolidation, the global arms industry is not about to vanish. Weapons and arms sales remain one of the largest industries of the world economy, notwithstanding the end of the Cold War. After falling sharply in the early years of this decade, actual global military expenditures declined by only $2 billion in 1996, according to the IMF. Over the first five years of the post–Cold War era, global arms sales totaled roughly $153 billion, an average of roughly $31 billion a year. Weapons spending in the industrialized nations and the former Soviet Union has declined, although demand for arms in the developing nations, especially the volatile Middle East and Southeast Asia, remains healthy. The global arms trade grew to nearly $40 billion in 1996, with the Middle East/North Africa accounting for nearly 40% of total imports. Southeast Asia accounted for 23%. Arm sales also remain brisk in the Indian subcontinent, with both India and Pakistan making known their nuclear capabilities in 1998.

Who is supplying the arms? The global market for weapons belongs to the U.S. government and American companies, which, combined, accounted for more than 46% of total arms sales over the 1991–95 period. The United States is easily the leading arms exporter, with total arms exports worth $17 billion in 1996. The United Kingdom was a distant second ($8.8 billion), followed by France ($5.6 billion), Russia ($3.4 billion), and Israel ($1.3 billion).

As the second table indicates, American companies dominate the global defense industry. Consolidation has been the most notable trend of the industry over this decade, with more than 20 mergers and acquisitions occurring since the end of the Cold War era. And because of military downsizing, many companies are shifting their focus to the civilian aircraft business, which remains globally brisk.

As the sole superpower of the post–Cold War era, the United States is the world's top cop. It is also, ironically, the world's top supplier of guns.

Military Spending as a Percentage of GDP

	1990	1995	1996
All countries	3.5	2.4	2.3
Industrial nations	3.3	2.3	2.3
Developing nations	3.2	2.6	2.5
Former Soviet Bloc	6.5	2.2	1.9

Source: IMF

Major Aerospace and Defense Companies
(By Sales, US$ Billions*)

Rank	Company	Country	Sales
1	Boeing/McDonnell Douglas	United States	45.8
2	Lockheed Martin	United States	28.1
3	United Technologies	United States	24.7
4	Raytheon/Hughes/Texas Instruments	United States	13.7
5	Thomson	France	12.2
6	British Aerospace	United Kingdom	12.0
7	Lagardere Groupe	France	11.0
8	GEC†	United Kingdom	10.7
9	Aerospatiale/Dassault	France	9.4
10	Daimler-Benz Aerospace†	Germany	7.3

*1997 sales estimates
†1996 sales

Source: Company sources

88 | Food and Beverages—Satisfying the Needs of New Consumers

Going global has become a strategic imperative for the world's leading food and beverage companies. Most industry leaders are well entrenched in the developed nations, but these markets are mature and highly saturated with products. In addition, power has increasingly shifted from the manufacturer to the retailer, while the growth of private or own-label brands continues to bite into the market share of more established companies. Accordingly, market-share gains are harder to achieve, and intense competition continues to squeeze profit margins.

For global leaders such as Nestlé, Unilever, Anheuser-Busch, and others, the future increasingly lies in the developing nations. Here, per-capita incomes are on the rise, diets and social norms are becoming more Westernized, and growth in personal consumption continues to accelerate. Rising affluence in the form of per-capita income growth is paramount, given that higher incomes correlate with increased spending on more value-added food and beverage items. Demographics are important as well, since the young populations of the developing nations are more prone to shift and change diets than older people. These factors and more make the developing nations ripe and attractive markets for many of the companies listed in the leaders tables in this section.

Successfully entering these new markets is one of the top challenges for these companies. Privatization in many developing nations has allowed some multinationals to snap up local companies, resulting in instant market access. Other routes of entry have included strategic alliances, building new facilities, and joint ventures. Heavy investment is required in distribution, retail, and packaging. Astute marketing and advertising are crucial as well.

There are not many global food brands, with Nestlé and Kellogg two exceptions. This stems from the fact that differences in culture, religion, and taste make food one of the toughest products to peddle on a global basis. The most successful global food companies, thus, are the ones that tailor their products to local tastes. One is Nestlé which produces some 200 different varieties of its Nescafé soluble coffee. Given these conditions, success in the industry lies with leveraging global capabilities while staying acutely attuned to local tastes and desires.

Top Food Companies
(By Sales, US$ Billions*)

Rank	Company	Country	Sales
1	Nestlé	Switzerland	47.9
2	Unilever†	United Kingdom/ Netherlands	37.0
3	Sara Lee	United States	19.7
4	Nabisco Holdings	United States	17.1
5	H. J. Heinz	United States	9.2
6	Campbell Soup	United States	7.9
7	Kellogg	United States	6.8
8	General Mills	United States	5.9
9	Ralston Purina	United States	4.5

*1997 sales estimates
†1996 sales estimates

Source: Company sources

Top Beverage Companies
(By Sales, US$ Billions*)

Rank	Company	Country	Sales
1	Pepsico	United States	20.9
2	Coca-Cola	United States	18.9
3	Seagram	Canada	11.7
4	Kirin Brewery	Japan	11.5
5	Anheuser-Busch	United States	11.1
6	Bass	United Kingdom	8.5
7	LVMH Moet Hennessey	France	7.9
8	Cadbury Schweppes	United Kingdom	6.7
9	Heineken	Netherlands	6.7

*1997 sales estimates

Source: Company sources

89 A World of Global Travelers

More people are traveling to more parts of the world, making tourism one of the most dynamic sectors of the global economy. In many countries, notably among the developing nations, the tourism industry is a key source of foreign exchange earnings and government revenue. Rising per-capita incomes, the growth of a global middle class, and lower transportation costs are the operative variables fueling growth in this industry. In 1997, the number of people traveling abroad rose to 613 million, up 2.9% from the prior year. Receipts (excluding airfares) totaled $448 billion, up 2.7%. Both figures represent record levels.

As shown in the first table, France ranked as the number-one destination in 1997, with 66.8 million arrivals, comfortably ahead of the United States (48.9 million) and Spain (43.4 million). Four out of the top five destinations in 1997 were in the "Old World," or Europe. To the east, Poland and the Czech Republic have emerged as popular destination sites for tourists. China tops the list in Asia.

The United States, however, earned the most in receipts as the second table shows, with total earnings rising to $75.1 billion in 1997. Italy ($30 billion) ranked second, France third ($27.9 billion). China was tops in the Pacific Rim, followed by Australia and Hong Kong.

By region, Europe ranks number one in attracting people, while Africa was on top in terms of growth in 1997. The latter registered a 7.4% increase in arrivals and nearly a 4.4% increase in receipts in 1997. This relatively robust level of growth was due largely to new arrivals to Egypt, Tunisia, and South Africa. The latter was number one in Africa in terms of arrivals. The "Old World" charm of Europe attracted 361,600 arriving tourists in 1997, or nearly 60% of total world arrivals, and 51% of total receipts. In general, Europe and the United States are the heavyweights of international tourism, although the fastest growing regions center on the developing nations. According to Boeing, the world's largest manufacturer of aircraft, China and East Asia is expected to lead the world in air-travel growth over the next decade. Asia's outlook in the near term, however, has been tarnished by the region's economic crisis. Above-average growth is also expected from Russia and the nations formerly of the Soviet Union, as well as Latin America.

The outlook for global tourism is promising, with a number of secular trends—falling transportation costs, expanding middle classes in many parts of the world—supporting growth over the next decade. The World Tourism Organization (WTO) expects the global tourist industry to expand by 4% annually throughout the first two decades of the next century. Given this rate of annual growth, the WTO projects that there will be just over 700 million international arrivals in the year 2000, 1 billion by 2010, and 1.6 billion, nearly three times the number of arrivals in 1996, by 2020.

The World's Top Tourism Destinations, 1997
(International Tourist Arrivals*/Millions of Arrivals)

Rank	Country	Arrivals	% of Total
1	France	66.8	10.9
2	United States	48.9	8.0
3	Spain	43.4	7.1
4	Italy	34.1	5.6
5	United Kingdom	26.1	4.2
6	China	23.8	3.9
7	Poland	19.6	3.2
8	Mexico	18.7	3.0
9	Canada	17.6	2.9
10	Czech Republic	17.4	2.8

*Excluding same-day visitors

Source: World Tourism Organization

The World's Top Tourism Earners, 1997
(International Tourism Receipts*, US$ Billions)

Rank	Country	Receipts	% of Total
1	United States	75.1	16.8
2	Italy	30.0	6.7
3	France	27.9	6.2
4	Spain	26.7	6.0
5	United Kingdom	19.9	4.4
6	Germany	18.9	4.2
7	Austria	12.4	2.8
8	China	12.1	2.7
9	Australia	9.3	2.1
10	Hong Kong	9.2	2.1

*Excluding transport

Source: World Tourism Organization

90 The Global Power Generation Market– Generating the Supply to Meet the Demand

Electricity is one of mankind's most precious commodities. Economic growth, industrial development, basic living standards—all depend on the generation of electricity from primary sources of energy including coal, oil, gas, nuclear, hydro, geothermal, and wind. In the United States (the largest consumer of electricity in the world) and many other industrialized nations, electricity is a basic staple.

But, as any visitor to the developing nations soon realizes, electricity is something not to be taken for granted. In the developing nations, energy is neither inexpensive nor plentiful. Power outages and brownouts are all too common in many emerging markets. Demand continues to outstrip supply, hampering the economic growth and industrialization of many countries.

The problem for most developing nations boils down to money, or the lack of capital required to install new power generation capacity. The industry is capital-intensive, though many of the most promising customers (the emerging markets) lack funds. The generating equipment market is dominated by the "Big Five"—General Electric of the United States; Siemens of Germany; ABB, the Swiss-Swedish engineering group; GEC-Alsthom, a British-French combination; and Mitsubishi Heavy Industries of Japan.

Asia is considered the prize market by many companies, notwithstanding current economic difficulties. The region is home to roughly three billion people and is on the cusp of an urban boom. Where Asia accounted for roughly 20% of the world's generating capacity in 1990, it is expected to represent one-third by 2010, according to industry sources. On a global basis, installed capacity is expected to rise 24.3% between 2000 and 2010.

Outside the developing countries, key industry trends in Europe and the United States center on the deregulation and liberalization of the power industry. In the latter, the Energy Act of 1994 has accelerated the pace of industry reform and deregulation. In the former, a 1996 European Union directive obligates member states to introduce competition in at least one-third of their electricity markets by 2003. The prospects of increased competition in both markets are expected to create new market opportunities for equipment manufacturers.

The Global Power Generation Market
(Worldwide Installed Capacity, Gigawatts)

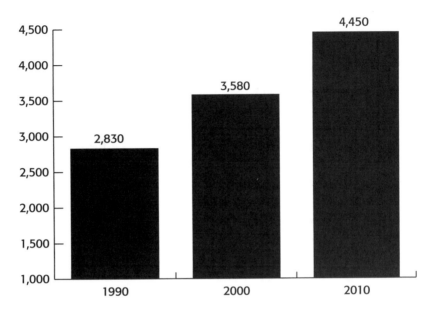

Source: *Industry sources and forecasts*

Electric Demand
(Consumption per Capita, Kilowatt-Hours)

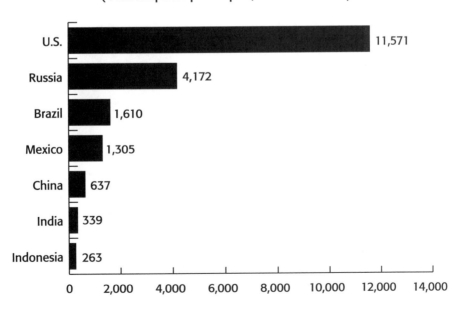

Source: IMD *World Competitiveness Yearbook, 1998*

91 The Global Media Industry and the Making of the Global Village

The media and entertainment sectors have long been more local than global. For years, news or entertainment that did traverse national boundaries was done via radio, namely the British Broadcasting Corporation (BBC). Then the Cable News Network (CNN) emerged in the 1980s, and global news events were splashed instantaneously all over the world's televisions. Just as globally potent has been the rise of MTV, the worldwide rock and roll network that helped globalize American pop culture. Think of CNN and MTV as just the tip of the global media iceberg.

In the 1990s, the development of a global electronic village continues, with satellites and rapid advances in digital technology bringing the world ever closer and nearer. To be sure, news and entertainment remain largely parochial or fragmented along national lines. But if a handful of global media operators have their way, in the future watching a football (soccer) game in the United Kingdom will be just as easy for an American as tuning in an American football game in Los Angeles. A Japanese executive working in New York will be able to come home at night and access the local morning news in Tokyo. On any given weekend, a German auto executive based in South Carolina will be able to dial up a German film from Frankfurt.

The global spread of music, movies, books, and information is being led by such companies as the News Corporation, owned by Rupert Murdoch; Time Warner, which now owns Turner Broadcasting and CNN; Viacom, whose television interests include MTV; and Walt Disney, parent of Mickey Mouse, one of the most recognizable brands in the world. Reuters and Bloomberg now provide global business news around the clock. All of these companies, along with many more, are trying to build integrated global media outlets, complete, in some cases, with production and distribution chains.

A large portion of the global entertainment industry lies with the $40 billion global music industry. The sector had experienced double-digit sales growth for roughly a decade until 1997, when global music sales fell to $38.1 billion, down from $39.8 billion the prior year. Accounting for the downturn were depressed sales in Asia. The region, thanks to its young population, had been a key new market for music companies, with India, Indonesia, Malaysia, the Philippines, Taiwan, and Thailand all experiencing double-digit music sales growth in 1996. Demand has weakened in the near term in most of these nations, although long-term fundamentals remain quite promising. Dramatic sales growth in Latin

America and Eastern Europe is expected with the recent improvement in economic conditions for both regions.

The global music industry is led by the "Big Five"—Sony (Japan), Polygram (the Netherlands), Time Warner (U.S.), EMI (the UK), and Bertelsmann (Germany). However, two of the world's largest music companies—Polygram and EMI—were sold or were on the verge of being sold in early 1998, a prospect that will inevitably shake up the industry.

As the accompanying chart makes clear, the bulk of music sales occur in Europe and North America, home to some of the world's best-known music stars. Yet, future growth will become more closely tied to the emerging markets, where local stars and acts are becoming just as popular and profitable.

The World Music Market
(Regional Shares by Dollar Value of Sales, 1997)

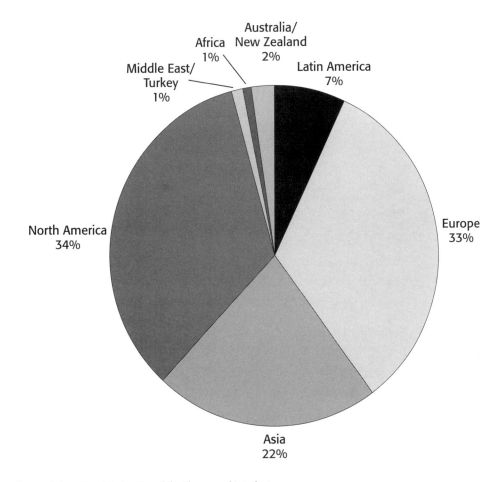

Source: International Federation of the Phonographic Industry

CHAPTER 6

Global Odds and Ends

Overview

This chapter contains 10 unrelated and wide-ranging entries that we feel are important trends of the world economy. They round out the entries of the previous chapters.

The trends that follow range from the world's top brands to the world's top religions. The former are critical, since global brand awareness is the first step toward capturing the hearts and wallets of the globe's new consumers. Sizing up our top 10 list will give investors a perspective on what companies are widely recognized around the world. The role of religion is also important to understand because in many parts of the world the predominant religion can shape the norms and traditions of the country and, therefore, the foundations of an economy.

One entry is devoted to the euro, Europe's new currency. Whether the euro emerges as a weak or strong currency remains the subject of great debate. However, there is near universal agreement that its introduction marks one of the most important international financial events of the past 50 years, if not the entire century.

We also take a look at world trade in illicit drugs, which is much larger than most people realize. Another entry highlights global carbon dioxide emissions and the impact of global warming on the world economy. The global "greening" of business promises to be very important in the future and is the focus of entry 97. The overseas Chinese are one of the most important business entities of Asia, although their presence and influence is neither widely recognized nor appreciated by investors; we shed some light on Asia's silent force in entry 94.

We take a look as well at immigration trends in the United States and the impact on the economy. The role of women in politics and at work is also featured in the entry on the global gender gap. Because Asia will play such a large role in the world oil markets in the decades ahead, one entry is devoted to Asia and oil, which could turn out to be a hazardous mix for the world economy.

Finally, the last entry of this chapter, and of this book, focuses on change, a fitting ending, in our opinion, since the global economy is all about change. Change is the one constant of the global economy and one all investors should not only accept but also embrace.

92 | Global Brand Awareness

Free-market reforms, rising per-capita incomes in many parts of the world, the collapse of communism, rapid advances in information technology, and urbanization have converged to produce more consumers in the world economy than at any other point in history. These global customers constitute new markets for fast food, entertainment, consumer staples, and a host of other products and services, ranging from computer software to footwear. What they eat, the clothes they wear, the music they listen to, and how they spend their leisure time will directly impact the fortunes of numerous multinationals. As a logical extension, the task for many companies is straightforward: secure the loyalty and income of the world's new consumers, a mandate made easier with a product or brand that is universally recognized. Brands are very important assets in an ever increasing competitive global economy.

What companies have global appeal and are therefore in position to win the business of new global customers? According to a survey conducted by Interbrand, a global consultancy firm, American companies producing American cultural products—movies, jeans, soft drinks, hamburgers, cigarettes, and, lately, software—hold a commanding lead in global brand awareness. The accompanying table recaps the results: of the top 10 most popular brands in the world in 1996, 8 were from the United States, with McDonald's ranked number one.

Ronald McDonald is not only an icon in Peoria, Illinois, but also a familiar and friendly face in Prague, the Czech Republic. By taking Ronald global, McDonald's has seen its international revenue rise sharply over this decade. Incredibly, a new McDonald's outlet opens someplace in the world every three hours; most of the new stores are overseas. Adapting to local tastes and norms is critical for companies like McDonald's, which explains why in the Indian market, where beef products are taboo, McDonald's offers the mutton burger.

Coca-Cola derives a significant share of revenue (more than two-thirds) from overseas. The company, which sells nearly half of all the soft drinks consumed on earth, is peddling not merely a beverage but an American experience. Coke vies with Marlboro cigarettes and the Marlboro Man as one of the most famous brands in the world. Philip Morris, the company that produces Marlboro cigarettes, derives more than half of its total revenue from international sales, as does Kodak, which continues to battle Japan's Fuji as the world's top film provider.

Newcomers to the list in 1996 include Disney, which, with the help of its successful films, has seen its foreign sales rise significantly this decade. Mickey Mouse, like Ronald McDonald before him, has gone global. The global appeal of Levi's jeans has also soared over the 1990s, with pent-up demand emanating primarily from nations once locked behind the Iron Curtain. For many consumers in Russia and Central Europe, owning a pair of jeans represents the ultimate emancipation from communism. Reflecting the rising power and popularity of global computing, Bill Gates and Microsoft have also gone global over the past decade. Gillette, the world's largest distributor of men's razors, garners nearly two-thirds of its sales from abroad.

Rounding out the top 10 in terms of global brand awareness are two non-American firms. Sony of Japan, the inventor of the Walkman and one of the most global companies in Japan, ranked number five in 1996. Mercedes-Benz of Germany, whose cars symbolize the ultimate in luxury, ranked number seven, the only car manufacturer to make the list.

The bottom line: Brands matter to the new and emerging consumer class of the world economy. The companies with superior brand image have a leg up on their competitors.

The World's Top Brands, 1996

Rank	Brand
1	McDonald's
2	Coca-Cola
3	Disney
4	Kodak
5	Sony
6	Gillette
7	Mercedes-Benz
8	Levi's
9	Microsoft
10	Marlboro

Source: Interbrand

93 The Euro—What It Is and What the Implications Are for Investors and Business

The U.S. dollar has long reigned as the world's premier currency, a position the United States inherited from Britain in the interwar period when the dollar surpassed the pound as the world's dominant currency. Today, the dollar plays a central role in the international monetary system, with more than 56% of the world's official reserve holdings in dollars at the end of 1995, up slightly from the level of 1985. In terms of daily turnover in the foreign exchange markets, roughly 84% is in dollar-denominated transactions. In short, no other currency, including the yen and deutsche mark, comes even close to rivaling the preeminence of the greenback.

However, the almighty dollar may have some competition in the future. A new currency, one with global significance, is in the process of being created in Europe. It is called the euro, and if all goes according to plan, stocks and government debt will be denominated in euros on January 1, 1999. By 2002, the euro is to replace all domestic currencies in use and circulation in member nations and is to be used in all financial and business transactions. At this juncture, 11 countries—Germany, France, Italy, Portugal, Spain, Ireland, the Netherlands, Austria, Belgium, Finland, and Luxembourg—have opted to participate in Europe's monetary revolution.

The question of how the introduction of the euro will impact global business has been the subject of great debate over the past few years. Will the euro emerge as a weak or strong currency, an outcome that will influence the global competitiveness of Europe? Will the euro emerge as a major international currency and rival the status of the dollar? Will billions in capital shift out of the dollar to the euro at some point, causing a major realignment of global exchange rates? Will the exchange-rate risk for investors decline or increase with the introduction of the euro?

There are endless questions, as well as endless answers. It is a fair bet that the euro will emerge as a primary international currency, one greater than what the German mark, Europe's de facto single currency, plays at this juncture. Supporting this assumption is the fact that the European Union accounts for one-fifth of world gross domestic product, nearly 20% of world trade, and has broad and liquid capital markets. The ultimate attractiveness of the currency, however, will depend on how well the European Central Bank (Europe's central bank) conducts monetary policies.

Beyond the financial markets, the introduction of the euro carries significant implications for corporations operating within the European

Union. In broad terms, the euro will mean greater price transparency, which in turn is expected to lead to lower prices across many sectors. Competition will intensify and trigger industry consolidation in many sectors. The ultimate benefit will flow to the consumer. For business, a single currency will obviate the need for spending on managing foreign exchange transactions, a sizable cost for many European companies. In addition, fewer currency fluctuations and the cost of dealing with them is expected to give a boost to small and medium-sized European firms that have long concentrated on the domestic market. A single market and single currency will help expand their business boundaries.

On balance, the introduction of the euro represents one of the most significant developments in the international monetary system since the beginning of this century. The intended and unintended side effects remain unclear. It is a safe assumption that even after the euro is in circulation, the dollar will remain a leading global currency. It will be some time before we know if the euro will challenge and alter the dollar-centered international monetary system that has been in place for the past half-century.

Symbol for the Euro—the New Currency of Europe

94 The Overseas Chinese—the Silent Force of Asia

Think of Asia or the Pacific Rim, and Japan immediately comes to mind. Japan, after all, is the largest economy in Asia and the leading producer and seller of some of the world's most visible products—Sony, Honda, Toyota, Panasonic, and other goods that have become household names around the globe.

But notwithstanding Japan's economic standing in Asia and the world, a second, silent force lies at the heart of Asia's economic success. It is the overseas Chinese, who, despite their relatively small numbers, control a disproportionate amount of Asia's wealth.

Migration from China to other parts of Asia has a long history, dating back to the fifteenth century. However, the Chinese migrants of the nineteenth and early twentieth century laid the basis for the prominent role the overseas Chinese play today.

And what a role it is. The 50 million or so ethnic Chinese people residing in Asia other than China (see the table) account for less than 10% of the region's population, yet generate an estimated $450–500 billion in economic activity. The sum is larger than the total output of many nations and is roughly half the total output of mainland China. Of Asia's billionaire class, some studies suggest that up to 86% of the region's super-rich are overseas Chinese. And while Japan is normally considered the top foreign investor throughout the region, Japanese firms face stiff competition from Chinese-dominated companies from Taiwan, Hong Kong, and Singapore. Companies owned and operated by overseas Chinese have staked out major investment positions in Vietnam, Thailand, Malaysia, and, above all, mainland China.

By country, the ethnic Chinese in Indonesia make up only 3.5% of the population, yet they control an estimated 70 to 75% of the wealth if listed by market capitalization. Of the nation's top 300 companies, nearly 70% are owned by ethnic Chinese. In the Philippines, the ethnic Chinese, just 2% of the population, own or control 50 to 60% of the capital of the companies publicly traded. Filipino Chinese control such sectors as banking, food processing, textiles, plastics, and footwear and have significant interests in wholesale and retail trade. Malaysia's ethnic Chinese population, roughly 30% of the total, is estimated to control around 60% of the market capitalization of Malaysia's public companies and account for roughly 60% of all private-sector administrative and managerial positions.

As for China, the overseas Chinese, by providing capital and connections to the outside world, have played an instrumental role in the economic transformation of the mainland. Much of the foreign direct investment to China has come from the Chinese diaspora, not the Americans, Japanese, or Germans. Combined, Taiwan and Hong Kong have accounted for the bulk of China's foreign direct investment over the past 15 years. Proximity, cultural links, linguistic abilities, and family ties all have helped cement commercial ties between the two parties.

How have the overseas Chinese carved out such a dominant commercial position? What are their secrets to success? In general, most ethnic Chinese companies are small or medium-sized, and family owned and operated. Informal organizations and networking are central to many firms, allowing companies to minimize their transaction costs, enter markets quickly, and raise capital on short notice. Other traits include risk taking, internal financing, and centralized decision-making. Large property holdings are common; in fact, among the top 500 ethnic Chinese–controlled public companies in Asia, roughly 20% have land and property development as their core activity. Thriftiness, avoiding politics, and an emphasis on education are also paramount to this commercial elite.

Obviously, it is not just the Japanese that play a dominant role in Asia. It is also the overseas Chinese. They are the silent, commercial elite of the region.

Overseas Chinese in Asia
(Millions of People)

Country	Number of Ethnic Chinese
Taiwan	20.3
Indonesia	7.2
Hong Kong	6.6
Malaysia	5.8
Thailand	5.8
Singapore	2.7
Philippines	0.9
Vietnam	0.7

Source: National sources

95 Immigrants and the U.S. Economy

Up until the 1980s, and beginning with the founding of the first English-speaking colonies in the Americas, immigrants to the United States came mainly from Europe. The largest waves of immigrants arrived during the first decade of this century, when almost 10 million people landed on America's shores. Because of this massive surge from across the Atlantic, almost one-quarter of Americans today have at least some German ancestry, the number-one ethnic group in America. The Irish rank number two according to a 1990 survey conducted by the Bureau of the Census, followed by the English. African Americans represent the fourth largest ethnic group in the United States, with 10% of the U.S. population having some African American roots.

How long the ethnic composition of America remains tilted toward Europe is in question, however. While America's ethnic origin is largely tied to the "Old World," the largest source of immigrants to the United States since 1980 has stemmed from the "New World," Asia and Latin America. In 1996, only 16.9% of new arrivals were Europeans, with the bulk from Mexico, 27.2% of the total, and Asia, 26.7% (see the first chart).

The Census Bureau estimates that roughly 9.3% of the U.S. population, or 24.5 million people, were foreign born in 1996. As the second graph illustrates, this represents a sharp upturn since the low point of 4.8% in 1970, although the percentage of foreign born in 1996 was still below the high mark of this century of 14.7% in 1910.

By state, California has the largest foreign-born population in terms of both absolute numbers (8 million people) and percentage of foreign-born people (25%) in total state population. In many states, political pressures are building to curb the inflow of immigrants.

However, the conclusions of a report conducted by the National Research Council shed a different light on immigrants and their impact on the U.S. economy. The Council estimates that the yearly influx of roughly 1 million immigrants adds up to $10 billion in total economic output, and that immigrant workers pay more in federal taxes than they collect in government services. Moreover, as fertility rates decline in the United States, immigrants are expected to account for most of the nation's rise in population over the next decade. These immigrant workers, in turn, will help provide the tax revenue to support the growing pool of American retirees. Immigrants have always been an underlying strength of the U.S. economy, a trend that is not likely to change in the near future.

Origins of U.S. Immigrants in 1996

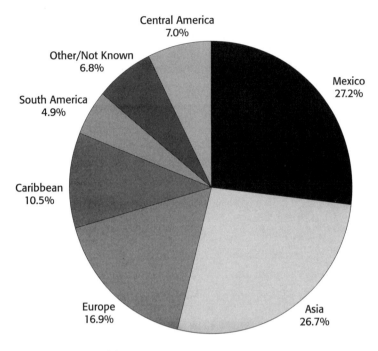

Source: U.S. Bureau of the Census

Share of the U.S. Population Who Were Foreign Born, 1900–96

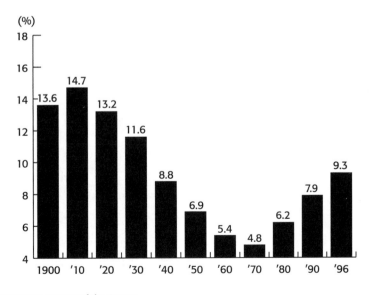

Source: U.S. Bureau of the Census

96   Asia and Oil—a Hazardous Mix for the World Economy?

As one of the most strategic commodities in the world, crude oil has a central function in the general well-being of the global economy. World oil prices rose sharply following Iraq's invasion of Kuwait in the early years of this decade, but for the most part, excluding a few blips in prices at certain times, crude oil prices have generally drifted lower or remained stable over most of the 1990s.

How long world oil prices remain tame is anyone's guess. Alternate sources of energy, new drilling and exploration techniques, global growth, and the discovery of new fields all influence the supply-and-demand balance of world oil, which in turn determines the price of "black gold."

In the future, another variable, Asia's rising thirst for oil, will come to bear more and more on the world markets. Asia and oil could become a hazardous mix for the world economy, given Asia's rising demand for oil at a time when regional supplies are declining. China, the region's largest oil producer, became a net oil importer in late 1993. Indonesia, the only member of OPEC (Organization of Petroleum Exporting Countries) in Asia, is expected to follow in China's footsteps and become a net oil importer by the early part of the next decade. Both nations, like the region at large, have sizable populations, confront rapid urban growth, and have yet to enter the automobile era, all of which entail rising oil demand and oil imports in the future.

Assessing Asia and oil boils down to three critical numbers, which are illustrated in the accompanying graph.

• The first number is 4.1%. This represents Asia's level of proven oil reserves relative to the world total. The region's reserves stood at 44.1 billion barrels at the end of 1995, down 1% from the prior year. As just a small fraction of the world's total, the region's level of proven reserves is less than Mexico's and Venezuela's, 50 billion barrels and 64.5 billion barrels respectively. And while the reserves of the world (estimated at 1 trillion barrels) are enough for 45 to 50 years at current world production rates, Asia's proven reserves are sufficient for only another 17 years.

• The second number is 10.8%. This represents Asia's oil production as a percentage of total world production. Like proven reserves, oil production lags the rest of the world by a large margin.

• The third number, 26.8%, is the most important. This figure represents Asia's total oil consumption as a percentage of the world total. Over a decade ago, in 1985, Asia accounted for 18% of global consumption. Since then, aggregate oil consumption in the region surpassed that of Europe in 1992 and exceeded that of the United States in 1994. According to some private forecasts, Asia will consume more oil than North America and Europe combined by the early part of the next decade.

Taken together, Asia's paltry level of proven oil reserves and modest production capabilities, weighed against its soaring thirst for oil, add up to a more prominent role for Asia in the world oil markets. The region is home to nearly 60% of the world population, continues to industrialize at a healthy pace, is on the cusp of an urban boom, and has yet to truly enter the automobile era. Accordingly, accommodating Asia's thirst for oil is one of the most intriguing and important challenges for the world economy.

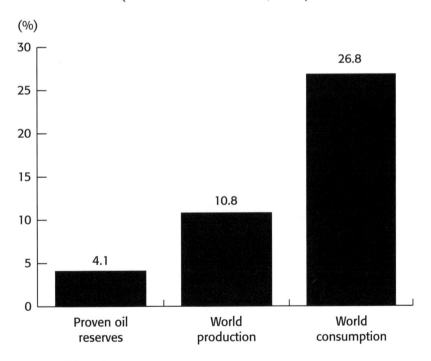

Asia and Oil
(Asia's % of World Totals, 1996)

Source: British Petroleum

97 Global Warming and the Consequences for Business

Caring for the world's precious environment is a significant challenge for all governments, and one with multiple consequences for investors and business. At issue is the fact that economic growth and industrial development increasingly threaten the natural environment we live in. Deforestation, urban smog, acid rain, airborne lead, polluted rivers—all are adverse consequences of development.

Of even greater importance is the buildup of greenhouse gases and the attendant global warming of Mother Earth. Scientists estimate that the earth's average surface temperature rose by 0.5–1°F over the last century. Due to even more fossil fuel usage, scientists estimate a continued warming of the earth during the next century, a prospect that could ultimately lead to substantial climatic changes around the world. At the center of the debates is the emission of carbon dioxide, the single most important greenhouse gas that is released when fossil fuels—coals, oil, and gas—are burnt. As shown in the accompanying graph, the United States and the industrialized nations are the main sources of carbon dioxide.

At the Earth Summit in Rio de Janeiro in 1992, more than 100 nations pledged that by 2000 their emissions of greenhouse gases would be no higher than in 1990. Most nations, however, either reneged or failed to live up to their commitments, including the United States. So they tried again at the Kyoto summit in 1997, and from this gathering, the delegates produced an arrangement which, if ratified by the nations participating, will legally bind the United States and other developed nations to cut emissions of carbon dioxide and five other greenhouse gases by 6 to 8% below 1990 levels over the next 15 years.

The Kyoto protocol still faces opposition in the U.S. Senate and among special interest groups, who believe the cost of compliance is too great and costly. The treaty does include provisions on emissions trading, which would allow a nation such as the United States to buy extra emission rights from a so-called emission surplus country.

One of the most significant flaws of the Kyoto treaty is that developing nations are not legally bound to limit emissions growth. That is unfortunate in that greenhouse gases are rising fastest in the developing nations, which means that overall emissions will continue to increase even if the developed nations succeed in reducing their aggregate level of emissions. Greater automobile use, rapid urbanization, notably in Asia, and accelerating rates of industrialization will eventually lead to greater energy usage and rising levels of greenhouse gases in such nations as Brazil, Russia, Poland, South Africa, and other emerging markets. Particularly worrisome is that coal, a key source of greenhouse gases, is likely to remain a chief form of energy in two of the world's largest nations—China and India.

Given these circumstances, action in the industrial nations to clean up the environment will be insufficient in itself. The developing nations must participate as well, though few governments have either the money or political will for such a massive undertaking. Efforts are under way to eliminate the sale of leaded petroleum in some nations. But for the most part, the developing nations have taken their cue from the rich nations and continue to drag their feet in addressing the problems of global warming.

The bottom line is that everyone recognizes the harmful effects of global warming on the environment and, by extension, on the world economy. However, more time has been spent debating the issue than actually implementing meaningful initiatives. The results of the Kyoto summit are encouraging, but whether or not governments will actually succeed in cutting emissions remains unclear. In the meantime the economic and social costs of inaction just keep right on rising.

Who Emits the Most?
(Carbon Dioxide Emissions, 1990)

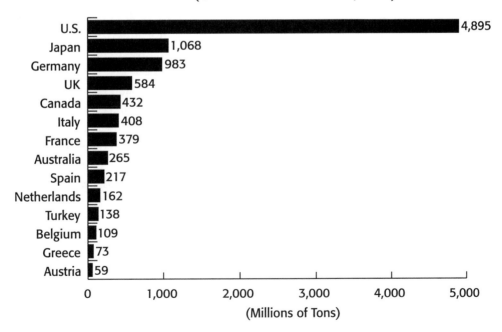

Source: © *OECD/IEA, 1997,* CO_2 Emissions from Fuel Combustion, International Energy Agency.
Reproduced by permission of the OECD.

98 The Global Market for Illegal Drugs and the Consequences for Business

The market for illicit drugs is among the largest in the world, with annual turnover estimated at $400 billion by the World Bank. We have included this entry on illicit drugs not to specifically highlight the features of the industry, but rather to make the point that this far-flung business carries numerous adverse consequences and social costs that impact the global economy and many individual economies.

Like other industries, the illicit drug industry has benefited from such global trends as the rapid diffusion of information technology, unfettered flows of trade and investment, improved global transportation facilities, and highly efficient capital markets. All of these factors have helped producers, in one fashion or another, to distribute their products and collect and bank the proceeds. And the proceeds are substantial: according to estimates from the World Bank, gross profit margins at the retail level for methamphetamine is 240% of wholesale prices. For crack cocaine, it is even higher—300%.

Strong demand weighs in favor of the industry, which is estimated to have more than 400 million customers. The industry's most popular products center on cannabis products—marijuana and hashish. Over the past few years, the most pronounced trend has been the rising demand for synthetic drugs, notably amphetamine-type substances.

In terms of supply, the coca bush is grown almost exclusively in South America, where more than 90% of worldwide coca bush cultivation takes place in three nations—Peru, Bolivia, and Colombia. Peru alone accounts for more than half the world total. The production of opium poppy is dominated by Afghanistan and Myanmar, which together account for roughly three-quarters of total world production. India, Pakistan, China, Laos, Thailand, and Columbia are also notable producers. As for cannabis, it is grown all over the world, including the United States. Countries with the largest cultivation areas relative to arable land are ranked accordingly: Peru, Afghanistan, Laos, Kyrgyzstan, Bolivia, Colombia, Myanmar, and South Africa.

Geography plays less of a role in the manufacturing of synthetic drugs. They are largely manufactured from chemicals that can be found or produced in various parts of the world.

It is important for investors to recognize the multiple consequences of the global drug trade. They range from the rise of transnational organized crime groups to widespread environmental damage. Money laundering has the potential to pollute the global banking industry and often leads to corruption within the public sector in some countries. At risk are the integrity of many local financial systems, which in turn are the life-lines of the real economy. Illicit trade in drugs can also affect a nation's money supply and the balance of payments, generating unexplained movements in capital inflows and outflows. Notably among small nations, illicit drug exports can lead to a rise in real exchange rates, which in turn can hamper the export prospects of other, legitimate industries. In Bolivia, Peru, Afghanistan, Myanmar, and Pakistan, illicit drugs make up a significant percentage of total exports according to the World Bank.

In addition to the variables already mentioned, drug proceeds can lead to widening income disparities, making the task of governing more difficult. Underlying consumption and investment trends can be skewed by illegal capital flows. Huge drug profits stoke official corruption in many cases, while drug injection has become a principal means of spreading the AIDS virus.

Thus, one of the world's most interesting industries is also one of the most dangerous.

World International Drug Trade in Context
(US$ Billions)

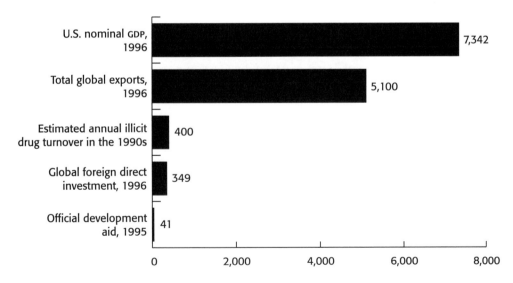

Source: World Drug Report; World Bank; International Monetary Fund; World Trade Organization

99 The Global Gender Gap

Whether in politics or at work, the status of women lags that of their male counterparts in many parts of the world, notably in the developing nations.

In all but a few countries, politics remains a male occupation. According to the Inter-Parliamentary Union, a Geneva-based world organization of parliaments, women constitute just 11.7% of the world's parliamentarians. In the United States, the percentage of women in politics was actually the world average (11.7%) at the start of 1997.

How well a female fares in politics depends on the country. A woman, for instance, has a better chance of being elected in Sweden, which has a system of proportional representation, as opposed to running for office in Japan. Politics is the traditional domain of men in Japan, where women account for less than 5% of the total legislature.

As illustrated in the first table, the Scandinavian countries top the list of nations with the highest representation of elected women. In addition to the unique political rules of Sweden, Finland has compulsory quotas for women.

Likewise, the gap between male and female educational and work accomplishments remains wide, though some progress has been forthcoming in narrowing the spread. In the developing nations, the most significant hurdle for women is overcoming illiteracy. Although female illiteracy has declined over the past two decades, the gap relative to males remains large, with the exception of Latin America. As shown in the second table, in sub-Saharan Africa and North Africa, illiteracy rates among females are greater than 50%. In South Asia, nearly two-thirds of females over the age of 15 are considered illiterate versus an illiteracy rate of 37% among males. In general, illiteracy among older women tends to be higher than younger women. Moreover, women in rural areas are more likely to be illiterate than women in urban areas.

Due in part to substandard educational achievements, women in the developing nations are most likely to be engaged in occupations that pay less than a job held by a male. In Latin America, the Caribbean, and parts of Asia, women predominate in services. In sub-Saharan Africa and South Asia, women are dominant in agriculture.

The global gender gap thus remains wide, particularly in the developing nations. Progress toward more equality has been forthcoming in many countries, yet the global gender gap persists. Women, then, remain one of the world economy's most underutilized assets.

Women in Politics

(% of Seats in National Parliaments Held by Women*)

Country	% of Women
Sweden	40.4
Norway	39.4
Finland	33.5
Denmark	33.0
Netherlands	31.3
New Zealand	29.2
Germany	26.2
Spain	24.6
China	21.0
Switzerland	21.0
Canada	18.0
Australia	15.5
Mexico	14.2
Poland	13.0
United States	11.7

*As of January 1, 1997; selected countries only

Source: Inter-Parliamentary Union

Adult Illiteracy Rate, 1995

(%, Aged 15 Years or Over)

Region	Female	Male
Developed nations	2	2
Sub-Saharan Africa	53	33
Latin America and the Caribbean	15	12
North Africa and Western Asia	56	32
East and Southeast Asia, Oceania	24	9
South Asia	63	37

Source: United Nations, World Economic and Social Survey

100 The Importance of World Religions

Robust levels of world trade, intense global competition, rapid movements of capital flows, the rise of multinationals, the diffusion of information technology, and the globalization of various industries are hallmarks of the world economy. Each variable influences the decisions of investors and the strategies of businesspeople.

Another important factor, and one not widely recognized or appreciated, is the role of religion. In many parts of the world, the prevailing religion shapes the norms and tradition of the community or country, which in turn directly impacts the economy. Islamic banking in the Middle East, for instance, forbids banks from earning interest on loans. In the Philippines, the Roman Catholic Church is one of the most powerful institutions of the country and plays a major role in shaping social and economic policies. Because of the Hindu reverence for cows, Indians abstain from eating beef, forcing multinationals such as McDonald's to adjust products to local conditions, lest their operations fail. The tenets of Islam forbid alcohol consumption, making the lucrative markets of the Middle East off-limits to many of the world's major beverage companies. Companies employing Muslim workers in Southeast Asia must work with and respect Muslim practices which dictate that followers pray five times a day. Buddhism, which is philosophically opposed to materialism, is the key religion in Thailand.

Meanwhile, religious strife can turn promising markets into disastrous ones for investors or companies alike. As one example, the economy of Israel has tremendous promise, although the potential of the nation has long been held hostage to political instability, with religious conflict at its core. India is periodically convulsed by religious strife between Hindus and Muslims, which does nothing to engender investor confidence. In May 1998, India's new Hindu nationalist-led government exploded three atomic bombs, boosting tensions with Pakistan and China, and damaging investment relations with India's major aid donors. Pakistan responded in-kind and saw the international community withdraw financial aid and assistance as a consequence. And then there is the volatile and unpredictable Middle East, home to the bulk of the world's Muslim population and major oil reserves.

All of these are examples of how religious norms, beliefs, and practices can influence the business environment and investment climate. Within this context, the accompanying table highlights the world's major religions. Top on the list are Catholics, who comprise nearly a quarter of the world population. Their greatest numerical strength lies in Europe and Latin America, in addition to the United States and key emerging markets such as the Philippines in Asia and Poland in Eastern Europe.

Muslims are followers and practitioners of Islam and represent nearly one-quarter of the world population as well. Their presence is dominant in North Africa, the Middle East, sub-Saharan Africa, Turkey, and Central Asia. Large Muslim populations are also in Pakistan, Bangladesh, and Indonesia. The latter is home to the largest Muslim population in the world.

Hinduism, another major religion of the world, is practiced largely where it was founded, in India. Large Hindu populations are also in East Africa, South Africa, and Southeast Asia. Anyone doing business in India must be aware of Hindu practices, since they permeate virtually every aspect of society, including what the Indians will eat and whom they will marry.

Combined, Catholics, Muslims, and Hindus make up almost two-thirds of the world population. Yet, in the not-so-distant future, and based on above-average population growth in such regions as North Africa and sub-Saharan Africa, Muslims are expected to exceed the number of Catholics. Other widely represented religions include Protestants (8.6%) and Buddhists (7.6%).

In general, religion clearly is an underlying force of the global economy, and one investors and businesspeople ignore at their own peril.

Religion by Affiliation

	% of World Population
Catholics	23.6
Muslims	22.9
Hindus	17.0
Protestants	8.6
Buddhists	7.6
Other Christians	10.1
Other religions	10.2

Source: United Nations

101 Living with Change in the Global Economy

It is a cliché to say we live in an era of technological change. The latter has been the one constant of the global economy for centuries. Over the past 100 years or so, such inventions as electricity, telephones, automobiles, airplanes, radio, televisions, and, recently, the computer have all produced profound change in how people live and work in the world economy. This is notably true of the United States, this century's economic and technological leader.

What is different today, however, from bygone eras is the pace or rate of change, a point demonstrated by the final graph. Note the lag between the time of an invention and the time it filters or proliferates into the mass market.

Household electricity in the United States, for instance, was invented in 1873, although it was not until after the First World War that electricity had spread to a quarter of the population. It took until 1940 for automobiles to spread to 25% of the people, even though the four-wheel marvel was invented in 1885. The lag between the invention of the aircraft and its mass-market appeal was nearly as great; the airplane was invented in 1903, but it took longer than a half century for more than 25% of the population to "take off." Electricity, automobiles, and airplanes all were adopted slowly by consumers and were, accordingly, slow to effect economic change. Even the radio and television, less expensive consumer items relative to the car and a plane ticket, took approximately a quarter century to spread to 25% of the population.

The computer and its penetration into everyday life in the United States has been different and much more dramatic. The personal computer was invented in 1975. But, rather than taking a half century or a few decades to spread to a meaningful segment of the market, it entered the mainstream much faster. It took just 15 years to penetrate a quarter of the U.S. population. Currently, lower prices for personal computers is only accelerating the pace of penetration of computers.

Predicting the consequences of this relatively new technology is a hazardous exercise. Recall that just a few years ago there was a great deal of talk about the paperless office and the cashless society brought about by new technology. However, checks and cash are still the norm in most nations, and, if anything, the computer has helped to generate more paper than anything else.

Yet, the world is changing, a point best symbolized by the exploding global use of the Internet, a network of computer networks. The Internet was established first to allow the world's scientists and military types to exchange information quickly and cheaply; however, this exclusive club of users now includes roughly 100 million people, with the number of users projected to soar to 500 million by the turn of the century.

The more widespread use of the Internet will lead to all types of changes and challenges for the world economy. Just as Johannes Gutenberg's invention of the printing press in the mid-fifteenth century helped disseminate information, ultimately ushering in a great period of learning and scientific discovery now referred to as the Renaissance, so the computer and the Internet have the potential to radically change the way the people of the world work and play. Whether the printing press, steamship, railroad, radio, or computer, the one constant of the world economy is change.

The Accelerating Pace of Change
(Number of Years It Took Technology to Spread to 25% of the Population*)

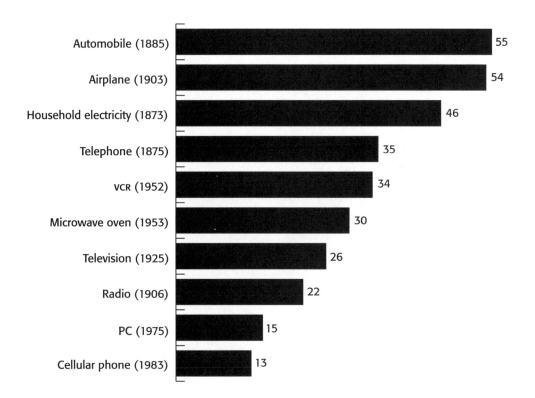

() = Year of invention

*Except for airplane: 25% of the 1996 level of air miles traveled per capita; automobile: number of motor vehicles reached 25% of the number of people aged 16 and older; cellular phone: number of cellular phones reached 25% of the number of registered passenger automobiles

Source: Dallas Federal Reserve Bank

Appendix: Key Terms and Organizations

Key Terms

Balance of payment: The measure and summary of a nation's total receipts from, and total payments to, the rest of the world.

Capital account: The change in assets abroad and foreign assets in a particular nation, other than official reserve assets.

Currency convertibility: The ability to exchange one national currency for another without any restrictions or limitations.

Current account: A measure of all sales and purchases of produced goods and services and unilateral transfers; the current account is the link between a nation's international transactions and its national income.

Dumping: The underpricing or invoicing of exports, usually below the cost of home-country prices.

FDI—foreign direct investment: The acquisition by an investor in one country of an asset in another country with *the intent to manage that asset*. In most cases, both the investor and the asset that is under management are companies. As such, the investor is known as the "parent company" while the asset is referred to as the "affiliate" or "subsidiary."

The three main categories of FDI are *equity capital* (the value of shares or voting power in a foreign company, usually 10% or more to be considered a controlling interest), *reinvested earnings* (the parent company's share of the affiliate's earnings which are reinvested in the affiliate rather than distributed as a dividend or remitted to the parent), and *other capital* (short- or long-term loans between the parent company and the affiliate). Because an international standard for calculating foreign direct investment is not yet available, the comparability of FDI data from different countries is limited.

Free Trade Agreement: Removes all barriers on trade among members, but each nation retains its own barriers on trade with nonmembers.

GDP—**gross domestic product**: The total value of goods and services produced in one country, without regard to whether the production is done by domestic or foreign factors of production.

GNP—**gross national product**: The broadest measure of the total value of goods and services produced by one country.

Most-Favored-Nation (MFN) Principle: The extension to all trade partners of any reciprocal tariff reduction negotiated by the United States with any other nations.

Nominal or current values: Values that have not been adjusted for inflation.

Purchasing power parity (PPP): The rates of currency conversion that adjust for national differences in the prices paid for goods and services.

Quota: A direct quantitative restriction on trade.

Real or constant values: Values that have been adjusted for inflation.

Tariff: A form of trade control; government tax levied on goods, either exports or imports.

Terms of Trade: The quantity of imports that can be bought by a given quantity of exports.

Key Organizations

Andean Pact: A regional trade organization including Bolivia, Colombia, Ecuador, Peru, and Venezuela.

ASEAN—Association of Southeast Asian Nations: Established in 1967, the association includes Brunei, Indonesia, Laos, Malaysia, Myanmar, the Philippines, Singapore, Thailand, and Vietnam.

BIS—Bank for International Settlements: The central banks' bank. Founded in 1930 and located in Basel, Switzerland, the BIS provides a number of highly specialized services to central banks, including monitoring the size of the Eurocurrency market and central bank intervention in the foreign exchange market, and, through them, to the international financial system as a whole.

Common Market: Removes all barriers on trade among members, harmonizes trade policies toward the rest of the world, and also allows the free movement of labor and capital among member nations.

Customs Union: Removes all barriers to trade among members and harmonizes trade policies toward the rest of the world.

E.U.—European Union: The 15 member nations include Austria, Belgium, Denmark, Finland, France, Germany, Greece, the Republic of Ireland, Italy, Luxembourg, the Netherlands, Portugal, Spain, Sweden, and the United Kingdom.

Group of 8 (G-8): Was originally composed of seven nations (G-7), including Canada, France, Italy, the United States, Germany, the United Kingdom, and Japan. The eighth member is Russia.

IFC—International Finance Corporation: Established in 1956 as part of the World Bank, the IFC is the world's largest source of financing for private enterprise in the emerging markets.

ILO—International Labor Organization: Founded in 1919, the ILO is a specialized United Nations agency that seeks to promote social justice and internationally recognized human and labor rights. The ILO publishes various statistics on the world labor force in its *Yearbook of Labor Statistics*.

IMF—International Monetary Fund: Created in 1944 at Bretton Woods, the IMF has as its main purpose to promote international monetary cooperation and exchange-rate stability. In addition, it compiles and publishes a broad range of international statistics.

ITU—International Telecommunications Union: The ITU, a specialized agency of the United Nations since 1947, is an intergovernmental organization that works with both the private and public sectors to promote the development of telecommunications.

Mercosur: The Southern Cone Common Market. A regional trade organization including Argentina, Brazil, Paraguay, and Uruguay. Established in 1991. Membership continues to expand.

NAFTA—North American Free Trade Agreement: Regional trade group, including the United States, Canada, and Mexico.

OECD—Organization for Economic Cooperation and Development: Founded in 1948, the OECD includes 29 members, all industrialized, market economies. Current members include the 15 nations of the E.U., and Australia, Canada, the Czech Republic, Hungary, Iceland, Japan, Mexico, New Zealand, Norway, Poland, South Korea, Switzerland, Turkey, and the United States. Associated with the OECD are the **International Energy Agency (IEA)** and the **Development Assistance Committee (DAC)**.

OPEC—Organization of Petroleum Exporting Countries: Algeria, Indonesia, Iran, Iraq, Kuwait, Libya, Nigeria, Qatar, Saudi Arabia, United Arab Emirates, and Venezuela.

UNCTAD—United Nations Conference on Trade and Development: Established as a permanent intergovernmental body in 1964, UNCTAD is a specialized agency of the U.N. which works to promote economic growth and development, particularly in the developing nations. It publishes a comprehensive review of international trade and investment statistics in its *World Investment Report*.

World Bank: Also known as the International Bank for Reconstruction and Development, the World Bank provides capital, technical assistance, and economic policy advice to developing nations.

WTO—World Trade Organization: Created in 1995, the WTO is the successor to the **General Agreement on Tariffs and Trade (GATT)**. Its role is promoting free trade through settling trade disputes between governments and organizing trade negotiations.

Index

About the Authors

Joseph P. Quinlan is a Vice President, Senior International Economist at Morgan Stanley Dean Witter in New York City. Quinlan has published more than 125 articles on international economics and trade and is the author of a previous book entitled *Vietnam: Business Opportunities and Risks* (Pacific View Press). He also lectures on global business and finance at New York University, where he has been on the faculty for the past six years. He was nominated as an Eisenhower Fellow in 1998. Quinlan resides in Buckingham, Pennsylvania, with his wife, Karen, and three children.

Kathryn L. Stevens is a graduate of Columbia University's School of International and Public Affairs. An Asia specialist, she has studied and worked in Taiwan, Japan, and Hong Kong. Previously employed by Morgan Stanley Dean Witter, Stevens now resides in New York City with her husband, Chris, and two small sons.